Trade, Investment, and Development in the Middle East and North Africa

Cover photos: Ships—© Nik Wheeler/CORBIS; map—© maps.com/CORBIS

Library of Congress Cataloging-in-Publication Data

Trade, investment, and development in the Middle East and North Africa : engaging with the world.
   p. cm. — (MENA development report) (Orientations in development)
   "The main authors of this book ... are Dipak Dasgupta and Mustapha Kamel Nabli ... earlier versions of the book, background papers, and main themes were presented at sessions at the Economic Research Forum (ERF) meetings in Cairo in 2001" —Ackn.
   Includes bibliographical references.
   ISBN 0-8213-5574-0
   1. Middle East—Commerce. 2. Africa, North—Commerce. 3. Investments, Foreign—Middle East. 4. Investments, Foreign—Africa, North. 5. Middle East—Economic conditions—1979– 6. Africa, North—Economic conditions. 7. Middle East—Foreign economic relations. 8. Africa, North—Foreign economic relations. I. Das Gupta, Dipak. II. Nabli, Mustapha K. III. World Bank. IV. Series. V. Series: Orientations in development.

HF3756.Z5T73 2003
330.956—dc22

2003057603

Contents

Boxes

Figures

Tables

Acronyms and Abbreviations

AFR	Africa
APEC	Asia Pacific Economic Cooperation
ASEAN	Association of Southeast Asian Nations
ASYCUDA	Automated System for Customs Data
ATUT	Agricultural Technology Utilization and Transfer Project
B2B	Business to business
BoP	Balance of Payments
CIF	Cost of insurance and freight
CPI	Consumer price index
DAC	Development Assistance Committee
DAI	Development Alternatives, Inc.
DEFRA	Department for Environment, Food and Rural Affairs
EAP	East Asia and Pacific
ECA	Europe and Central Asia
ECAA	European Civil Aviation Area
EU	European Union
FAO	United Nations Food and Agriculture Organization
FDI	Foreign direct investment
FEU	Forty-foot equivalent unit
FOB	Free on board
GATS	General Agreement on Trade in Services
GATT	General Agreement on Tariffs and Trade
GCC	Gulf Cooperation Council
GDP	Gross domestic product
GNI	Gross national income
GNP	Gross national product
GOIEC	General Organization for Import and Export Control
GSM	Global system for mobile communication
GTAP	Global Trade Analysis Project
HIC	High-income countries
ICT	Information and communication technology

IIT	Intra-Industry Trade Index
IMF	International Monetary Fund
ISIC	International standard industrial classification
IT	Information technology
LAC	Latin America and the Caribbean
LC	Letter of credit
MENA	Middle East and North Africa
MERCOSUR	Mercado Común Sur (Argentina, Brazil, and Uruguay)
MFA	Multifibre Agreement
NAFTA	North American Free Trade Agreement
ODA	Official Development Assistance
OECD	Organisation for Economic Co-operation and Development
OPEC	Organization of Petroleum Exporting Countries
PAFTA	Pan-Arab Free Trade Area
PPP	Purchasing power parity
QIZs	Qualifying industrial zones (Jordan)
RIAs	Regional integration agreements
SAR	South Asia
SITC	Standard Industry Trade Classification
SSA	Sub-Saharan Africa
TU	Traffic unit
UAE	United Arab Emirates
UEA-GCC	Unified Economic Agreement between the Countries of the Gulf Cooperation Council
UNCTAD	United Nations Conference on Trade and Development
UNDP	United Nations Development Programme
UNESCWA	United Nations Economic and Social Commission for West Africa
UNIFEM	United Nations Development Fund for Women
VAT	Value added tax
WCU	World Customs Union
WDI	*World Development Indicators*
WITS	World Integrated Trade Solution database
WTO	World Trade Organization

Overview

For the countries of the Middle East and North Africa (MENA), trade and private investment are needed to provide new engines of growth and dynamism. With more trade and investment, countries in the region will be able to achieve faster growth, reduce poverty, create more jobs, and improve the knowledge, skills, and productivity of their work force.

The most important development challenge in the coming decade is to create enough jobs for the rapidly growing work force. During 2000–10 the number of new entrants to the labor force will average 4.2 million a year, twice the number for the previous two decades. The best and most sustainable way for all countries in the region to address this challenge is to accelerate their trade and investment integration, with the help of their partners.

Implicit in this is a transition—from an old model of economic organization and activity to a new one. The old model—driven by the public sector, supported by oil, aid, and workers' remittances—cannot any longer generate faster growth or jobs, as the performance of the past two decades attests. A new model, which is much more reliant on trade and private investment, promises to support faster growth and jobs needed in the region.

Most governments in the region have already started to undertake this shift, and the region is in a state of transition. Early reformers include Jordan and Tunisia, which have opened to trade and created a more hospitable investment climate, with encouraging outcomes. Egypt and Morocco have also been taking greater steps at trade and investment reform. Among the resource-based economies, Algeria and the Islamic Republic of Iran have started to reopen their trade regimes and encourage private investment. In the Gulf, smaller countries have accelerated reforms. The United Arab Emirates, especially Dubai, are following an impressive outward-oriented strategy with large gains. Yet, compared with the rest of the world, trade and investment climate reforms in the region have been decidedly weak.

Many countries are seeking to strengthen their trade partnerships with Europe, their largest trading partner, through the Euro-Med trade agreements, while intraregional trade is being promoted through the Pan-Arab Free Trade Area (PAFTA) and the Gulf Cooperation Council (GCC) customs union. Several other smaller regional trade groupings also have been established. A number of countries are seeking membership in the World Trade Organization (WTO). Jordan and the United States have signed a free trade agreement, and more such agreements may be forthcoming.

Yet, the results on the ground remain disappointing. The 1990s were marked by stagnant or declining trade and private investment—MENA was the only region in the world to experience a reversal. There is strong pressure to produce better results.

The pressure is needed, for the transition to a new model is never easy, given the politically powerful and better organized potential losers and the weakly organized potential winners. It is no surprise, then, that trade and investment reforms have been hesitant and cautious, and outcomes weaker still. While some structural and external political economy factors (conflict, sanctions, limited WTO membership and participation, limited market access in agriculture, exclusions of services in trade agreements, and others) help to explain some of the results, weak policies and reforms also bear a large responsibility.

The region now needs to deepen and accelerate its reform, finishing the process that it has started. It needs to make three fundamental shifts in its sources of growth: from oil to nonoil sectors; from public, state-dominated to private, market-oriented activities; and from protected, import-substitution to competitive, export-oriented activities. Intensifying trade and investment is at the core of all three shifts.

Why Intensify Trade Now? There's Little Choice

Waiting is costly. Policies preserving the old model, which may have been merely inefficient and expensive, are fast becoming unsustainable—for four reasons, each pointing to the urgency of reforming trade and investment. The first is the prospective decline in oil and other sources of income derived from the rest of the world. The second is the growing competition in world markets. The third is the slowing of labor migration opportunities. But the most urgent and compelling reason of all is the enormous pressures building in domestic labor markets, from the existing and growing pool of unemployed, and from the millions of new entrants to the labor markets who are young and better educated. Alternatives for employment in the public sector or in small, protected domestic markets are exhausted, and this only heightens the need for change.

Oil, aid, and workers' remittances are unlikely to be able to support enough employment and income in the coming years. Countries face a steady decline in per capita oil revenues, strategic aid inflows, and workers' remittances. Rising competition in world markets is creating more pressure, both in skill-intensive activities and in employment-intensive activities, such as garments, textiles, and light manufacturing. And countries in and outside the region are constraining the free movement of labor.

These developments will only increase the pressure on employment. Of all regions, MENA faces the greatest challenge in providing jobs. Average annual growth in the labor force is expected to be 3.4 percent a year in 2000–10, twice the growth in other developing countries. A potential demographic gift runs the risk of turning into deeper social crises in the absence of adequate growth in jobs. Already, unemployment rates, which have risen in the past two decades, are among the highest in the world. At the same time, the public sector cannot provide anymore the jobs needed by the scale of new entrants to the labor force. Queuing for public jobs no longer presents a viable option.

Countering Unfounded Pessimism with the Tremendous Potential for Trade, Investment, and Employment

Pessimism about the region's trading potential is deterring many MENA countries from accelerating their trade and investment. This pessimism is pervasive, barring a few exceptions, such as in Jordan, Tunisia, and the United Arab Emirates. As a corollary, political leaders do not favor policies to make the needed transition from the safety and comfort of the old model to the uncertainty of gains from a new model. Compounding the pessimism is fear about the ability to compete in world markets. There is nothing especially unique about the MENA countries in this respect. But the pessimism is unfounded.

The region's characteristics are favorable to trade. Exports other than oil are a third of what they could be. Manufacturing imports are one-half of what would be expected. The region is small, with 2 percent of world income and 5 percent of world population. Its incomes are low, in the bottom half of the world income distribution. Wages are also fairly low, in the bottom half of world wages. And it is near a high-income region, across the Mediterranean from the European Union (EU).

MENA countries can also attract more investment from abroad and encourage more private investment at home, both of which are crucial for trade and development. If exports other than oil were higher, and were in a better investment climate, domestic private investment in traded goods and services would be much higher. And the foreign direct investment (FDI) inflows that the region could expect would be five to six times what they are today—some 3 percent of gross domestic product (GDP), as compared with 0.5 percent.

Even if only half the region's trade and private investment potential were realized over the next 10 years, per capita GDP growth would jump from 1 percent to about 4 percent a year—half from more private investment, and half from the greater productivity that openness would encourage. Importantly, this would meet the growth in jobs required in the region in the coming decade, both to absorb the new entrants to the labor force and to address the stock of unemployed.

Expanding trade and investment holds the promise of substantial dividends in job creation, for export opportunities would add millions of jobs, many of them for women if the structural barriers to women's participation are removed. The share of nonoil merchandise exports in GDP was about 6 percent on average (compared with more than 20 percent in East Asia and the Pacific). Bridging only a small part of this gap would increase employment by more than 4 million over the next five years, equivalent to cutting the unemployment rate by 4 percentage points of the labor force.

International trade is cutting up the manufacturing production chain and permitting finer gradations of specialization within that chain, for skills and labor costs and productivity. Small, resource-poor countries in the region stand to benefit from such production chains—and given their size, the prospects are virtually unlimited in world markets. Larger countries will also benefit from such specialization. Their domestic markets and proximity to major international markets will drive a much larger range and scale of domestic manufacturing possibilities. The prospects for specialization in manufacturing thus remain immense in all MENA countries. The manufacturing sectors of most MENA countries are small by international standards—almost half the typical levels in other lower-middle-income countries. And the prospective gains from more open trade are large over time.

Services will also grow, with pronounced shifts out of low-productivity public and private services and agriculture. Complementary human resource improvements and broader improvements in governance and gender equity will be essential—to enable shifts to more knowledge-based activities.

Trade is thus likely to be a key source of growth in the MENA region in the next decade and beyond. It is also likely to be relatively skill intensive, suited to the changing characteristics of educated youth entering labor markets of this region. And it can improve female participation in labor markets, as has been the case elsewhere around the world. But these effects can come only with a better investment climate to nurture new investment and new firms, as is evident in China, India, Indonesia, Malaysia, Mexico, and Vietnam. Halfhearted attempts at trade reform in the absence of deeper domestic investment climate reforms fail to create much positive impact on jobs. They can even be devastating—with large job losses from imports, and few gains from new jobs in new industries.

The Road to Capturing the Gains from Deep Economic Integration

Decisive action, and the support of the region's trading partners, is needed to capture the large gains possible from regional and global economic integration—and to take advantage of the opportunities missed for the past two decades. Policies must address not just at-the-border constraints, but also a full range of behind-the-border trade and investment constraints.

Making Trade Reforms Successful

Effective trade reform rests on (1) eliciting an adequate supply or private investment response, from both domestic and foreign investors, (2) inducing technological or productivity gains from a more open economic system, and (3) minimizing output and job losses in the transition. This, in turn, requires that the content, pace, and sequencing of reforms be tailored to specific settings. Indeed, many successful countries (such as China, India, and Vietnam) have often undertaken what look at first to be incomplete (or nonorthodox) approaches to liberalizing trade and investment. But they have produced outcomes that are often better than in other cases where reforms have been more orthodox and complete (as in Argentina or Brazil).

Sequencing and Pacing Reforms

The debate on sequencing and speed of reforms, intense in the 1980s for Latin America, gained even more attention for the transition countries of Eastern Europe in the 1990s. The reasons for supporting gradual reforms range from allowing the costs of reform to be spread over time (avoiding the danger of reversals), to institutional arguments for creating adequate capacity and learning, and to political economy arguments of building support for reforms. The counterarguments for faster ("big bang") change are to gain credibility, ensure complementarity among different parts of the reforms, reduce uncertainty, and capture opportunity.

The evidence on the pace and sequence of trade reforms from experiences around the world (including from neighboring Eastern Europe, Asia, and Latin America) suggests the following:

- First, to build momentum, programs must start boldly and then follow through with further measures. This proves more durable than an initially hesitant approach, which creates doubts about the credibility of the program. So, trade reforms must encompass broad-based liberalization and widen its domain successively and quickly—so that more individual sectors or groups are able to perceive the benefits and spread the costs more evenly. Evidence from the region suggests that accelerated trade reforms would bring fairly immediate gains in aggregate consumption of 3 to 5 percentage points, creating visible benefits for consumers and domestic support for change.

- Second, programs that decisively reduce import quotas or import licensing monopolies succeed more than those that retain such privileges. That step sends a clear signal that no rent-seeking, special enclaves deserve more protection than others. Also, such actions provide widespread benefits to consumers and others through lower prices and higher-quality goods.

- Third, there must be across-the-board cuts in tariffs, setting as little administrative discretion as possible, and progressively lower ceilings within a time-bound program. Indeed, lowering all tariffs to as uniform a rate as possible is the best way to do away with a discretionary and administrative approach.

- Fourth, reforms must go well beyond at-the-border trade policies to eliminate behind-the-border impediments in customs, standards, ports, and other barriers. Indeed, trade reform cannot work without such complementary reforms.

- Fifth, trade reforms must be accompanied by consistent and bold investment deregulation to free up new entry and allow private investment to respond. That investment response is probably the most decisive element in the success or failure of the entire program.

- Sixth, the financial sector needs to allow the shift in resources from previously protected and unproductive state enterprise–dominated sectors to the new exportable sectors.

- Seventh, a case for gradualism can nevertheless be made for sectors in which job losses are likely to be significant.

Reforms in Resource-Poor Countries: Egypt, Jordan, Lebanon, Morocco, and Tunisia

Although there are differences, countries in this group are relatively advanced in their broad direction of reforms. The challenge now is for these resource-poor countries to move on to a new round of more decisive and credible trade liberalization. There is little reason for gradualism, after more than a decade of adjustment time for domestic industry, enormous pressures in domestic labor markets for new jobs, and huge potential benefits of accelerated reform.

Exchange rate policies. Exchange rate polices need to be supportive of an accelerated round of trade reform. Significant adjustments of real exchange rates, through nominal rate adjustments or domestic demand measures, need to precede trade reforms. Tunisia has a managed float, with a real exchange rate target. Jordan and Morocco have pegged exchange rate polices. Morocco's persistent overvaluation in the past contributed significantly to its poor export performance during the 1990s, but it has improved more recently. Egypt's recent shift to a floating exchange rate offers the opportunity to slash tariff protection across the board since the depreciation that has occurred will protect import substitution industries. In Lebanon sustainable macroeconomic reforms are needed before the country can reap benefits from trade reforms.

Tariffs and nontariff barriers. Countries need to accelerate tariff reductions and apply them across the board, reduce peak tariffs, and simplify a still complex tariff structure. For example, the simple average tariff rates in Morocco and Tunisia at 33 percent and 30 percent, respectively, remain more than double the average for all low- and middle-income countries, while Egypt's (21 percent) remains well above. Reforms should move to cut these rates. That includes avoiding any trade-diversion effects of regional trade agreements by providing only marginal tariff advantages—if any—to regional trade partners. Tariff peaks need to be drastically reduced. For example, tariffs in Morocco and Tunisia on agriculture remain extremely high (up to 358 percent), while taxation peaks for other products remain distorted with high protection for domestically produced items and multiple and complex rates (up to 29 rates in Egypt and 22 in Tunisia).

Although nontariff barriers have been progressively eliminated, a few remain. Tunisia replaced import licensing with administrative barriers, such as *cahiers de charge*, which still impede trade. In addition, quality standards and systematic technical controls are often used, as in Morocco, which has a multiplicity of such controls. Replacement of nontariff barriers with their tariff equivalents would create transparency and reduce lobbying for import licenses and rent seeking.

Domestic standards and inspections often lack any international equivalence, and many countries enforce quality norms that provide little health or safety protection. In Egypt, testing and certification procedures are lengthy and costly (Nathan Associates cited in Kheir-El-Din, 2000). More recent measures have helped, but the standards regime still remains the most significant trade barrier. Standards and inspections ought to be aligned with WTO principles.

Managing fiscal consequences. Fiscal consequences of tariff reduction are often cited as one important reason by countries for not cutting tariffs faster. This is wrong. Most revenue losses can be recouped through domestic taxes, such as a value added tax (VAT) and with faster growth in aggregate. Experiences around the world and in the region itself also suggest that trade tax revenue losses are frequently overstated, and revenues may indeed increase with trade liberalization as more revenues are captured because of reduced evasion, faster growth in import volumes, and tariffs that replace nontariff barriers. For example, in Morocco, customs duties are an important source of revenues for the national budget, and accounted for 4.2 percent of GDP in 1995—just before tariffs started to be reduced under the association agreement with the EU. In 1996–2000, revenues from customs duties fell to 3.3 percent of GDP, a significant loss, but smaller than feared. Most of the decline in import tariffs was compensated for by a nearly 25 percent rise in imports, so that customs duties also continued to generate revenues. But revenues from a new VAT on imports rose in the same period to 3.3 percent of GDP, more than compensating for the decline in import tariffs.

Euro-Med agreements. Instead of the Euro-Med agreements' scheduled tariff reductions, which are too slow, negotiations should focus on achieving greater benefits from trade partners in return for offers of accelerated trade reform. For example, Tunisia's trade liberalization has focused on the association agreement, initially yielding significant gains in some products (capital goods and intermediates) but escalating effective protection for others. The reduction of tariffs on heavily protected items was backloaded and they are only now beginning to be implemented. And countries would also gain by extending such tariff reductions on a most-favored-nation basis.

Customs reforms. Customs reforms, which are proceeding well in Jordan and Morocco, need to be accelerated in Egypt and Tunisia. Customs procedures remain complex and time consuming. In recent surveys

Tunisian firms report that it can take three weeks or more to comply with administrative bottlenecks. The costs are especially large for small firms. A similar situation prevails in Egypt. Procedures are complex, inspections are excessive, and release times are long.

Services and new businesses. Critical service sectors need to be opened to competition, especially in telecommunications, financial services, transport, education, and health. Commitments to market access require reexamination, especially in Jordan and Tunisia. In Jordan and Morocco, port and road transport deregulation is critical in view of the high transport costs. Privatization and regulatory reform in air transport is also urgent, especially in air-freight services. Tunisia requires further telecommunications liberalization. Jordan, Egypt, and Tunisia may need to actively encourage competition from foreign banks, by opening up their banking sectors.

All countries in the MENA region need deregulation to reduce bureaucratic procedures and transaction costs for new firms. The number of steps required to open a business is excessive and costly.

Reforms in Labor-Abundant, Resource-Rich Countries: Algeria, the Islamic Republic of Iran, the Republic of Yemen, and Syria

The resource-rich countries have a more complicated task in shifting from state-dominated and protectionist economic systems to open, market-led systems. Much of the core support for reform has to come from the very sectors that stand to lose initially from trade policy reforms—the dominant, protected public enterprises and private sectors.

With the current situation inherently unstable, there are significant pressures for more credible and consistent change. The largest pressure comes from labor markets. The current system is unable to generate enough jobs for a young, educated, and rapidly growing labor force. Unemployment rates are among the highest in the world, and real wages are falling. Falling per capita oil rents compound the problems. At some point reform becomes inevitable. It is encouraging that some countries are indeed beginning to start such deeper reform.

What should the countries in the group of larger, resource-rich countries do to initiate and sustain effective trade reform? They first need to achieve macroeconomic stability—as most have—at a reasonable level of oil prices. But they also need to deal with the massive distortionary effects of oil rents on traded goods and services. This means managing the booms and busts better, avoiding the stop-go cycles of structural reform and backtracking, and progressively reducing the rent-seeking effects of oil. For example, during the 1979–81 boom, more than 40 percent of Indonesia's oil windfall was saved abroad, and supporting exchange rate policies allowed the nonoil sectors to grow despite the oil boom.

Specifically, these countries might:

• Establish fiscal rules that insulate government spending from windfalls and downturns, by setting up explicit rules-based mechanisms for saving or drawing down temporary oil funds.

• Set aside an increasing proportion of oil revenues as longer-term surpluses for future generations (as a provident fund for old-age pensions for the current generation or for social safety nets for job losses in the transition), the scale depending on the prospects for exhaustion of the resources.

• Adopt appropriate macroeconomic policies to reduce misaligned real exchange rates.

To be credible these measures need to be backed by constitutional-type reforms so that the rules cannot be easily changed. Many of these countries distribute a significant part of the oil rents as production subsidies or low energy prices to consumers, with the same distortionary macroeconomic effects as public spending. Energy prices need to be raised progressively to world levels. Diversification and growth of nonoil traded goods and services will be impossible without some combination of these measures.

Domestic pricing deregulation for key traded goods and services is another precondition to effective trade reform. Price controls, regulations, and subsidies, so pervasive in these economies, muffle the price signals through which trade policy reforms work. For example, manufacturing, agricultural products, and key services such as transport remain subject to extensive domestic price controls, particularly in Algeria, the Islamic Republic of Iran, and Syria.

Across-the-board cuts in tariffs spread the costs of reform across all sectors, increasing the benefits and reducing resistance. The goal should be a uniform tariff rate of about 10 percent (a target lower than in resource-poor countries because offsetting oil revenues should permit lower trade taxes).

Import duties can be replaced by a stronger nonoil tax base, boosting overall government revenue. In some countries, for example, the complexity of the VAT and other taxes and high rates of evasion result in low yields. The tariffication of extensive nontariff barriers would be more effective. Customs reforms are also vital.

All countries would benefit from deregulation of services and the introduction of competition to state-owned and -operated activities—in ports, transport, telecommunications, and finance. The waiting time for a fixed telephone land-line is 10 years in Syria and 6 years in Algeria. The advent of cellular telephones has reduced the access problem, but is not a complete solution. Freight costs are about twice benchmark levels. Algeria, the Islamic Republic of Iran, and Syria severely limit foreign bank activity in varying degrees, with state-owned banks dominating (up to 95 percent of assets). The result is poor services, high costs, extensive lending to state enterprises, shaky balance sheets, and weak financing of new activities and trade. Financial sector reform ranks high on the agenda of services requiring critical attention.

Deregulation of domestic and foreign investment is also critical for export activities. Attracting more FDI will require deep-seated reforms and improvements in the business climate. The Republic of Yemen, as a very low-income country, represents a special case in which improvements in governance (property rights, land registration, security) with respect to the private investment climate and the supply of key public services are especially critical.

Public enterprises in manufacturing and services, which employ large sections of the labor force, are often the greatest obstacles to effective trade reform in many of these countries. They are threatened by many of the trade measures and by the change to a private-sector-led economy. They also form a natural coalition with others who stand to lose from trade reforms, especially a smaller group of rent-seeking constituencies that directly benefit from many of the current trade restrictions.

Trade policy reformers will need to isolate and break up these natural constituencies of support for the status quo. One way is to isolate them by removing the main sources of their rents in trade, typically by removing administrative discretion, setting tariff rules, and eliminating licensing and quota barriers. That would release large and visible benefits to consumers, through lower prices and greater availability of consumer goods. However, it would be important to deal carefully with state enterprises and potential job losses, by allowing some state enterprises to remain in operation with harder budget constraints. A progressive reduction in the size of state enterprises could avoid large job losses.

Reforms in Labor-Importing, Resource-Rich Countries: The GCC States

The resource-rich GCC countries face two main challenges. The first is accelerating nonoil growth to generate adequate employment opportunities for the young job seekers, who constitute nearly a quarter of the population. The second is reducing vulnerability to oil price fluctuations. On both accounts, the smaller GCC countries have done well. But challenges remain. Per capita incomes in Saudi Arabia have fallen (in nominal terms) from a high of about US$17,000 in the early 1980s to about US$9,000, an almost unprecedented drop.

The GCC countries have embarked on deeper reforms that promise to sustain these basic policy directions and accelerate their integration with the global economy. They have established a US$335 billion customs union, which will allow them to forge a larger common market with lower trade barriers to the rest of the world, with a standard 5 percent external customs tariff. The goal is to form a homogeneous unit to facilitate intragroup trade and collective negotiations with the WTO and trade partners and to attract foreign investment.

Challenges in trade lie mainly in four interlinked areas. First, labor markets suffer from wage rigidities, skills mismatches, and institutional factors. Some GCC countries are replacing foreign workers with nationals by setting quotas on expatriate workers and raising employment costs for expatriates. These policies could be counterproductive in the long term because wage flexibility and skilled workers are needed for growth of the nonoil sectors. Mandatory systems are not a good substitute for wage flexibility. Education and skills training improvements are also critical.

Second, the government wage bill, defense and security spending, and subsidies and entitlements are straining government budgets. The traditional role of the government as dominant employer and wage policy setter needs reconsideration, as do subsidies for food, health, education, agriculture, and basic industries. Explicit subsidies are small by international standards (2 to 3 percent of GDP), but implicit subsidies through low energy prices and long-term loans are significantly larger. Revenue policies will also need attention, especially fees for utility services and the introduction of broad-based consumption taxes.

Third, structural policies to diversify economies will need continued attention, especially privatization since most of the larger, nonoil industries remain in public hands. New regulatory standards are needed for financial markets and to spur development of local equity markets.

Fourth, making the GCC customs union work will require establishing common customs rules and procedures, harmonizing technical and regulatory procedures (standards, security, inspection, and licensing), increasing transparency, and minimizing administrative barriers.

Managing Transition Costs and Job Losses

In many MENA countries, some sectors will likely suffer significant job losses—such as agriculture, public enterprises, and capital-intensive manufacturing. Business expansion takes time, and in some cases the investment climate may not be sufficiently attractive—leaving restructured and export-oriented companies without incentives to expand and to absorb labor released by the shrinking sectors. So job destruction may outpace job creation, because lowering trade barriers may initially hurt sheltered domestic producers and displace unskilled workers in import-competing industries.

Although import-competing industries are usually capital intensive, MENA industries—like those in many middle-income countries—are also often intensive in unskilled labor. They are also often protected disproportionately because they face potentially stiff competition from lower-cost producers. In Morocco before the trade liberalization, the nominal tariff and import license coverage in apparel and footwear was among the highest in manufacturing. And in Egypt, clothing imports are still discouraged by tariff rates set at four times the weighted average.

Whether there would be significant job losses in a particular sector depends on four factors:

- The underlying aggregate growth in the economy, with higher aggregate growth offsetting the downward pressure on these sectors.

- The ability of the trade liberalization program to insulate some sectors from overall trade liberalization measures, by providing partial time-bound protection.

- Possible compensatory measures to allow enterprises to manage the transition more smoothly—such as providing enterprises funds to restructure operations, such as in the Tunisia *mise à niveau* program and similar programs in Morocco and Egypt, although these should be used sparingly given doubts about their efficacy.

- The ability to restrain job losses in state-owned enterprises without derailing the objectives of reform (allowing losses to mount temporarily in state-owned enterprises while downsizing operations as an implicit compensation measure).

The investment response of new firms and new entry into new sectors are, however, the most critical—with quick payoffs in new activities. Mexico jumpstarted the *maquiladora* border investments to generate new jobs—while negotiating longer phase-ins of trade liberalization for employment-heavy sectors, such as automobiles, agriculture, and pharmaceuticals, and leaving the state banking and oil sectors relatively untouched.

All this highlights the need for careful design in the pace and sequencing of trade and investment climate reforms—and for close monitoring and early corrections, but without backtracking, which can be costly for the credibility of the program. In China, India, Indonesia,

Mexico, Vietnam, and elsewhere, transition issues have generally been handled well through:

- Liberalizing early in key areas and inputs, and addressing key bottlenecks (such as customs or inspections) to jump-start new export-oriented activities.

- Embarking on large-scale and upfront domestic investment deregulation to foster new entry and job growth.

- Delaying state enterprise downsizing and job losses, but exposing them to competition and reducing the scale of their operations so that losses are held in check by hard budget constraints.

- Instituting compensatory mechanisms for firms that can restructure.

- Maintaining competitive exchange rates.

- Phasing reforms in with the macroeconomic cycle.

A similar strategy is possible for all countries in the MENA region, so the political and economic fear of large job losses should not be a significant reason for deferring the reform agenda.

Liberalizing Services

International experience suggests that better-quality and lower-cost backbone services—such as finance, transport, and information and communications—and important production inputs—such as electricity—reduce the cost of exporting and strengthen linkages with global production networks. Regulatory reforms that inject more competition in markets for services and network industries, in turn, force operators to improve efficiency and pass on the lower production costs to users. Similar outcomes can be achieved by lowering trade barriers in services and making room for increased foreign investment.

Despite recent initiatives, MENA is far from a situation in which services do much to promote trade and investment. Indeed, today's regulatory constraints and low efficiency are substantial impediments to trade and investment. Inefficient and costly services, provided mostly by the public sector, raise the cost of MENA merchandise exports and limit attractiveness to investment, while impeding trade expansion within the region.

With the right enabling environment in place, liberalization of key services—especially telecommunications and transport—could facilitate the development of export capacity in other services—especially in tourism-related services and the information and communication technology sector. In addition to its benefits for trade, liberalization in services can create more investment opportunities for the domestic private sector and attract more job-creating foreign investment as well. Stepped up investment can offset the short-term adjustment costs from the reduction of protection for import-competing industries. Sound design of private participation schemes in infrastructure services, coupled with procompetitive regulatory regimes and strong regulatory capacity, are key.

Making Agriculture More Dynamic

It is in the MENA region's interests to subscribe to an equitable, liberal, and open rules-based multilateral trading system within the WTO framework. But sustainable development requires gradual reforms in agriculture and in rural areas. It also requires much faster opening of market access in richer countries and a commitment from MENA's trading partners to mitigate the substantial welfare losses from freer global trade. Closer to home and within the context of trade relations with the EU, revitalized regional trade agreements can begin to address market access and trade reforms.

With substantially better access for its exports, and with substantial trade and domestic price reforms, MENA could have welfare and efficiency gains that are large (some US$2 billion a year). It could also have large savings in water use, with food security achieved through trade rather than protection. Already, trade is playing a vital role with the very substantial food imports that are saving huge water resources (equivalent to the annual flows of the Nile River, by some estimates). But there is much more opportunity, for a shift out of production of the still heavily protected, costly, and water-intensive activities such as beef, dairy, sugar, rice, and wheat into more labor-intensive and less water-intensive export crops such as cotton, fruits, and vegetables. Improvements in agricultural trade should lead to faster and more sustainable growth, reducing poverty along the way.

The consequences of trade-related job losses are a serious issue in agriculture. The benefits of freer trade will go mainly to better-off farmers in irrigated areas and urban consumers. But large losses will be borne by the more vulnerable segments of the rural population—small field crop producers, subsistence farmers in rainfed areas, and poor livestock herders. Their earnings losses will have to be dealt with in ways different from those envisaged for the "average" displaced manufacturing worker. The displacement process should avoid putting the burden disproportionately on women. Packaging the transition process to accommodate those constraints and designing adequate safety nets could ensure that trade reform in agriculture is politically viable.

Anchoring Reforms in Regional Integration Agreements

Anchoring reforms in revitalized regional trade agreements and in multilateral forums, such as the WTO, will help lock in reforms with domestic constituencies and strengthen the credibility and commitment to reform generally. An important part of the trade and broader economic reform strategy in MENA countries will thus be to revitalize regional trade agreements. There are several ways to make these trade agreements work better.

First, trade with Europe, the natural geographic trading partner for the MENA region, falls far short of its potential. With new members expanding the size and scale of the EU market, the potential gains for a number of MENA countries are expanding as well. The Euro-Med agreements and the Barcelona Process could be strengthened by accelerated commitments by MENA countries to reduce trade barriers, liberalize services, and phase in domestic agricultural reforms. The EU could offer immediate, expanded access to its markets for agriculture, as well as increased temporary migration, funds for managing transition costs, and more efficient rules of origin.

Second, substantial expansion in regional trade is possible if the barriers to trade and investment are progressively eliminated. Intraregional trade agreements could be strengthened by mutual agreements to reduce product exclusions in agriculture and services and to harmonize customs and regulatory processes (standards, investment and other licensing processes, visa restrictions).

Third, MENA countries would do well to maintain open access to world markets, anchoring their trade and investment reforms in a multilateral framework such as the WTO, which will give them greater credibility. But first more countries in the region will have to become full members of the WTO.

Getting Support from MENA's Main Partners

MENA's trading partners need to rethink the challenges in this region, including the devastating effect of persistent conflict and sanctions and the disincentives of strategic aid. There is strong evidence to suggest that the incidence of violence and conflict has had a hugely negative influence on trade and investment integration, rivaling the influence of poor domestic policies. Persistent conflict has had large neighborhood effects throughout the region, affecting not just the conflict-ridden countries but all their neighbors.

Trade barriers compound the problems. This region has the lowest proportion of its population covered by membership in the WTO. Sanctions have created their own distortionary effects. Agricultural exports (of less water-intensive crops such as fruits and vegetables) have also faced large market access barriers and tariff escalation for processed food. Labor flows have been restricted.

The support of regional partners for faster and deeper integration will thus be important in revitalizing the incentives and effectiveness of regional trade agreements and in making trade and investment reforms work. That support will include opening their markets for the region's exports of agriculture, and permitting greater flows of temporary migration—and harmonizing trade and investment processes. Building more fences around this region is not a viable solution.

Tackling the Broader Reform Agenda

Faster growth of output, productivity, and jobs is available if MENA countries tackle deep-seated barriers to trade and investment. Reforms need to go beyond the shallow at-the-border trade policy reforms and the signing of numerous trade agreements—the staples of the 1990s—to much deeper domestic policy reforms. Liberalizing trade in goods as well as liberalizing services will yield much bigger gains in welfare. Accelerating tariff and nontariff reforms and moving to appropriate exchange rate regimes and improving the investment climate are also critical.

But a broader agenda of reforms, elaborated in companion volumes to this report, will need to complement the reforms identified here:

- Improving governance to increase the voice of citizens and the accountability of government. Improved governance is implicit and critical to reduce the array of barriers to trade and private investment discussed here, but such reforms cannot be isolated from or be successful and sustainable without broader governance reforms.

- Putting gender issues at the center of development. Women's gains from trade and investment reforms cannot proceed without the removal of a large number of social barriers, nor will the overall gains to trade and investment reform be achievable without greater participation from half the citizens of this region.

- Tackling the unemployment and labor market issues and absorbing a growing labor force into a more dynamic economic system. Trade and private investment is one critical instrument to enlarge labor demand, and indeed the central reason for shifting to a more open system, but a larger array of labor market issues will need to be addressed.

CHAPTER 1

Shifting to New Sources of Growth

The countries of the MENA region (see box 1.1) need to achieve faster growth, reduce poverty, create more jobs, and improve the knowledge, skills, and productivity of the work force. Greater openness and trade are likely to be an engine of change in all these areas, given the limits to alternative domestic sources of growth. This chapter discusses why international trade and private investment are so important for addressing the region's economic challenges.[1]

The main messages are as follows:

- The region needs to make three shifts in its sources of growth: from oil to nonoil sectors; from state-dominated to private, market-oriented investment; and from protected import-substitution to export-oriented activities. Intensifying trade is at the core of all three shifts. Today's protected activities, driven by the public sector, cannot support fast enough growth—as the experience of the past two decades suggests. The region's growth has collapsed since the mid-1980s, with falling oil prices and little integration with the rest of the world.

- Oil, aid, and workers' remittances, factors that have helped sustain the old development model, are unlikely to support enough growth in employment and income in the coming years. The region faces a steady decline in per capita oil rents, strategic aid inflows, and workers' remittances. Rising competition in world markets also is putting more pressure on employment-intensive activities, such as garments, textiles, and light manufacturing. That situation makes it vital to improve trade policies and strengthen competitiveness.

- Of all regions, MENA faces the greatest challenge in providing jobs. Average annual growth in the labor force in 2000–10 is expected to be 3.4 percent a year, twice that in all other developing countries, with about 42 million net entrants. What should be a demographic gift of rapid labor force growth is turning into rising unemployment, already among the highest in the developing world, with high social costs.

BOX 1.1

The Middle East and North Africa Region

In World Bank geographic classification, the following 21 countries or territories constitute the Middle East and North Africa (MENA) region: six Gulf Cooperation Council
(GCC) members (Bahrain, Kuwait, Oman, Qatar, Saudi Arabia, and United Arab Emirates [UAE]), and 15 other countries or territories: Algeria, Djibouti, the Arab Republic
of Egypt, Iraq, the Islamic Republic of Iran, Israel, Jordan, Lebanon, Libya, Malta, Morocco, the Republic of Yemen, the Syrian Arab Republic, Tunisia, and West Bank and
Gaza. This report focuses on a subset of 16 countries that covers most (more than 90 percent) of the population and geographic size of the region: 10 low- and middle-income
countries (Algeria, Djibouti, Egypt, Islamic Republic of Iran, Jordan, Lebanon, Morocco,
Republic of Yemen, Syria, and Tunisia) and 6 partners in the GCC. Others are not covered in any depth because information is limited (Iraq, Libya), or they have special characteristics (West Bank and Gaza), or they are high-income (Israel, Malta). Although the
countries in the region show considerable diversity in economic structure and circumstances, which are examined in the next chapter, certain commonalities and features allow
a focus on broader regional trade and development issues in this chapter.

- MENA countries have good potential for expanding trade. Exports
  other than oil are a third of what they could be given the characteristics of the region, which are favorable to trade. Openness to manufacturing imports is half of what would be expected. It is small, with 2
  percent of world income and 5 percent of world population. Its incomes are low, in the bottom half of world income distribution.
  Wages also are fairly low, in the bottom half of world wages. And it is
  close to a high-income region, the European Union (EU), which is
  just across the Mediterranean.

- MENA countries also have great potential for attracting more investment from abroad and encouraging more private investment at home,
  both of which are crucial in trade and development. If exports other
  than oil were higher, and if the investment climate were better, domestic private investment in traded goods and services would be much
  higher. And the foreign direct investment (FDI) inflows that the region could expect would be five to six times what they are today—
  some 3 percent of gross domestic product (GDP), up from an average
  of 0.5 percent. That level could be achieved even without being at the
  high-achieving end for many other fast-integrating countries, such as
  Chile and the Czech Republic.

- If only half the region's trade and private investment potential were realized over the next 10 years, that would be enough to raise its per capita GDP growth from about 1 percent to about 4 percent a year— half from more private investment and half from the greater productivity that openness would encourage.

- Expanding trade also holds the promise of substantial dividends in job creation, for export opportunities would add millions of jobs. For example, if the region could achieve faster nonoil export growth of about 15 percent a year, it would probably be sufficient to generate some 4 million jobs or 4 percent of the labor force, directly and indirectly in the export sectors alone, during the next five years. The employment effects are conditioned critically, however, on a more favorable investment climate. Women's participation and employment would gain sharply, provided barriers to their entry and participation in the economy are dismantled.

Faster Growth from Trade and Private Investment

From the 1960s to the early 1980s, a prominent government, high public spending, and protected national markets promoted growth and social development—aided by higher revenues in oil-producing countries and aid inflows, labor migration, and workers' remittances in non-oil-producing countries. The region grew by about 4 percent a year per capita, with impressive improvements in social conditions—comparable to those in fast-growing East Asia. But by the end of the 1980s, this model of growth came to an end. With falling oil prices, and a costly and inefficient public sector, public spending became unsustainable, social safety nets came under stress, and public and private investment collapsed as the limits of costly import substitution in small national markets were reached (figure 1.1).

It was clear to policymakers by the late 1980s that a new model had to rely on exploiting profitably opportunities from global trade integration and encouraging private investment in more open, competitive, market-oriented settings.

But the policy responses of countries were, however, mostly cautious and hesitant, and the actual outcomes even weaker (Dasgupta, Keller, and Srinivasan 2002). Macroeconomic stabilization was reasonably successful in most countries. Fiscal and current account deficits were reduced. Exchange rates corrected for large overvaluations. And inflation was brought under control. But structural reforms—reducing trade barriers, promoting private investment, removing inefficient public regulation,

FIGURE 1.1

Divergent Per Capita Growth in MENA versus East Asia, 1965–2000

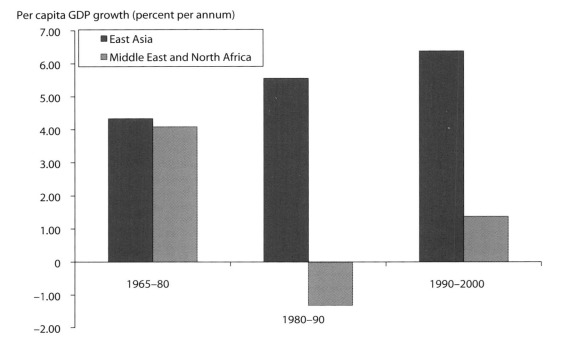

Sources: Staff estimates and World Bank 2003a.

and privatizing inefficient public enterprises—remained far from complete and were sometimes reversed. Accompanying these policy reforms
were efforts at trade cooperation—evident from trade agreements with
the EU and the Pan Arab Free Trade Area (PAFTA). But the results on
the ground, and especially growth, remained disappointing (figure 1.2).

The sources of growth suggest that much of the disappointing out-
come lies in poor productivity and the collapse in private investment
(Dasgupta, Keller, and Srinivasan 2002).

Why? Two main reasons have contributed: (1) The region has failed
to integrate with the world economy, and (2) private investment has not
responded to the halting progress in policies.

The underlying reason for poor performance is the lack of commitment by the leadership in governments of the region to new policy directions. There also is a deep, underlying pessimism about trade
prospects and their effects on jobs. National leaders see significant short-
term political and economic costs in changing policies. And a large and
influential civil society—comprising large sections of public sector employees, unions, civil society, media opinion leaders, and private enter-

FIGURE 1.2

Real Oil Prices and Growth, 1976–99

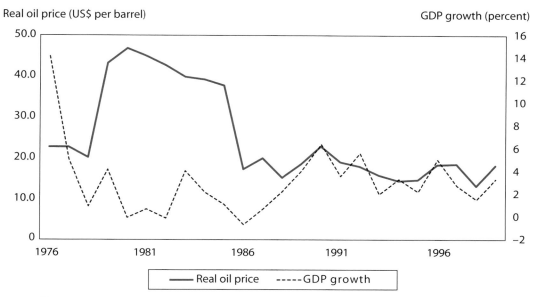

Real oil price (US$ per barrel)   GDP growth (percent)

prises—remains deeply wedded to the security and benefits of the old order. Unlike the transition in Eastern Europe, there is no deep commitment to reforming trade and investment—or to fostering markets more generally—within or outside government. This situation has severely limited the credibility and extent of critical reforms needed to make the new trade integration and private investment model work.

In comparison to the intensity of reforms elsewhere, the MENA region has fallen behind. In a winner-take-all environment, rewards in the new global economy go to the most hospitable environments. In MENA the response of private investment to new opportunities in global markets remains hobbled. Adding to the problem is the persistence of almost continual conflict in the region over the past two decades. The result: missed opportunities in trade and private investment both at home and abroad, which are discussed at some length in the next chapter.

Fortunately this overall picture of weak policy reforms and outcomes is neither static nor monolithic. Jordan and Tunisia have opened to trade and created more hospitable investment climates, with encouraging outcomes. Morocco's initial reforms met some success in the late 1980s. Egypt, for a brief period, stimulated public and private investment, with the promise of faster progress in the mid-1990s. In the Gulf many

smaller countries accelerated reforms. The United Arab Emirates, especially Dubai, have followed an impressive outward-oriented and private
investment–led growth strategy that so far has been successful (box 1.2).

BOX 1.2

The United Arab Emirates—Breaking Out from a Resource Curse

Seven small emirates with a combined population of about 3 million people—similar in
size to Jordan, Lebanon, and Tunisia—make up the UAE, formed in 1971 as a confed-
eration of Abu Dhabi, Ajman, Dubai, Fujairah, Ras Al-Khaimah, Sharjah, and Umm Al-
Qaiwain. The UAE has the world's third-largest recoverable oil reserves—about 98 billion barrels, 10 percent of the world total. It also has large natural gas reserves (4 percent
of the world total). Oil production capacity is about 3.7 million barrels a day, and actual
production is about 2 million barrels a day under Organization of Petroleum Exporting
Countries (OPEC) quotas.

Per capita GDP in the UAE was about US$26,000 in 2001 in purchasing power par-
ity (PPP) terms, rising significantly since 1989 (US$17,000). Real GDP growth averaged
some 7 percent a year since 1993. Much of this growth was led by rapid diversification
to the nonoil sectors—first to energy-intensive petrochemicals, fertilizers, cement, and
aluminum, and more recently to tourism, entrepot (reexport) trade, and manufacturing.
Growing by 9 percent a year in real terms in the 1990s, these nonoil sectors accounted
for 70 percent of GDP and 43 percent of exports in 2000. The growth of employment
in the nonoil sectors has averaged about 8 percent a year, with private fixed investment
growing at about 11 percent a year in the 1990s.

What accounts for this rapid nonoil export growth and diversification led by private
investment, in a small, rich, oil-producing country? Four factors have been crucial.

First, the leaders of the emirates have all been deeply committed to trade and openness as engines of development, each reliant on their comparative advantages—Abu
Dhabi in energy-based industries; Dubai in commercial, telecommunications, tourism,
and financial services; Sharjah in textiles and light manufacturing; and the northern emirates in agriculture, quarrying, cement, and shipping.

Second, they have pursued quite open trade, investment, and labor policies. Effective
trade tariffs average 4 percent. Expatriate workers account for 90 percent of the labor
force (mostly from the Indian subcontinent, the Middle East, and the Philippines). And
free trade zones permitting 100 percent foreign ownership of companies were established to capture the strategic advantages of location. Dubai's Jebel Ali free trade zone is
the largest, and the 12 free zones increased their share of total nonoil exports from about
22 percent in 1999 to 57 percent in 2000, with 3,000 companies operating, US$8 billion
in trade, and US$1.4 billion in net exports.

BOX 1.2 (continued)

Third, the emirates' trade-related services and infrastructure compete aggressively, with the best internationally benchmarked standards in ports, airports, customs, shipping, telecommunications, power, water, roads, banking, finance, and stock markets. They are among the top 20 economies in Internet usage and the most wired in the MENA region: 29 percent of the population use the Internet compared with 16 percent in Bahrain, 8 percent in Kuwait, 3 percent in Saudi Arabia and Oman, and 1 percent in Morocco and Egypt.

Fourth, these policies have combined with better governance and structural reforms more broadly—reducing rents and emphasizing education and economywide productivity improvements instead.

Some challenges remain: creating job opportunities and skills training for a rapidly growing young labor force, dealing with Multifibre Arrangement (MFA) abolition in textiles and garments, reducing the direct role of the state, and encouraging greater private participation in public services.

Sources: Fasano 2002; IMF 2003; Ministry of Information and Culture UAE 2002.

Policymakers elsewhere in the region are beginning to reexamine their strategies. Algeria and the Islamic Republic of Iran have started to significantly reopen their trade regimes and encourage private investment. Syria's earlier hesitant steps are being reexamined with a view to strengthening the trade and investment climate. Lebanon is beginning to consider ways of addressing the massive economic disincentives of the difficult public debt and macroeconomic situation. Even in larger, oil-based countries, such as the Republic of Yemen and Saudi Arabia, nonoil trade and private investment have become central issues, because oil contributes little to job creation.

Expanding trade and investment remains critical to economic revitalization everywhere in the region (box 1.3). The challenge is to strengthen the consensus, ability, and capacity of policymakers to implement needed reforms in key areas. Other fundamental institutional changes are likely to be equally essential in modernizing and reinvigorating the region's economic prospects in the medium to long term: better and more accountable governments, greater citizen participation and voice, a greater role for women, and a better-educated and skilled work force for the transition to more knowledge-based economies. (These changes are addressed elsewhere [UNDP 2002; World Bank 2003b].) The focus of this study is on the reform agenda for trade and investment.

BOX 1.3

Straddling Three Continents—and Three Millennia

The MENA region straddles the trading routes of three continents. Given this geography, trade has been a powerful engine of progress. Examples in history are legion (Hourani 1991):

- Knowledge of seasonal trade winds in the Indian Ocean and Arabian Sea combined with innovations in navigation (the compass, derived by the region's traders from China), shipping (the galleon-shaped dhows), and finance (the first promissory notes and bills of exchange) raised regional trade to preeminence.

- Citrus fruits from China were shipped to Rome, and traders started citrus groves in North Africa. Frankincense trade brought merchants tons of coined silver each year from Rome and fine porcelain from China.

- Spices were introduced to Europe by the region's traders, and it was their prosperity, efficiency, and monopoly that spurred European expansion around the Atlantic and Africa to India and the East, beginning in 1497.

- Coffee was shipped from Ethiopia to Arabia, and the world's first coffeehouse opened in Mecca in the 15th century. The first in Europe was reputedly hosted by a Viennese spy who had tasted coffee during the Ottoman wars. By the early 1700s London had more than 2,000 coffeehouses, and France was not far behind.

- In Africa both coasts saw flourishing trade by the region's traders, including the salt–gold trade between North Africa and Ghana, and the devastating slave trade.

- Knowledge of chemistry and mathematics spread to Europe from the region, helping lay the basis for the scientific revolution.

- Trade reached its peak in the 10th century with the growth of large cities, unrestricted by borders and abetted by new methods of organizing trade. With multiple trading routes—inland, caravan, sea, and river—multinational competition was stiff (Arab, Iranian, Jewish, and Indian traders).

- In the Mediterranean, trade linked Spain and the Maghreb with Egypt and Syria, with Tunisia as the entrepot for silk, gold, metals, and olive oil. Later, trade with Venice and other Italian cities became more important.

Three main lessons apply. Trade was an essential handmaiden to economic prosperity at different times. The state reduced risks and costs and gave traders room to innovate. When trade started to decline, opportunities eventually bypassed this region. "The Middle East flourished economically and politically as long as the ancient routes were used, but decayed when they were closed, often by political change." (Beaumont, Blake, and Wagstaff 1988).

Why Intensify Trade Now?

The old model of economic development in the region has been sustained to a large extent over the past two decades by oil earnings, aid inflows, and workers' remittances. The decline in oil earnings in the 1980s created pressure to shift to a trade and private investment–led model, but the volatility of oil prices since (periods of temporarily high prices that have often obscured the longer-term decline in revenues) and a much smaller population base (than is prospectively ahead) have sustained the old model. The appropriate macroeconomic policy responses of reducing fiscal excesses and undertaking exchange-rate corrections at times of more acute pressures, together with official debt reductions, have also helped cushion the adjustment. In similar fashion, aid inflows remained relatively high (and volatile) and have supported the old model's continuance.

Finally, worker migration—at least until the early 1990s—reduced the pressures to address the growing unemployment at home. The old model thus managed to sustain itself through the 1980s and the 1990s. There was no sudden and deep crisis that made it imperative for countries to shift to a new model.

But all three factors mentioned above are now under much greater pressure. The choice not to change to a new trade and private investment–led model of development is becoming far more constrained. Three factors in the international environment point to the urgency of accelerated trade and investment reform. The first is the prospective decline in oil and other sources of income derived from the rest of the world. The second is the growing competition in world markets. The third is the slowing of labor migration opportunities. All three are also now juxtaposed against the much larger labor market pressures at home. In some senses, an incipient social crisis is now evident. Annual new entrants to the labor market are now twice as numerous as in the previous two decades. At the same time, the domestic alternatives of employment in the public sector or in small protected domestic markets of the old model have been exhausted.

Declines in Oil Revenues, Strategic Aid, and Other Rents

Oil and gas exports provide a large, continuing stream of resources to the region. The world relies on the region for some 50 percent of traded energy, and the region accounts for some 35 percent of global oil production and a slightly smaller share of natural gas. But oil revenues will decline for all countries in the region, continuing the pattern of the past two decades. Aid inflows are the other important source of rents or quasi rents. The MENA region receives the second highest per capita aid inflows (after Sub-Saharan Africa), much for conflict prevention, military assistance, and other politically driven reasons.

These resources raised incomes and consumption to levels higher than these countries could otherwise afford. The decline in oil and aid flows should now encourage them to diversify, by providing a reason to reform and to correct real exchange rates. But the adjustment will not be easy, for two main reasons:

- *The political economy problem of institutional rent distribution.* Large current inflows of rents reduce the pressure for states to undertake fundamental reforms needed for growth of nonoil sectors. Instead, the inflows encourage rent seeking and lobbying by public and private recipients to maintain their access to rents (through the budget and financial sectors).

- *The Dutch disease problem.* The excess consumption is in nontraded goods and services, bidding up their prices and reducing the profitability and incentives for producers of traded goods and services. The resulting exchange rates, overvalued and uncompetitive, provide marked disincentives for the growth of traded sectors. The overvalued exchange rates tend to persist until countries face a macroeconomic crisis. In the past three decades, MENA countries had substantial real-exchange-rate misalignments, with large negative impacts on exports (Nabli and Veganzones-Varoudakis 2002).

Few countries have avoided the twin curses of resource rents and made a smooth adjustment to declining rents.

The decline in per capita oil rents or revenues between 1980 and 2000 is consistent across all countries and groups (figure 1.3). It reflects the steady decline in oil prices from the peaks of the early 1980s and in the sales in a cartelized market (where the share of the oil cartel countries is eroded over time). The long-term outlook is for real oil prices to decline steadily from the current levels to those that are about the same as prevailing in the 1970s (figure 1.4). Known oil resources will be depleted in some countries in the region, such as Algeria and the Islamic Republic of Iran, in about four decades, and in some others, such as Egypt and the Republic of Yemen, much sooner. Exports will fall as domestic energy consumption ratchets up and the population grows. With declining oil production, the decline in per capita oil rents will be steeper than in the past two decades. The picture for aid flows is similar: they decline steadily except in temporary periods of strategic importance and conflict resolution (figure 1.5). For example, aid flows to the region reached a peak in the early 1980s following the 1979 peace accord, but fell fairly

FIGURE 1.3

Falling Per Capita Oil Rents in MENA Countries, 1980–2000

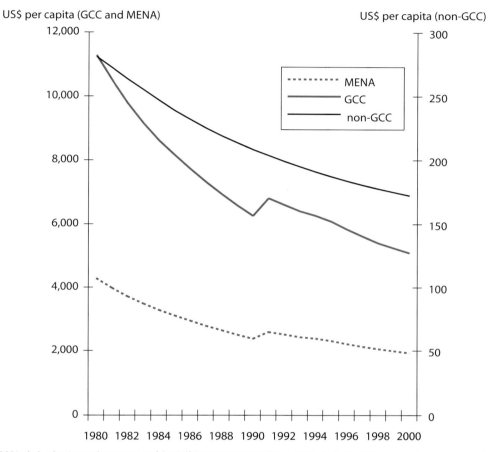

Note: GCC includes the six member countries of the Gulf Cooperation Council. Non-GCC includes the 10 lower-middle-income countries in the MENA region.
Sources: Staff estimates and World Bank 2003a.

sharply thereafter; another increase is evident in the wake of the first Gulf war in the early 1990s, and then a rapid fall; a third rise and subsequent fall is evident after the 1995 Oslo peace agreement.

Rising Competition in Global Markets

The region also faces intensified competition in world markets—at both the skill- and labor-intensive ends. Many important existing industries and activities are affected, such as textiles and garments, light engineering, and manufacturing. As well, the competition indirectly affects

FIGURE 1.4

Period Average Real Oil Prices, 1970–2015
(US$1990 prices)

Dollars per barrel (1980 prices)

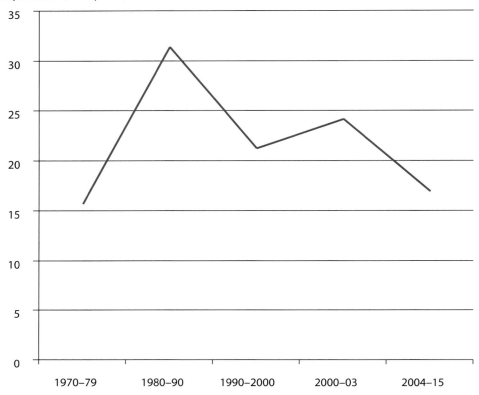

Sources: Staff estimates and World Bank 2003a.

prospects for services such as ports, shipping, distribution and finance, and agriculture. Done right, trade reform can strengthen these areas. But done wrong or not at all, intensified competition from abroad will chip away at many of them.

A major competitive threat is the upcoming accession of some Central and Eastern Europe or Europe and Central Asia (ECA) region countries (the Czech Republic, Hungary, Poland, the Slovak Republic, and others) to the EU—and the customs union agreement of Turkey with the EU. Both provide accelerated entry and competition in MENA's major export market. Other regional groupings and free trade agreements—such as the North American Free Trade Agreement (NAFTA) and the free trade association for the Americas—also pose challenges. The Latin

FIGURE 1.5

Aid-to-GDP Ratio in the MENA Region, 1980–2000

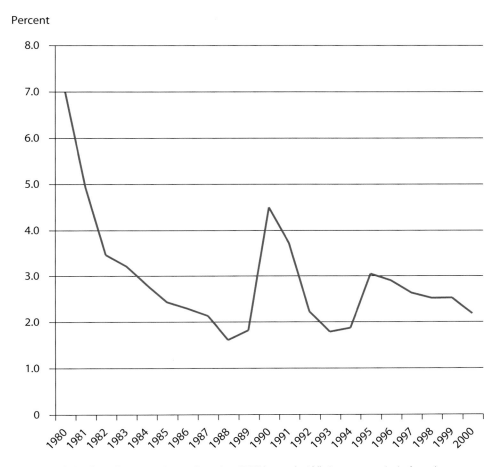

Note: MENA includes all Development Assistance Committee (DAC) low- and middle-income countries in the region.
Sources: Staff estimates and World Bank 2003a.

America and the Caribbean (LAC) region competes directly with MENA at the higher skill range and is ratcheting up its competitiveness. Both ECA and LAC have enjoyed faster trade reforms and integration with global markets in recent years, and are gaining rapid market share growth in world trade. Meanwhile, MENA lags behind. At the skill-intensive end, MENA thus faces rising competition in its major industrial country markets from these two middle-income regions with similar labor skill profiles (figure 1.6).

At the opposite end is the competitive challenge from low-wage, high-productivity countries, such as Bangladesh, China, India, Indonesia, and Vietnam, in labor-intensive products and manufactures, espe-

FIGURE 1.6

Other Competitors Are Growing Nonmineral Exporters in World Markets, 1990–98

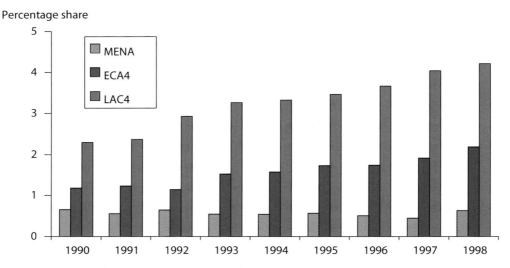

Percentage share

Note: ECA4 = four Europe and Central Asia countries (Czech Republic, Hungary, Poland, Turkey); LAC4 = four Latin America and Caribbean countries (Bolivia, Brazil, Chile, Mexico).
Sources: Staff estimates and United Nations Conference on Trade and Development (UNCTAD), various years.

cially with the abolition of quota preferences in textiles and garments by 2005 (figure 1.7). This is particularly important in garments and textiles, of major importance to the MENA region for manufacturing employment (10 to 52 percent) and export earnings (5 to 23 percent). More than a million workers are employed in these sectors in the MENA region, with about 400,000 in Egypt, about 200,000 in Morocco, and about 270,000 in Tunisia. These labor-intensive sectors have been among the few in which the MENA region has been gaining market share—partly because of protected quota markets in the EU and elsewhere, now slated for abolition by 2005.

Adjusted for labor productivity, labor costs in the garments sector in MENA countries are significantly higher than in populous countries of Asia (Bangladesh, China, India), higher than in Asian newly industrialized economies (Indonesia, Malaysia, Thailand), but lower than in Eastern European countries (Hungary, Poland, and Turkey).

Preferential access for MENA countries to European and U.S. markets will not be completely removed after the abolition of the MFA, although it will be somewhat diluted with extension of such privileges to a larger group of countries. Only quotas will be removed on January 1, 2005, while peak tariffs by industrial countries will continue to apply, al-

FIGURE 1.7

World Market Shares of Textiles and Garments, 1980–99
(percent)

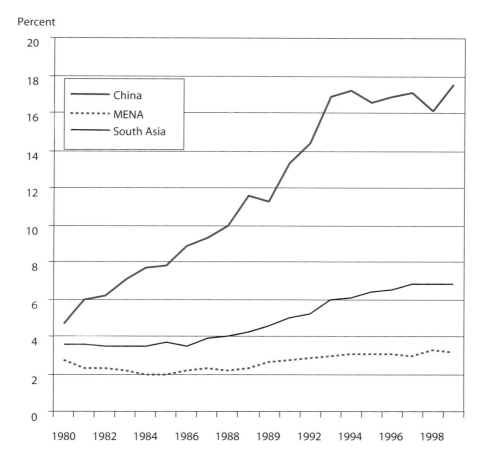

Percent

China ━━━━
MENA ·············
South Asia ━━━━

Sources: Staff estimates and UNCTAD, various years.

though subject to periodic negotiations in the World Trade Organization (WTO). The textile and clothing exports from GCC countries will be most subject to risk, as the quota-free world in 2005 will offer little justification for exports from these countries, which enjoy neither the geographic closeness of the Mediterranean to the EU market nor the low costs of Asian exporters.

With the MFA abolition, product prices would be expected to fall in quota-restrained markets (because hitherto restricted efficient exporters will supply more) and to rise in unrestrained markets (because efficient exporters "dumping" in unrestrained markets would have no incentive to do so) (Martin and Suphachalasai 1990). In the key export markets of the EU and the United States, the end of quota restrictions in 2005 would tend to lower the price of textiles and clothing in these markets.

This does not mean an erosion of the trade integration and openness prospects for the MENA region. Indeed, the strengthening of MENA's association agreements with the EU is an opportunity. And fortunately the region is small enough to continue to take advantage of global markets and multilateral and regional trade liberalization. The imperative for the region is to take actions now to strengthen its trade and related reforms—and thus its competitive position against the growing threats in world markets at both ends of the spectrum.

Falling or Stagnant Opportunities for Labor Migration

Labor migration—from the poorer and populous countries to the richer, labor-scarce Gulf countries and to Europe—and workers' remittances are important for many countries in the region. Migrant workers' earnings contribute to some 6 percent of gross national product (GNP), provide up to 7 to 8 percent of lifetime employment opportunities for the labor force, and are equivalent to some 50 percent of nonoil exports—larger than in most other developing regions of the world. Inward migration also is an important component of the labor force and production structure of the richer, labor-receiving countries in the GCC.

When oil prices and labor demand were high (in the 1970s), labor migration from poorer to richer countries was booming. But since the mid-1980s, opportunities have been decreasing because of falling oil prices or rising unemployment in receiving countries. And migration has slowed both to the GCC and to Europe. With lower oil prices, rapidly rising domestic supplies of national labor, and competition from lower-cost labor from the Indian subcontinent and elsewhere, the GCC will demand less labor from the labor-abundant countries of the region. In the rest of the world, the barriers to mobility are rising, reducing the prospects for migration to substitute for trade (box 1.4).

The Domestic Job Market: Rising Labor Forces and Dwindling Employment Alternatives

The opportunities in domestic job markets also are falling, especially given the structural imbalances in the region's emerging labor market. The first imbalance is an extraordinarily rapid rise in new entrants to the labor force in the past three decades (figure 1.8). In the face of slow job creation, open unemployment rates have risen to around 15 percent of the labor force. That contrasts with other middle-income and high-income countries, in

---

BOX 1.4

Is Migration a Substitute for Trade?

Trade is fundamentally a substitute for migration (and vice versa) between poorer and richer countries (Schiff 1994, 1996). With relatively free labor mobility, convergence of incomes proceeds faster than with trade alone, and welfare gains are larger and more direct as people move from poorer to richer countries. So the best policy is to promote greater labor mobility by reducing the policy barriers to labor mobility. But labor mobility in practice is far from free, with receiving countries imposing significant and rising restraints for a number of political economy reasons that are generally far more restrictive than for trade.

Migration can complement trade. Even if migration is generally restricted, it can still be used as an important policy tool and safety net in richer countries to complement trade policies in poorer countries, especially in a temporary adjustment phase (Diwan and others 2003). It can support trade in the medium term—by allowing a window of trade reforms to proceed in poorer countries (when the employment outcomes may be still fragile), boosting integration between receiving and sending countries (language, familiarity, proximity, networks, and investment), and using demographic transition differences. This is probably the case for the MENA region today.

At certain adjustment stages, trade and migration may be essential and temporary complements. Trade liberalization may increase unemployment in the short term. Unskilled workers in previously protected sectors may be displaced. And demographic transitions may swell labor out-migration pressures as countries restructure for faster growth. In labor-receiving, rich, industrial countries, demographic transitions in the opposite direction (sharply falling population and working-age population, as in Europe and Japan) may gain by accommodating rising in-migration, boosting growth, productivity, and trade.

What about the GCC labor-receiving countries? They would do well to avoid restraining migration too heavily: their future ability to grow remains dependent on rapid diversification and growth of a thriving private sector that will need to draw on migration. And encouraging job growth for nationals would probably be best served through such faster growth, enhanced local skills training (as is happening with private institutes and training), and changing incentives (linking public wage setting and jobs to productivity).

---

which entries to labor markets are slowing and unemployment rates are now half or less than those in MENA (figures 1.9 and 1.10).

The second structural imbalance is a deep skills mismatch. MENA is seeing the fastest rise in educated new entrants to the labor force—measured by the change in average years of schooling per head. The problem is the high and growing unemployment among educated cohorts, espe-

FIGURE 1.8

Rapidly Rising New Entrants to the Labor Force, 1980–2010

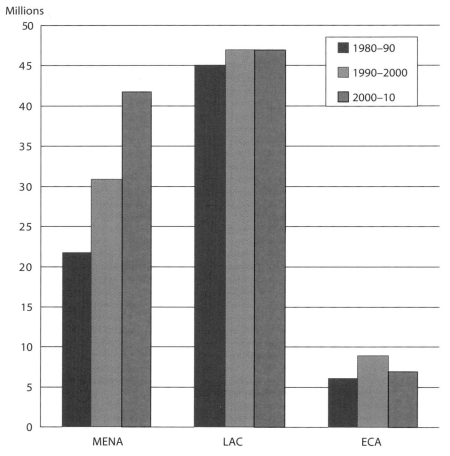

Notes: ECA = Europe and Central Asia region; LAC = Latin America and the Caribbean region.
Sources: Staff estimates and World Bank 2003a.

cially acute among secondary school leavers (figure 1.10). The mismatch has two sides. Demand for educated workers is weak because of a gap in the development of services employment. Skills in the labor force do not match the skills the private sector demands, because of weaknesses in higher education. Unemployment among women is particularly high (figure 1.11). Women's jobs are found only in government or a few gender-specific occupations, and their participation rates are among the lowest in the world.

The third imbalance is sector specific: Agricultural employment in water-intensive crops is still high in MENA countries, reflecting the steep protection of such crops and production as sugar, livestock, rice, dairy,

FIGURE 1.9

Unemployment Rates Are Rising Rapidly in MENA, 1980–2000

Percent of labor force

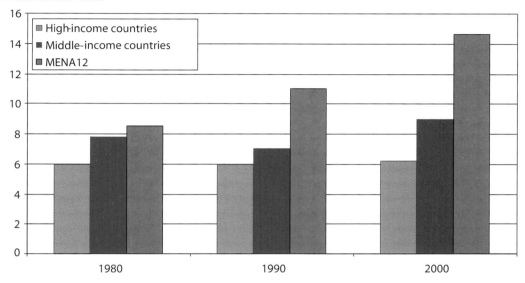

Legend:
- High-income countries
- Middle-income countries
- MENA12

Note: MENA12 refers to available data for 12 countries in the region (Algeria, Bahrain, Egypt, the Islamic Republic of Iran, Jordan, Morocco, Oman, Saudi Arabia, Syria, Tunisia, the United Arab Emirates, and the Republic of Yemen.)
Sources: Staff estimates and World Bank 2003a.

and wheat (discussed in chapter 6). But private services employment is smaller than that in comparator regions (figures 1.12 and 1.13).

Without enough jobs for a young and rapidly growing, educated labor force, social tension is a major threat to the stability and prosperity of the region. The alternatives are not promising. Public employment with implicit or explicit job guarantees for graduates of secondary and tertiary education—from Egypt to the Gulf states—has all but come to an end. The queuing for public jobs and pressures on governments to provide these jobs remain strong, inducing attempts to expand public employment schemes in fits and starts.

In Egypt, for example, the waiting period before graduates can apply for government jobs was extended from an initial two to three years to five to six years in the 1980s, before the official guarantee of public employment was halted. In the 1990s, after fiscal consolidation and debt writeoffs, public employment expanded again until it hit another fiscal and balance-of-payments crisis in 2000. Even in the smaller, oil-rich Gulf states, the rising unemployment of graduates who cannot be absorbed in public employment was leading to street demonstrations in 2001, as took place in Bahrain and Oman.

FIGURE 1.10

MENA Has the Greatest Problem in Educated Unemployed, 1998

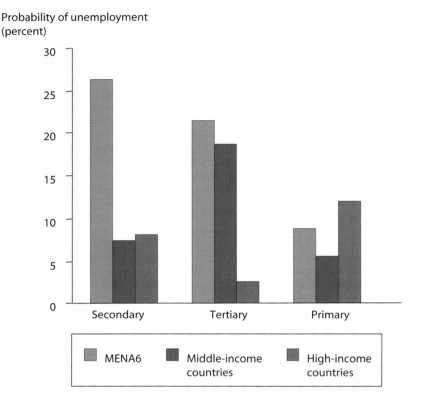

Note: MENA6 refers to available data for the following six countries—Algeria, Egypt, Jordan, Morocco, Syria, and Tunisia.
Sources: Staff estimates and World Bank 2003a.

If the public sector cannot provide jobs, neither can the private sector in small, protected home markets. Service employment remains weak, as does manufacturing employment throughout the region. Isolated home markets simply cannot provide the scale of world markets to create growth and jobs. Protection-induced industrial growth and job creation has also reached a saturation point. As a result of the growing imbalance between the fast-growing labor force and the slow pace of job creation, real wages have been falling throughout the region for the past decade or more.

Faster Trade and Investment Integration—to Meet Key Development Challenges

A deep pessimism about the region's trading potential is deterring many MENA countries from accelerating their trade and investment. This

FIGURE 1.11

Female Unemployment in MENA Is Severe

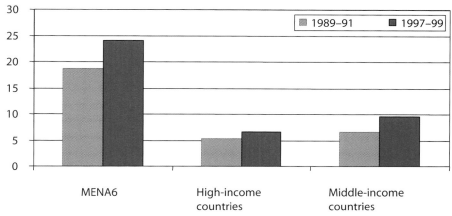

Note: MENA6 refers to available data for the following six countries—Algeria, Egypt, Jordan, Morocco, Syria, and Tunisia.
Sources: Staff estimates and World Bank 2003a.

pessimism is pervasive in the region, barring a few exceptions such as Jordan, Tunisia, and the UAE. But this pessimism is unfounded. The potential for accelerated trade and investment integration is large. Even if only half the potential is realized in the coming decade, it is likely to double or triple the rates of per capita economic growth. This growth would come from higher private investment and from greater economywide productivity. The pattern of growth also would be much more labor-demanding—creating an engine for job expansion.

The Potential for Trade

The MENA region should be trading a lot more than it does. Policy reforms that remove some of the key barriers to trade and investment, discussed in more detail in other chapters, should allow the region to achieve its potential and spur much faster growth in output, jobs, productivity, and wages. No other area is as ripe for the picking as trade is in this region.

Nonoil exports. The simplest starting measure of trade potential is the gap in the performance of nonoil exports. Total nonoil exports of the MENA region amounted to about US$28 billion in 2000 (excluding reexports). For a middle-income region with nearly 300 million people and with good re-

FIGURE 1.12

Agricultural Employment Is High in Water-Scarce MENA, 1980–98

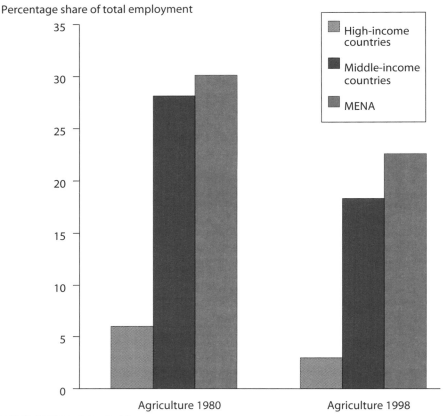

Percentage share of total employment

Legend:
- High-income countries
- Middle-income countries
- MENA

Sources: Staff estimates and country data.

source endowments, this is a small fraction of its potential. Finland, with 5 million people, has almost twice the nonoil exports of the entire MENA region. And the Czech Republic and Hungary, with populations of about 10 million, each had greater nonoil exports than the region.

Nonoil exports of the MENA region are vastly smaller than those from other subregions with similar populations and resource endowments. For example, a group of five Eastern European countries—the Czech Republic, Hungary, Poland, Russia, and Turkey, with a similar population of 270 million—had nonoil exports of US$151 billion, five times more than MENA's. Three Southeast Asian countries—Indonesia, Malaysia, and Thailand—had nonoil exports of US$197 billion, seven times more than MENA's. And four Latin American countries—Bolivia, Brazil, Chile, and Mexico—had nonoil exports of US$213 billion, eight times more than MENA's (figure 1.14).

FIGURE 1.13

Private Service Employment Is Low, 1980 and 1998

Percentage of total employment

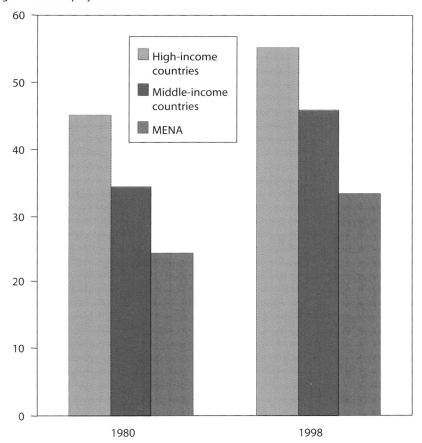

Sources: Staff estimates and country data.

The analytical basis for such a comparison can be extended more carefully by conditioning per capita nonoil exports on per capita incomes (as a proxy for overall skills and institutional endowments capacity to export)—and on natural resource endowments (measured by the value of resource-based exports, mainly oil and minerals) and population. For some 42 mostly middle-income countries (including the MENA countries), the results suggest a strong positive association of per capita nonoil exports with per capita incomes, and a negative association with natural resource endowments and population size. That is expected, because higher skills and institutional endowments should support higher exports, while greater natural resource rents should show up in less intensity of effort to export nonnatural resource exports (figure 1.15). And larger countries tend to

FIGURE 1.14

Trade Potential of Nonoil Exports, 2000

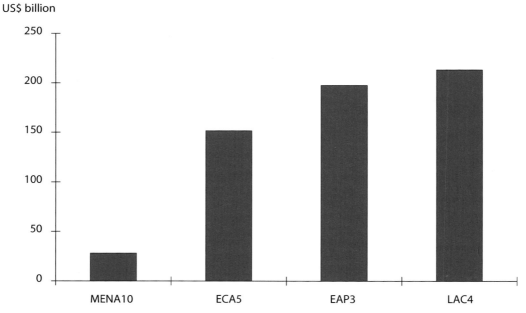

US$ billion

Note: EAP3 = three countries (Indonesia, Malaysia, and Thailand) in the East Asia and Pacific region; ECA5 = five countries (the Czech Republic, Hungary, Poland, Russia, and Turkey) in the Europe and Central Asia region; LAC4 = four countries (Bolivia, Brazil, Chile, and Mexico) in the Latin America and Caribbean region; MENA10 = Algeria, Egypt, the Islamic Republic of Iran, Jordan, Lebanon, Morocco, Saudi Arabia, Syria, Tunisia, and the Republic of Yemen.
Sources: Staff estimates and World Bank 2003a.

trade less. For the MENA countries, their nonoil exports are, on average, one-third of their predicted levels. Only Jordan and Morocco had exports close to what would be predicted. The world's three biggest underperformers are MENA countries (Algeria, Egypt, and the Islamic Republic of Iran), and the other MENA countries are all underperformers.

Manufacturing imports. Trade has impacts much bigger than is captured by simply looking at export performance. When firms can get imported inputs at world prices and quality, the knowledge embodied in goods and services is transferred from the rest of the world to the domestic economies—the productivity and knowledge then enhances spillover of trade. When consumers can buy goods and services produced more efficiently in the rest of the world, they benefit from lower prices and better quality. But the largest benefit of trade is that it allows countries to specialize in the production of goods and services that rely more intensively on its most abundant resource—for MENA, labor—and import more of its least abundant resource—for MENA, capital and (increasingly knowledge-intensive) goods and services. Barriers that impede

FIGURE 1.15

MENA Nonoil Export Potential, Conditioned on Per Capita Incomes, Natural Resources, and Population, 2000

(actual-to-predicted nonoil merchandise exports, per capita US$)

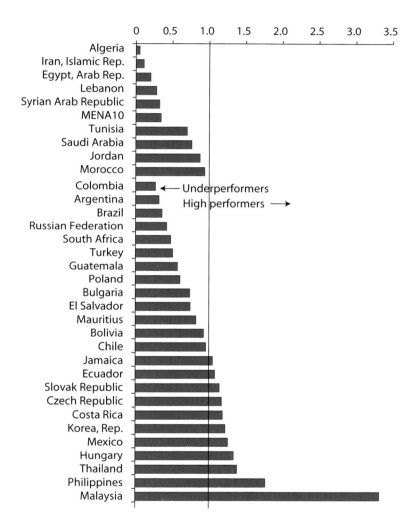

Note: Regression is based on 42 countries, but values for 8 low-income countries (Bangladesh, Cameroon, Côte d'Ivoire, Ghana, India, Indonesia, Pakistan, and the Republic of Yemen) are not reported because of negative values. The regression equation is as follows: PCNOXs = −134.3 + 0.19*GDPPPPPC − 0.54*PCNatRes − 74.7*Log(Pop); Adj R^2 = 0.60; Sample Size 42. MENA10 = Algeria, Egypt, the Islamic Republic of Iran, Jordan, Lebanon, Morocco, the Republic of Yemen, Saudi Arabia, Syria, and Tunisia.
Sources: Staff estimates and World Bank 2003a.

trade therefore impede potential gains in knowledge, consumer welfare, and labor productivity.

That is why it is important to measure the trade potential of the region more broadly than by simply looking at export performance, but also by focusing on imports. The relative openness of countries to imports can be measured by comparing actual imports versus a predicted level of imports conditioned on per capita incomes (where a higher level of incomes should be associated with a higher level of imports) and population (to the extent that larger countries tend to trade less). For the same group of 42 mostly middle-income countries, per capita manufacturing imports of the MENA region were about half of their predicted levels in 2000, confirming again that the region trades far less than its potential (figure 1.16). Once again, Algeria, the Islamic Republic of Iran, and Syria have extremely low actual levels of imports, implying relatively closed trade regimes. Other countries also fall surprisingly below predicted levels, including Egypt, Jordan, Morocco, Saudi Arabia, and Tunisia. Only Lebanon is more open than expected.

Results of gravity models. Gravity models, based on geographical factors such as distance to major markets, reinforce the findings described above. MENA trades much below its potential (see box 1.5).

The special role of tourism. Countries in the MENA region, given their antiquities and world heritage sites, climatic advantages, natural attractions, and proximity to a high-income region, should be well placed to benefit from tourism. Tourism receipt averages in recent years have been more than US$4 billion a year in Egypt (27 percent of total exports), US$2 billion in Morocco (20 percent of total export earnings), about US$1.5 billion in Tunisia (17 percent of total export earnings), and some US$0.7 billion each in Jordan and Lebanon (20 percent and 35 percent of total export earnings, respectively). These levels are among the highest in the world relative to total exports. Yet Algeria, the Islamic Republic of Iran, the Republic of Yemen, Saudi Arabia, and Syria receive flows of tourism far below their potential (figure 1.17). Even in the current high-tourism countries, the numbers of arrivals and their spending are below potential. For example, the Czech Republic, Hungary, and Poland together receive some US$12.5 billion annually in tourism receipts (compare with US$9 billion for Mexico and US$6 billion for Indonesia annually). As everywhere, tourism is vulnerable to safety and security issues, followed by the quality of services. In the next 10 years, if conflict in the region can be reduced sharply, the prospects for tourism remain good and will boost employment. The reforms in trade and investment will benefit tourism both directly and indirectly.

The Potential for Foreign Direct Investment

The MENA region, excluding the Gulf countries, received net inflows of FDI of about US$2.2 billion in 2000—slightly more than 1 percent of

FIGURE 1.16

MENA's Import Potential, Conditioned on Per Capita Income and Population, 2000
(actual-to-predicted manufacturing imports, per capita US$)

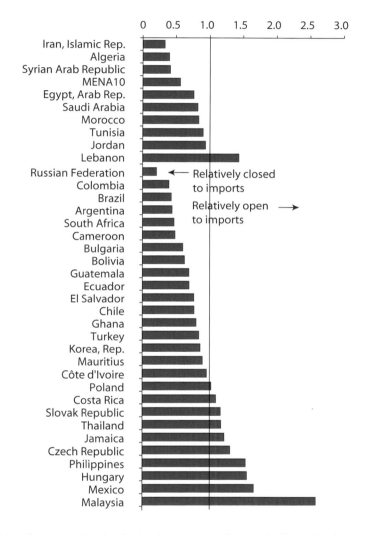

Note: Regression is based on 42 countries; values for 6 low-income countries (Bangladesh, China, India, Indonesia, Pakistan, and the Republic of Yemen) are not reported because of negative values. The regression equation is as follows: PCMgM = 237.5 + 0.14*GDPPPC − 124.8*Log(Pop); Adj R^2 = 0.65; Sample Size 42. MENA10 = Algeria, Egypt, the Islamic Republic of Iran, Jordan, Lebanon, Morocco, the Republic of Yemen, Saudi Arabia, Syria, and Tunisia.
Sources: Staff estimates and *WDI*.

the US$158 billion to all developing countries, and one-sixth of their share (7 percent) in the GDP of all developing countries. The group of five Eastern European countries (the Czech Republic, Hungary, Poland, Russia, and Turkey) together received some US$19 billion, nine times more than MENA. The three East Asian countries (Malaysia, the Philip-

BOX 1.5

What Geography-Gravity Models Show

Per capita incomes, natural resources, and size are not the only factors that drive trade. Given its close proximity to Europe, a major developed region, the MENA region should be trading a lot. Smaller countries tend to trade more with the rest of the world, and geographic proximity to high-income neighbors encourages trade. Distance from major industrial country markets is less than for other major regions, with a long coastline and well-developed shipping and transport arrangements (across the Mediterranean). The region's low incomes and wages raise the opportunities for convergence through trade with high-income neighbors in the EU and elsewhere (Ben-David, Nordstrom, and Winters 1999).

These factors therefore suggest a considerable potential for trade within and between the region and the outside world, especially Europe. A formal test of this potential is to apply a gravity model of trade, which combines some of the main factors identified above (although not the relative wage factor because of data and quality comparison difficulties) plus other proximate ones. According to this model, the trade flows between any two pairs of countries (bilateral trade) should be affected by their economic size (or GDP), by the distance between them (affecting transport and transaction costs), and by such other factors as exchange-rate volatility, common currency, common colonial history, trade agreements, common borders, physical size, population, whether landlocked or not, and telecommunications services (as a proxy for services generally) (Nugent 2002). The conclusion is that practically all countries in the MENA region—Algeria, Egypt, Islamic the Republic of Iran, Jordan, Morocco, Tunisia, and some of the Gulf countries—are large underachievers in trade (see figure below). They trade far less than their potential, both with each other and with their most important neighbor and trading partners in the EU and North America. No other region has as big a gap as MENA in potential and actual trade.

With its main trading partners—the EU and the United States (or NAFTA countries)—actual trade in MENA was 16 to 17 percent, or one-sixth, of predicted nonoil trade.

Within the MENA region, trade was better, rising significantly in 1992–97, but it still remained substantially below expected levels, especially when compared with that expected under existing trade agreements.

The Maghreb and Mashrek subregions trade little with each other and their main external trade partners. Only the GCC countries showed high and rising trade with the MENA region and with each other. But even for the GCC countries, the actual trade with the EU was only one-quarter of what would be expected.

BOX 1.5 (continued)

MENA Trade Potential: Actual-to-Predicted Trade from Gravity Model, 1992–97
(actual–to–predicted trade ratios)

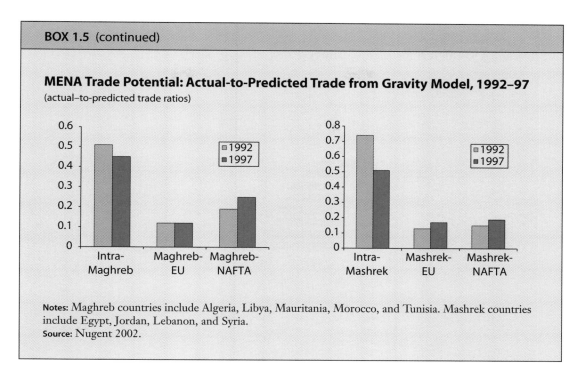

Notes: Maghreb countries include Algeria, Libya, Mauritania, Morocco, and Tunisia. Mashrek countries include Egypt, Jordan, Lebanon, and Syria.
Source: Nugent 2002.

pines, and Thailand) received more than US$8 billion in inflows, four times more than MENA. And the group of four Latin American countries (Bolivia, Brazil, Chile, and Mexico) received about US$50 billion, more than 22 times the inflows to the MENA region. These comparisons provide some indication of the huge potential for expanding inflows of FDI to the MENA region. A large part of these inflows came from (neighboring) high-income Europe.

Egypt accounted for about half the MENA total (US$1.2 billion), and Jordan and Tunisia about a quarter each (US$750 million and US$560 million, respectively). The rest received small amounts or even had significant outflows (the Republic of Yemen).

The potential for higher inflows by country can be determined by conditioning FDI inflows on nonoil trade performance (measured by ratios of nonoil exports to PPP GDP), natural resources, and population. FDI inflows are known to be closely related to trade flows, so the predicted levels of FDI should be associated with trade. Natural resource endowments often also lead to higher levels of foreign investment, albeit of a different type of flows. And size may matter, with larger countries expected to receive higher investment inflows (market-seeking investments); but because this is already accounted for by measuring FDI inflows relative to GDP, the residual population variable may or may not be significant. The results for 42 countries are pretty much in accord

FIGURE 1.17

Actual versus Predicted Tourism Receipts, 2000

(actual-to-predicted per capita tourism receipts, US$)

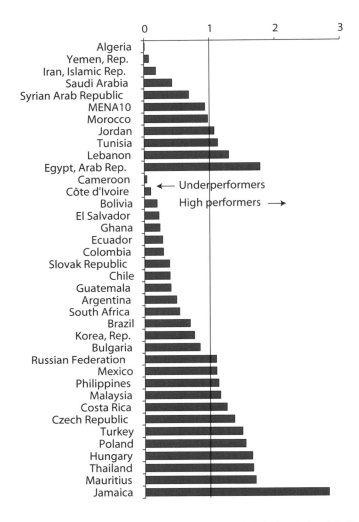

Note: Regression is based on 42 countries; values for 5 low-income countries (Bangladesh, China, Indonesia, India, and Pakistan) are not reported because of negative values. The regression equation is as follows: PCTourism = 172.7 + 0.012*PCGDPPP – 43.6*Log(Pop); Adj R^2 = 0.45; Sample Size 42. MENA10 = Algeria, Egypt, the Islamic Republic of Iran, Jordan, Lebanon, Morocco, the Republic of Yemen, Saudi Arabia, Syria, and Tunisia.
Source: Staff estimates.

with expectations: trade and natural resources raise FDI flows, but size turns out to be a negative influence.

How do the actual inflows of FDI to MENA countries look in relation to expected inflows, once nonoil trade, natural resources, and population are factored in? First, only Jordan, Lebanon, and Tunisia (small, resource-poor countries) do as well or slightly less than expected (figure

FIGURE 1.18

Foreign Direct Investment Potential, Conditioned on Openness, Natural Resources, and Population, 2000

(actual-to-predicted net foreign direct investment, per capita US$)

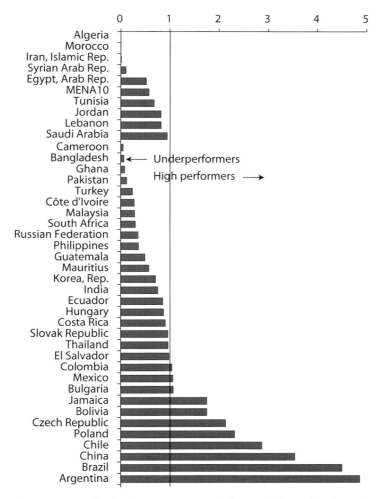

Note: Regression is based on 42 countries; values for 2 low-income countries (Indonesia and the Republic of Yemen) are not reported because of negative values. The regression equation is as follows: FDIPC = 76 + 0.07*NOXPC + 0.04*NRXPC − 10.9*Log(Pop); Adj R^2 = 0.27; Sample Size 42. MENA10 = Algeria, Egypt, the Islamic Republic of Iran, Jordan, Lebanon, Morocco, the Republic of Yemen, Saudi Arabia, Syria, and Tunisia.
Source: World Bank 2003a.

1.18). Morocco is a surprise in how little it receives in FDI inflows (at least for 1998–2000); Egypt receives more, possibly given its larger size, but still well below expected levels. Second, among the countries with large natural resource endowments, Saudi Arabia is the only country that receives relatively high FDI led by its oil sector. All the larger oil-producing countries (Algeria, the Islamic Republic of Iran, the Republic of

Yemen, Syria) receive very low FDI relative to expected levels. Third, for the MENA countries as a whole, FDI inflows are only about half what they should be receiving. In comparison, Chile receives three times as much FDI as expected, and the Czech Republic twice as much. Others such as Argentina, Brazil, and China receive FDI inflows four to five times their expected levels. The FDI gap for MENA also shows investment climate barriers in these countries, since the gap in potential already takes into account their low nonoil trade. If their nonoil trade were higher and if the investment climate were better, the region should expect FDI inflows at least five to six times the current level—or some 3 percent of GDP on average, compared with the current 0.5 percent of GDP. This level would be expected, without even being at the high-achieving end for many other fast-integrating countries (such as Chile and the Czech Republic).

Potential Impact on Growth and Productivity

Greater trade liberalization and expansion will be expected to lead to faster growth (and faster job creation). In the 1990s rapidly integrating developing countries achieved per capita growth of about 5 percent a year, nearly twice the growth in high-income countries (figure 1.19). In contrast, nonintegrating developing countries, such as many of those in the MENA region, experienced slow per capita growth, and as a group even negative growth, in the 1990s. The link between trade integration and growth is reasonably robust (Dollar and Kraay 2001; Frankel and Romer 1999). If MENA countries can integrate rapidly with the global economy, growth is expected to pick up—and with it, aggregate employment. MENA countries need employment growth of at least 4 percent a year to make a dent on existing unemployment and employ the increments to the labor force (Nabli and Keller 2002), which are rising by 3.4 percent a year.

It may be prudent to assume that the region will achieve only half of its trade and more of its investment potential over 10 years. This would raise the nonoil export ratio of the region from about 6 percent of its GDP to about 13 percent by the end of 10 years—reaching roughly half the average ratio of nonoil exports to GDP of all developing countries today. The nonoil export growth rate underlying this scenario is about 15 percent a year, nearly twice the expected world export growth, but the climb in MENA's share of that market remains small because of the low starting levels. Merchandise imports, now 20 percent of GDP, would also be expected to rise by about 7 percentage points over the decade (with incremental financing of additional imports from higher nonoil exports and higher FDI).

FIGURE 1.19

Fast-Integrating Countries Grow Faster, 1990s

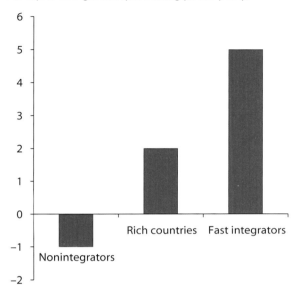

Per capita GDP growth (purchasing power parity)

Source: Dollar and Kraay 2001.

The effect would be to raise the merchandise trade ratio from about 46 percent of GDP (2003) to about 58 percent over a decade (2013)—and nonoil merchandise trade from about 26 percent of GDP to about 39 percent. The increase in the nonoil merchandise trade ratio over the decade would be a substantial gain and about half of the average (100 percent) increase for fast-integrating developing countries in the 1990s (Dollar and Kraay 2001). FDI inflows are correspondingly assumed to rise by some 2.5 percentage points of GDP, and private productive investment rates (inclusive of FDI) by some 7 percentage points of GDP (from the current 12.5 percent of GDP to about 20 percent of GDP).

These broad assumptions are useful for calibrating the likely impacts on growth and productivity with an aggregate source of growth model. The MENA region has three basic sources of growth (other than exploiting oil or other nonreproducible assets more intensively):

- Deepening capital investment per laborer.

- Deepening human capital per laborer.

- Increasing total factor productivity.

If policies are reasonably successful in achieving the trade and investment outcomes described above, and a reasonably modest turnaround in productivity growth of about 1.4 percent a year is achieved as a result of greater trade, the net effect would be to raise annual growth from about 1.4 percent per capita in the 1990s to about 4 percent per capita in the coming decade (table 1.1). This growth is consistent with the experience of other countries in the world, where correspondingly faster growth was achieved with greater trade and investment orientation (World Bank 2002).

The 1990s were marked by a fall in capital per laborer in MENA primarily because of low and falling rates of growth in private investment relative to the growth of the labor force. With gains in trade intensification and major improvements in the investment climate, faster growth in private domestic investment and FDI are expected to lead to a significant improvement in capital deepening. Given a fast-expanding stock of labor force (of about 3.4 percent a year), achieving such gains will be difficult but critical. Historically, capital per laborer increased in the MENA region by as much as 7.9 percent per annum in the 1970s (driven by public investment); it slowed to 2.1 percent per annum in the 1980s; and it collapsed to negative levels in the 1990s. Therefore, business climate reforms to elicit a more robust private investment response are likely to be central to the success of trade reforms in the MENA region. Moreover, the shift this time from public to private investment will be critical.

Improving total factor productivity also is a key driver of growth. It is reasonable to hypothesize that the total factor productivity gains from opening trade and investment would be significant. Opening trade would

TABLE 1.1

Potential for Faster GDP Growth, Accumulation, and Productivity from Trade and Investment Climate Reforms in MENA, 2003–13

(percentage per annum per laborer, except when noted)

Category	Physical capital		Human capital		Total factor productivity		Growth of GDP per labor (labor force weighted)		Growth of GDP per capita	
	1990s	2003–13	1990s	2003–2013	1990s	2003–13	1990s	2000–13	1990–2000	2003–13
MENA	−0.3	2.4	1.2	1.2	−0.2	1.4	0.7	3.0	1.4	4.3
East Asia	8.4	—	0.7	—	3.2	—	7.0	—	7.1	—
South Asia	3.3	—	0.9	—	0.9	—	2.7	—	3.2	—
Organisation for Economic Co-operation and Development (OECD)	2.0	—	0.6	—	0.4	—	1.6	—	2.1	—
World	4.8	—	0.7	—	1.6	—	3.9	—	4.7	—

—Not projected.
Notes: All growth estimates by regions and world are labor force weighted. GDP per capita growth rates differ from GDP per labor growth rates because of differences between labor force and population growth rates.
Source: Staff estimates.

improve productivity by encouraging shifts in resources to more productive and internationally competitive activities (the stock effect), by improving the access to higher-quality inputs (Coe, Helpman, and Hoffmaister
1995), and by spillovers from FDI and greater competition. Edwards
(1997) points to the robustness of substantial positive impact of trade on
productivity. The gains from trade openness should be substantial, as evident from a sample of 42 developing countries, with an additional 1 percent of GDP originating from such productivity gains in fast-integrating
countries in the 1990s (compared with 0.6 percent in slow-integrating
countries) (figure 1.20). The relationship between total factor productivity
gains and openness—other significant drivers were initial levels of productivity and education, which should also help the MENA region—was
strong and significant. Historical experience of individual countries confirms the total factor productivity and growth enhancing effects of reforms
(figure 1.21) in Indonesia and Mexico, both oil producers. For the next
decade for MENA, therefore, it is reasonable to assume that total factor
productivity gain of 1.4 percent per laborer will be achieved, reversing the
negative total factor productivity growth in the previous two decades, as
the economies open up to trade and private investment.

Substantial employment effects can be expected from GDP growth of
about 6 percent annual rate resulting from faster trade integration and

FIGURE 1.20

Total Factor Productivity Change, 1980s to 1990s

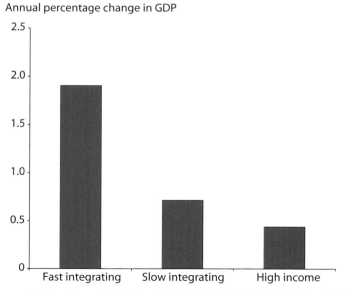

Annual percentage change in GDP

Note: The regression equation is as follows: $\Delta TFP90\text{--}80 = -1.32 + 1.03INTGDUM^{**}-0.4InitialTFP70^{**} + 0.16$ Education*; Adj $R^2 = 0.29$; N = 42 Countries.
Source: Staff estimates.

FIGURE 1.21

Trade and Investment Reforms Boost Total Factor Productivity and Growth

(contributions to growth in percentage points)

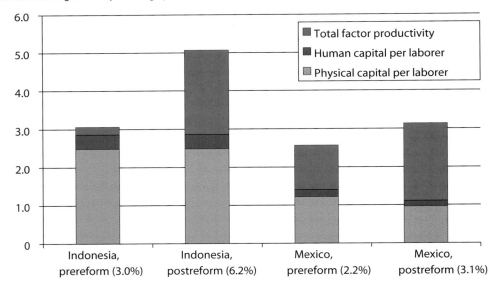

Notes: For Indonesia, prereform period is 1983–87 and postreform period is 1987–92. For Mexico, prereform period is 1988–94 and postreform period is 1995–2000. Annual GDP per laborer growth rates are given in parentheses in x-axis labels.
Source: Staff estimates.

improvement in the investment climate. Faster GDP growth will itself generate equivalently faster growth in employment. However, the technological progress and productivity growth assumed will mean that the gains will be distributed more widely and that employment growth will therefore be at a slower pace. Moreover, likely real wage increases will also dampen employment growth as firms respond to higher wages. Offsetting these pressures will be greater labor intensity of production driven by greater trade orientation of the production structure. The net effects of these factors are a resulting employment growth of between 4 and 4.5 percent a year. This would be adequate to absorb the new entrants to the labor force and to cut unemployment rates by half over the next decade.[2]

Exporting more merchandise goods and manufactures will create new jobs. In just the next five years, if the MENA region can achieve 15 percent real annual nonoil export growth for the region through improved policies, this would boost the region's nonoil exports to about US$60 billion, from the present level of US$28 billion (excluding reexports). And this could generate some 2 million additional jobs directly in such nonoil export activities, and another 2 million indirectly, from domestic goods and services supply inputs to these activities and from the multiplier effects on domestic final demand. So closing even a small part of the export gap could generate about 4 million jobs over five years from direct trade effects alone. This simplified projection abstracts from a much more complex set of factors, but the magnitude is indicative of the potential.

Other examples abound of the effects of expanding trade on jobs. For Mexico, thanks to NAFTA and radical economic reforms, trade more than tripled, from US$82 billion in 1990 to about US$280 billion in 1999, making it the seventh-largest trading nation in the world. The pace of job creation has been particularly swift in manufacturing (box 1.6).

Job creation has also been strong in export processing zones in the Dominican Republic, El Salvador, and Mauritius (Rama 2001). Indonesia is another country in which a major trade and investment policy reform produced employment benefits in the mid-1980s. Manufactured exports and FDI boomed, as did manufacturing employment (figure 1.22). Indonesia is especially relevant to some MENA countries. It was a resource-dependent economy until the mid-1980s, when it found a new engine of growth in manufactured exports (Iqbal 2002). Within the MENA region, Tunisian exports of textiles and clothing have boomed in "offshore companies" supplying foreign markets, and employment in these industries increased steeply. Morocco is another example of a country that gained significantly from an initial burst of economic reforms in the early 1980s. Manufacturing sector employment and exports rose sharply in the early 1980s in response to a series of trade and investment liberalization measures (figure 1.23). But the Moroccan boom faltered in the 1990s as the impact of the initial reforms package dissipated and macroeconomic effects allowed the real effective exchange rate to appreciate, hurting exports.

Cross-Country Evidence

Analysis of 59 developing countries—including about 140 observations, spanning five-year periods from the early 1960s to the late 1990s—reveals a positive medium-term association between employment in industry (as a share of the total working-age population) and openness to trade (figures 1.24–1.26). Productive capacity—measured by the economywide capital-to-labor ratio—turns out to be a significant factor affecting industrial employment across countries. Differences in real labor costs in manufacturing—measured in common currency—also explain variations in employment ratios across countries. All else equal, a 10 percent increase in real labor costs lowers the industrial employment ratio by an estimated 2 to 3 percent on average. High real interest rates also appear to depress industrial employment—although in a statistically less robust way.

BOX 1.6

Export Growth and Employment Generation in Mexico—the NAFTA Effect

When the Mexican administration was negotiating NAFTA in 1993, one of the strongest arguments put forward was Mexico's potential for job creation as a response to export expansion. It also was hoped that trade openness would encourage productivity growth and that these efficiency gains would lead to higher and more equitable growth through the creation of jobs. Structural reforms, launched in 1985, laid the groundwork for Mexico's NAFTA membership and fundamentally changed the business landscape.

The centerpiece of reforms was trade liberalization, beginning with Mexico's entry to the General Agreement on Tariffs and Trade (GATT) in 1986, then slashing Mexico's average applied tariffs to 13.3 percent in 1993–95 from 24.1 percent in 1984–85. There is little question that NAFTA boosted Mexico's exports. Its share of (strongly growing) U.S. imports nearly doubled, from 5.4 percent in 1985 to 10.2 percent in 1998. The United States was traditionally Mexico's main trading partner, but links became even closer after the trade reform. Of all Mexican export revenues, 60 percent were earned in the United States in 1980, compared with 85 percent in the mid-1990s.

Since NAFTA, Mexico has one of the highest concentrations of trade in a single market destination in the world. But along with the trade intensification with the United States, a major shift occurred in the composition of Mexican exports, fostering diversification out of oil and toward manufactures. In 1985 oil exports accounted for 55 percent of total Mexican exports; in 1999 they accounted for only 7 percent. At the same time, exports of manufactures increased from 38 percent of total exports to 90 percent. *Maquiladora* (foreign-owned assembly plants in Mexico) and non-*maquiladora* manufacturing firms shared equally in the export boom, each accounting for about half of total Mexican manufactured exports before and after NAFTA. Metal products and machinery (including automobiles and auto parts) were the biggest beneficiaries, accounting for almost 70 percent of all manufactured exports in 1998, with exports of automobiles in 1997 matching oil exports.

Shortly after its accession to NAFTA, Mexico suffered a financial crisis resulting in a sharp depreciation of the peso. The

crisis hurt manufacturing employment, but the depreciation of the peso boosted competitiveness. So in the years after the Mexican crisis, manufacturing employment rebounded strongly (see box figure). And the upturn was sustained. From 1985 to 1993, manufacturing employment grew by 8 percent a year on average, but it grew by more than twice that from 1994 to 1999, after the implementation of NAFTA.

Source: World Bank staff.

FIGURE 1.22

In Indonesia Exports Have Promoted Employment in Manufacturing

(employment in manufacturing and manufacturing exports/GDP)

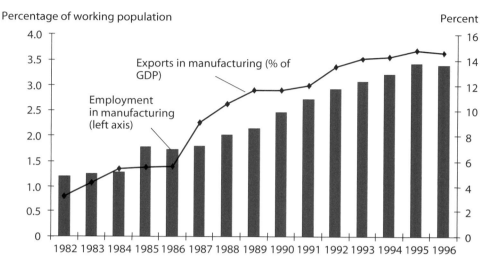

Source: Staff calculations.

FIGURE 1.23

The 1980s Saw a Sharp Increase in Manufactured Exports and Employment in Morocco

(employment in manufacturing and manufacturing exports/GDP)

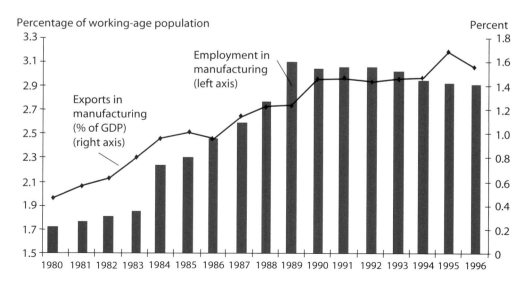

Source: Staff calculations.

FIGURE 1.24

Trade Openness Is Associated with Higher Industrial Employment
(employment in industry, as a ratio of total working-age population, in logarithm)

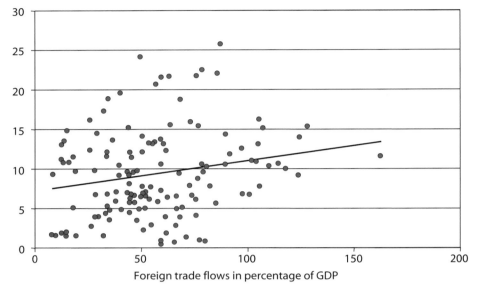

Foreign trade flows in percentage of GDP

Source: World Bank staff.

When accounting for the structural factors that explain differences in industrial employment across developing countries, greater openness to trade turns out to contribute to significantly higher employment ratios in the medium term (figure 1.25). This is true for traditional measures of trade openness (foreign trade as a share of GDP) and for various measures of export performance—as, for example, nonoil merchandise exports as a share of GDP (figure 1.26). The medium-term benefits of trade expansion for employment could thus be substantial, as described earlier. Higher employment and incomes in industry also would boost domestic expenditure in nontradables, so the second-round multiplier effects from trade expansion could further contribute to economywide job creation.

Agricultural exports also will create substantial new jobs. Chapter 6 discusses at some length the issues in the sector, including the potential shift to more efficient and less water-intensive crops such as fruits and vegetables. These shifts in cropping patterns also will tend to be much more labor-intensive than the current ones, both in the production process

FIGURE 1.25

The More So When Accounting for Other Structural Factors that Affect Employment

(employment in industry after controlling for factors other than nonoil merchandise exports, as a ratio of total working-age population, in logarithm)

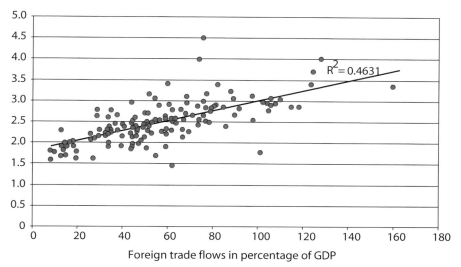

Foreign trade flows in percentage of GDP

Source: World Bank staff.

FIGURE 1.26

Nonoil Merchandise Exports Also Directly Boost Industrial Employment

(employment in industry after controlling for factors other than nonoil merchandise exports, in percentage of total working-age population)

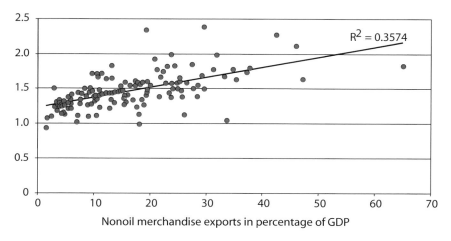

Nonoil merchandise exports in percentage of GDP

Source: World Bank staff.

and in the postharvest, transport, processing, and marketing stages. The net job creation effects in aggregate will tend to be small because agriculture as a whole will probably lose jobs in the transition to other sectors, because of the already high employment in the sector with relatively low productivity and the scarcity of water resources. But without the creation of new jobs in export crops, this structural shift will become even more difficult. Consequently, the opening of agricultural market access in EU markets is an especially critical issue. Results from the accession of Portugal and Spain to the EU show dramatic gains—agricultural exports to the rest of the EU that became three times larger after unrestricted market access with accession—that suggest how important the effects might be for the MENA region for new agricultural exports, and jobs, that result from improved market access.

Expanding and liberalizing services will create more jobs and raise incomes and productivity. The MENA region already is a heavily service-oriented economy. But formal services are dominated by low-productivity government services and jobs, at twice the average for most other middle-income developing countries. These low-productivity jobs also tax the rest of the economy, because of service conditions and the bureaucratic controls they impose on productive activities. Services also are dominated by small, informal, low-productivity sectors, such as retail trade, distribution, housing, and construction.

Few of the service jobs are in high-productivity and fast-growing sectors critical to trade expansion such as transport, telecommunications, infrastructure, finance, private education, health, and information technology. An examination of models for Egypt and Tunisia suggests that services liberalization, when combined with merchandise trade liberalization, will yield welfare gains (or faster growth) some 30 to 40 percent greater than goods trade liberalization alone because of the productivity-enhancing effects (Hoekman and Messerlin 2002). Moreover, the employment effects are likely to require far less adjustment because employment expansion effects dominate in services relative to manufacturing and agriculture.

The Critical Role of Investment Climate

The potential gains from trade integration in terms of faster growth and especially employment are, however, critically dependent on the private investment response, which, in turn, depends on improvements in the investment climate. MENA has not benefited from an improved investment climate so far, especially in manufacturing. The success of a new trade integration model will rest heavily on such an investment climate change. It is already built in to the projections on gains in growth, productivity, and employment described in the preceding sections.

A better investment climate would allow domestic investment to rise in traded goods sectors. Trade liberalization also would allow large international corporations to use cheaper labor in MENA countries and locate processing plants there, through direct investment. Both effects of the investment climate change multiply the effects of trade liberalization on jobs. It is important to illustrate why this matters.

Because of the lack of adequate measures of investment climate change and the investment response, the inflow of FDI can stand as a reasonable proxy for the overall investment climate—and a measure of the supply response to trade reforms (figures 1.27 and 1.28). Analysis similar to that shown earlier splits the observations in the sample into different groups: developing countries with large FDI inflows, and small FDI recipients, with the cutoff at the sample median of 0.7 percent of GDP. While the impact of trade expansion on employment in manufacturing is highly significant in the group of large FDI recipients (figure 1.27), the estimated coefficients of trade turn out to be not significant in the other group of countries that receive only small amounts of FDI (figure 1.28). This is true whatever the indicator of trade in the regressions.

Potential Impact on Women's Participation

The shift from an old to a new growth model also will gain from greater participation of women and benefit them in turn, provided the formidable barriers to women's participation are removed. During the past two decades, women have accomplished or are in the process of accomplishing two key transitions: fertility reduction and education gains. The third key transition that needs to follow is employment and labor market participation. Increased women's participation is critical in MENA. Women represent a huge, untapped resource, whose greater economic participation could lift aggregate growth and productivity in the countries of the region over and above the earlier projections. The effect could be as much as adding 0.6 to 1.0 percentage point to aggregate per capita growth if women's participation improved even modestly. It also would directly lift the prospects for successful trade and investment, by strengthening the quality of the labor force for newly competitive and fast-growth-potential industries, such as information and communication technology (ICT) or tourism and other services, because of often better education and skills profiles. And it would improve the overall sustainability of the development process with more visible gains and rising incomes for women. The potential economic and social impacts and benefits are thus large indeed.

FIGURE 1.27

Investment Climate Matters: Trade Creates More Jobs in Developing Countries that Attract Large Amounts of Foreign Direct Investment

(employment in industry after controlling for factors other than nonoil merchandise exports, as a ratio of total working-age population)

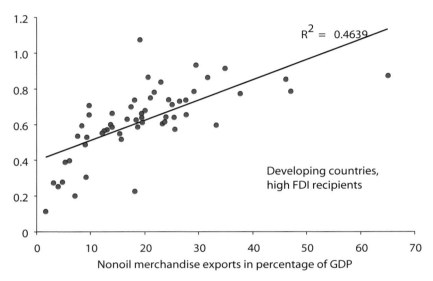

Source: Authors' calculations.

Women's participation and employment would potentially benefit (box 1.7) from trade and investment climate reforms. Experience around the world suggests that women often gain a large proportion of the jobs that are created from more open and competitive trade and investment climate reforms. Private enterprises in traded sectors around the world often prefer to employ women because of their lower wages (given the gap that exists in MENA that is larger than in other parts of the world) and higher skills and productivity. Women's entry into entrepreneurship and small businesses also is likely to be a key driver of new start-ups, businesses, and activities, key to the new model of growth from trade and investment reform. The experience of MENA is likely to be no different from the rest of the world in these directions—provided the still considerable economic and social barriers to women's participation are addressed. A companion volume will address gender issues in more detail.

To maximize these gains, complementary measures will need to address many constraints to an increased women's role in labor markets, in the small business sectors, and in entrepreneurship activities. In many parts of the Middle East, laws fundamentally discriminate against women by constraining their conditions for employment, restricting their ownership of productive resources, or limiting their rights to travel and free

FIGURE 1.28

But Trade Expansion Does Not Significantly Add to Jobs When Foreign Direct Investment Is Low or Investment Climate Is Weak

(employment in industry after controlling for factors other than nonoil merchandise exports, as a ratio of total working-age population, in logarithm)

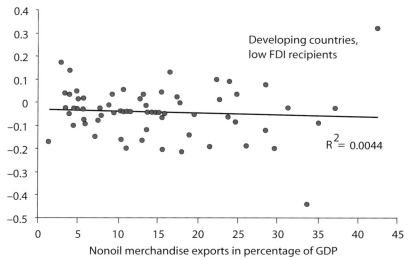

Source: Authors' calculations.

movement. Evidence suggests a gender-differentiated impact of trade liberalization; whether it is positive or negative depends on the initial conditions of the economy, the sectoral distribution of men and women in the labor market, the sexual division of labor in the households, and supply- and demand-side constraints (El-Kogali and Nizalova 2003). One example of weakness is that, of the region's 170,000 active clients of microfinance lending—indicative of small business participation—fewer than half were women. Even within this region, the differences are striking between high participation (between 80 and 100 percent) in Lebanon, Morocco, and the West Bank and Gaza, and far lower rates in Egypt, Jordan, or the Republic of Yemen. The process of trade and investment impetus will therefore require a more gender-aware and country-specific approach when analyzing the impacts of trade reform. This will permit the design of mitigating measures to counter any adverse consequences (such as possible downsizing and restraints on public sector employment, which has traditionally provided the main source of jobs to women; or in agriculture, in which negative impacts of restructuring could be large, as is discussed more fully in chapter 6). It also will permit countries to address key constraints to encourage wider participation and gains for women's employment. Further research is needed

BOX 1.7

Do Women Benefit from Trade Expansion?

Trade expansion has been associated with a rise in women's labor force participation in export-processing industries in Asia, Europe, and Latin America and the Caribbean and in export agriculture in Africa (UNIFEM 2002). Similarly, traded services—such as data entry, financial services, and tourism—often have a high proportion of women (Fontana, Joekes, and Masika 1998). Younger, educated women benefit more than men from employment gains in the initial stages of trade expansion, which could have wider benefits for women's sense of autonomy, status in the household, and incentives to invest in female education (Joekes and Weston 1994). The experience of NAFTA and Mexico is illustrative. Research suggests that NAFTA has favored job creation in sectors where women have traditionally played an important role. Overall, women's share of employment in *maquiladora* industries in Mexico has remained well above one-half.

The experience of the MENA region is expected to be no different, provided traditional norms do not hold back women's participation. Strengthening of working conditions will allow women to gain even more from trade expansion opportunities.

The gains to women's participation from trade expansion, so far mostly in garments and textiles, are already evident in Egypt, Jordan, Morocco, and Tunisia. But traditional, male-dominated norms may have held back some potential gains to women in Egypt, in contrast to Morocco (Assad and El-Hamidi, forthcoming). Other research in the region suggests that women may lose from trade liberalization if it is accompanied by significant downsizing in public sector jobs, which have had a larger share of jobs reserved for women, while private enterprises still often do not employ women. Agriculture also represents an important sector in which structural transformations from trade could have both positive and negative consequences (discussed in chapter 6).

on a number of issues, including a better understanding of the barriers to labor mobility, access to specific labor market segments, impacts of liberalization, and burdens on time management.

Conclusion: Trade, Investment, and Employment

Trade intensification is likely to be a key source of growth in the MENA region in the next decade. Most important, it has the potential to generate millions of new jobs for a rapidly growing, young labor force. Trade also is likely to be relatively skill intensive, suited to the changing characteristics of educated youth entering labor markets of this region. And it can be a powerful instrument to improve female participation in labor

TABLE 2.1

Characteristics of Natural Resource Endowments

Resource endowment	Number of countries	Cropland (ha/hd)	Per capita GDP growth, 1970–93	Rents as a percentage of GDP, 1994		
				Total	Cropland	Mining
Resource poor						
Large	7	0.15	3.7	10.6	7.3	3.2
Small	13	0.16	2.1	9.9	5.4	4.5
Resource rich						
Large	10	0.56	1.3	12.7	5.8	6.9
Small						
Nonmineral	31	0.57	0.7	15.4	12.9	2.5
Hard-mineral	16	0.66	−0.2	17.5	9.6	7.9
Oil exporter	8	0.44	0.8	21.2	2.2	19.0
All countries	85	0.48	1.1	15.0	8.8	6.3

Note: Resource-poor in 1970 (cropland per head < 0.3 hectares, large = 1970 GDP > US$7 billion). ha/hd = hectares per head.
Source: Auty 2001, pp. 4 and 131.

mostly large net exporters of labor.[1] They either have no natural resources, or have some limited natural resources (oil or minerals). Most of the countries in this group have generally had better trade performance than other low- and middle-income countries in the region.

- *Labor-abundant, resource-rich countries.* Algeria and the Islamic Republic of Iran have large populations and are resource rich. The Republic of Yemen and Syria also are resource rich, with smaller populations.[2] All four countries are net exporters of labor. They have generally had the weakest trade performance of all low- and middle-income countries in the region, suggesting the dominant effect of natural resource availability in determining trade orientation.

- *Labor-importing, resource-rich countries.* Bahrain, Kuwait, Oman, Qatar, Saudi Arabia, and the UAE, constituting the GCC countries, are all large net importers of labor and extremely resource-rich countries.[3] They have generally been the more successful trade integrators in the region, reflecting their smaller size and higher incomes.

The typology is not watertight. For instance Egypt is much larger (in absolute size) and relatively more labor abundant, but also has some significant natural resources including oil and Suez Canal revenues (and benefits from strategic aid inflows, which are large). Similarly, Saudi Arabia has structures more similar to larger, resource-abundant countries because of its larger size. But it remains a large net labor importer. The very-low-income countries, Djibouti and the Republic of Yemen, probably belong to a separate subclass, with very low endowments of capital per worker.

Trade Outcomes

Trade integration outcomes have product dimensions (goods and services) and factor dimensions (labor and capital flows), with some traditional substitution effects. But the globalization of production and the emergence of intraindustry trade can make factors and products complementary. This section focuses on trade in goods, while later sections of this chapter discuss the factor channels of integration and services.

Failing to Ride the Wave of Global Trade Integration

The recent globalization of trade is neither new nor complete.[4] Globalization, measured by trade-to-GDP ratios, rose through much of the 19th century and the first 25 years of the 20th century (figure 2.1). It collapsed because of the world wars, the prolonged depression, and the raising of national trade barriers, falling to a low of near 5 percent of GDP by the late 1940s. Only by the mid-1970s did global trade recover to the heights of the early part of the 20th century. After remaining flat for the next decade—hindered by the adjustment to oil shocks—trade integration resumed in the mid-1980s. It is far short of its full potential, reaching only 13 percent of GDP in the United States.

In the 1950s MENA trade was higher than the world average, but it has since moved in the opposite direction (figure 2.2). MENA's oil resource boom helped realize high initial export-to-GDP ratios—and high GDP growth rates. But with the windfall revenues invested at home in infrastructure and services, the export-to-GDP ratio declined steadily. The sharp gain in the terms of trade in 1973–85, when real oil prices quadrupled, merely accelerated the already declining trend because of the cutbacks in exports of oil required to sustain higher oil prices. Since 1985, when world trade accelerated, the MENA region has only arrested its decline. Small oil exporters in the GCC have had some success in diversifying their export base (Bahrain, Oman, and the UAE). But for the resource-poor exporters (Egypt, Jordan, Morocco, and Tunisia) and the larger and resource-rich countries (Algeria, the Islamic Republic of Iran, Syria), the pace of trade integration continued to slide.

Trade has fallen from about 100 percent of GDP in the mid-1970s to about 60 percent in the late 1980s, and has since remained stagnant (figure 2.3). In contrast, most other regions show sharply rising trade ratios after the mid-1980s. Note too that Africa and MENA both share relatively high starting trade ratios because of their oil and natural resource exports. Once oil is excluded, trade integration is lower still. The nonoil

FIGURE 2.1

Long-Term Trends in World Trade Integration

Export-to-GDP ratios

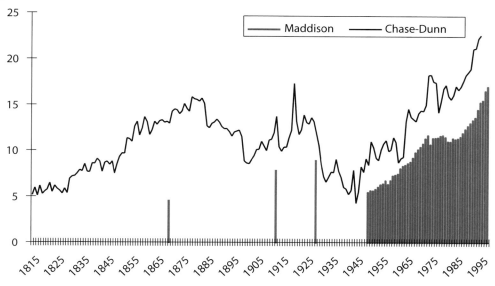

Note: From Maddison, export-to-GDP ratio in constant 1990 PPP prices is used. From Chase-Dunn, population-weighted aggregate of export-to-GDP ratio in local prices is used.
Sources: Data from Chase-Dunn, Kawano, and Brewer 2000; Maddison 2001; WTO 2001.

trade-to-GDP ratio fell from about 53 percent of GDP in the early 1980s to 43 percent by 2000 (and the changes in this period are similar to those for total trade).

There is some divergence in outcomes within the MENA region but not much (figure 2.4). The class of labor-abundant, resource-poor, and relatively diversified economies (Egypt, Jordan, Morocco, and Tunisia) generally does better than the labor-abundant but resource-rich countries (Algeria, the Islamic Republic of Iran, Syria), the latter experiencing a major and continuous decline in their trade openness ratios. The labor-importing, resource-rich GCC countries generally maintain a higher level of openness. But there is still a large neighborhood effect of declining or stagnant trade integration affecting the entire region's trade outcomes.

Another way to describe the declining trade integration of MENA countries is through the speed of integration, which simply measures the difference between the growth of real trade and the growth in GDP. A positive index suggests accelerating trade integration (higher values indicating faster integration), while a negative index suggests countries

FIGURE 2.2

Long-Term Trends in Trade Integration, World and MENA

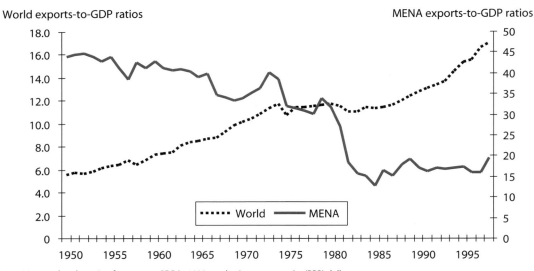

Note: Measured as the ratio of exports to GDP in 1990 purchasing power parity (PPP) dollars.
Sources: For PPP GDP, Maddison 2001; for exports, WTO and International Monetary Fund's (IMF) *International Financial Statistics* for current dollar values. Volume measures are constructed by weighting oil and nonoil share of exports (available from World Bank sources) with world oil price and U.S. consumer price index (CPI).

where trade integration is falling. All regions other than the MENA region showed a positive acceleration in trade integration in the 1990s, and only the MENA region showed a persistent decline in trade integration in the 1990s (table 2.2). The divergences between the three country types also are evident.

High Degree of Product and Geographic Concentration

The progress in product diversification, measured by a product concentration index, has been slow (figure 2.5). Although MENA country exports have become more diversified, fuels continue to be the most significant exports. In 1978, 94 percent of exports were fuels and related products, and the share had fallen to only about 82 percent by 2001. The labor-abundant, resource-poor producers (Jordan, Morocco, Tunisia) have done best (table 2.3). Tunisia and Morocco have seen a large fall in their trade product concentration, comparable to or better than that in Chile or Malaysia. Lebanon and Jordan, already well diversified, saw further declines in the concentration. Egypt's apparent diversification is largely a reflection of newer oil and gas finds and exports from the Sinai—not of underlying better diversification performance. The diver-

TABLE 2.4

Geographic Destination of Middle East and North Africa Countries' Exports in 2000

	Exports as percentage of total exports											
Country	World (U.S.$ million)	All industrial countries	Industrial Europe	North America	Asia and Pacific	All non-industrial countries	Africa	Asia	Europe	Middle East	Latin America	Area not specified
All MENA	254,295	53.6	26.1	9.4	18.1	46.4	1.7	28.0	2.4	6.8	1.3	6.1
Labor abundant, resource poor	22,459	65.4	56.1	6.7	2.1	30.9	2.5	8.6	3.1	9.7	1.4	9.2
Labor abundant, resource rich	57,870	57.2	41.4	7.0	8.8	42.8	0.7	20.5	5.4	5.5	3.1	7.7
Labor importing, resource rich	161,278	48.0	11.6	11.4	25.0	52.0	1.9	35.5	0.9	7.3	0.8	5.6
ECA4	29,102	74.8	68.2	68.2	0.7	23.9	1.2	2.2	16.4	3.3	0.9	1.5
EAP5	129,287	54.5	15.5	21.1	18.2	45.3	1.3	36.7	1.6	2.6	2.6	0.2
LAC4	66,892	60.1	19.1	36.5	5.4	37.9	1.4	8.4	1.3	2.3	24.6	1.3
All developing countries	2,075,378	53.9	23.7	17.2	13.0	46.1	1.7	28.7	6.3	5.1	4.2	0.1

Note: EAP5 = five countries (China, Indonesia, Malaysia, Republic of Korea, and Thailand) in the East Asia and Pacific region; ECA4 = four countries (Czech Republic, Hungary, Poland, and Turkey) in the Europe and Central Asia region; LAC4 = four countries (Argentina, Brazil, Chile, and Mexico) in the Latin America and Caribbean region.
Source: IMF 2001.

the nearly 68 percent of Eastern European country exports that go to Europe. In the labor-abundant, resource-rich countries, that ratio falls to about 40 percent. For the labor-importing, resource-rich countries of the GCC, the European share is even lower (only 12 percent of total), with Japan and the rest of Asia as their single largest destination of exports, primarily for oil.

Fewer Dynamic Export Products

Dynamic products are defined here as exports that exceed annual growth of 15 percent at the three-digit level, roughly about twice as fast as overall growth in world exports in the period. A decline in number of items that qualify as dynamic exports from the MENA region is evident, from 84 to 66 between 1988 and 2000 (table 2.5). Algeria, Egypt, Kuwait, Lebanon, Morocco, Oman, and Tunisia have been losing their presence in the dynamic products list for the past two decades, while the Islamic Republic of Iran, Syria, and the UAE have been gaining. The resource-poor countries are traditionally the largest contributors, but their share of dynamic export products has fallen (by half). The lowest contribution is from the labor-abundant, resource-rich countries, whose share has been stagnant (without the Islamic Republic of Iran, there would have been a large decrease). The same is true for the high-income GCC countries (without the UAE, there would have been a drastic decrease). Overall, there has been a steady loss of dynamism. Dynamic products accounted for about 9.8 percent of nonfuel exports in 1988 and 9.4 percent in 1995. But by 2000 the corresponding figure was 2.6 percent, indicating the loss of importance for dynamic export products in MENA nonfuel exports (figure 2.6).

Intraregional Trade Remains at Low Levels

Comparative data also suggest that MENA countries trade little with each other (Al-Atrash and Yousef 2000). Intraregional trade has remained at low levels, despite many formal trade agreements to promote such trade. Among other regional groupings it has increased, in many cases dramatically, as in the Andean Pact countries, Southern Cone countries, and NAFTA countries (table 2.6).

TABLE 2.5

Country Frequency of Dynamic Nonfuel Exports, 1980–2000

Country	1980–88	1988–95	1995–2000
Algeria	9	1	0
Bahrain	2	0	2
Egypt, Arab Rep. of	6	13	7
Iran, Islamic Rep. of	1	3	6
Jordan	0	2	1
Kuwait	3	1	0
Lebanon	5	3	2
Libya	0	1	0
Morocco	15	15	5
Oman	3	0	0
Saudi Arabia	14	13	12
Syrian Arab Rep.	0	0	2
Tunisia	18	18	11
United Arab Emirates	8	10	17
Yemen, Rep. of	0	1	1
MENA Total	84	81	66
Labor abundant, resource poor	44	51	26
Labor abundant, resource rich	10	5	9
Labor importing, resource rich	30	24	31

Source: Staff estimates.

FIGURE 2.6

Falling Growth and Shares of Dynamic Nonfuel Exports in MENA

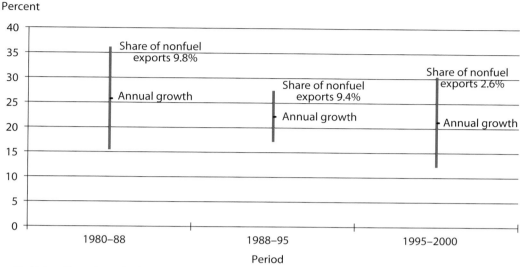

Percent

Note: The high and low points in the figure are defined as ranging from half a standard deviation above and another half below the average growth rate for each period (36 percent to 15 percent in 1980–88, 27 percent to 17 percent in 1988–95, and 30 percent to 12 percent in 1995–2000).
Source: Staff estimates based on World Integrated Trade Solution (WITS) Database (UNCTAD and World Bank 2002).

TABLE 2.6

Trends in Intraregional Trade, 1970–98
(share of total exports)

Category	1970	1975	1980	1985	1990	1995	1998
MENA countries	5.2	4.9	4.5	7.8	9.4	6.7	8.2
Andean Pact countries	1.7	3.6	3.5	3.1	4.0	11.3	11.4
Australia and New Zealand	6.1	6.1	6.4	7.0	7.6	9.9	8.6
Southern Cone countries	11.4	11.1	14.3	6.7	10.6	21,6	25.5
East Asia	19.2	21.3	22.4	20.7	20.7	26.4	22.2
NAFTA	36.0	34.6	33.6	43.9	41.4	46.2	51.0
EU	59.5	57.7	60.8	59.2	65.9	62.4	56.8

Note: Andean Pact countries include Bolivia, Colombia, Ecuador, Peru, and República Bolivariana de Venezuela. Southern Cone countries include Argentina, Bolivia, Brazil, Chile, Paraguay, and Uruguay.
Source: Al-Atrash and Yousef 2000.

Foreign Direct Investment and Global Production

Low and Stagnant FDI Flows

Accompanying the shrinking trade integration picture are low FDI inflows into the region from the rest of the world. Integration with global
private capital flow markets also has been relatively stagnant, in sharp
contrast to comparable country groups. Net FDI inflows to MENA
(measured as a share of PPP GDP) were consistently less than half a percentage point of GDP for most of the period (figure 2.7). In the early
1980s this put MENA roughly on par with comparable groups. But in
the next 15 years, the average of the other comparators had risen to between 1.0 and 2.5 percent while MENA continued to trail at about 0.5
percent.

Low and Slowly Rising Base for Intraindustry Trade

The recent poor record in capital flow integration (FDI inflows) has also
been accompanied by a modest share in intraindustry trade, typically led
by FDI. Intraindustry trade, the fastest rising portion of global trade, allows countries to specialize in production chains and seek comparative

FIGURE 2.7

Net Foreign Direct Investment Flows to MENA and Other Regions

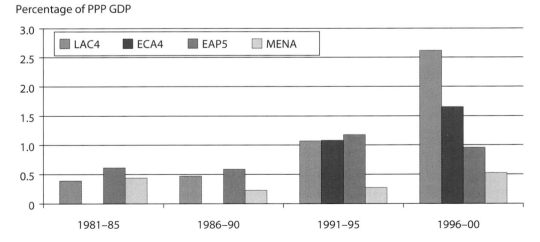

Notes: EAP5 = five countries (China, Indonesia, Malaysia, the Republic of Korea, and Thailand) in the East Asia and Pacific region; ECA4 = four countries (the Czech Republic, Hungary, Poland, and Turkey) in the Europe and Central Asia region; LAC4 = four countries (Argentina, Brazil, Chile, and Mexico) in the Latin America and Caribbean region.
Source: World Bank 2003

advantage in specific parts of those chains. It also produces extra gains from international trade because a country can reduce the number of similar goods it produces and reach economies of scale with higher productivity and lower cost. Its level can thus be considered to indicate a country's ability to exploit international trade integration more fully. MENA's share of intraindustry trade is low for all manufactures, at 13.5 percent in 2000 (table 2.7). Compare that figure with an intraindustry trade share of 77.3 percent for NAFTA in 1992–94, 90 percent for the Asia Pacific Economic Cooperation (APEC) region, and 89 percent for the EU (Havrylyshyn and Kunzel 2000).

TABLE 2.7

Intraindustry Trade Ratios for MENA Countries, 1988 and 2000

Country	Chemicals		Machinery and transport		Other manufactures		All manufactures	
	1988	2000	1988	2000	1988	2000	1988	2000
Algeria	0.086	0.066	0.037	0.012	0.135	0.064	0.077	0.035
Bahrain	0.032	0.064	0.248	0.089	0.286	0.334	0.237	0.180
Egypt, Arab Rep. of	0.058	0.131	0.027	0.070	0.203	0.353	0.090	0.181
Iran, Islamic Rep. of	0.015	0.160	0.019	0.027	0.021	0.116	0.019	0.075
Jordan	0.060	0.121	0.096	0.090	0.100	0.270	0.089	0.159
Kuwait	0.043	0.078	0.095	0.069	0.033	0.063	0.063	0.069
Lebanon	0.104	0.056	0.079	0.052	0.369	0.296	0.262	0.168
Libya	0.119	0.066	0.025	0.028	0.006	0.041	0.034	0.042
Morocco	0.132	0.115	0.139	0.319	0.156	0.218	0.145	0.242
Oman	0.022	0.146	0.336	0.095	0.173	0.246	0.257	0.144
Qatar	0.035	0.021	0.053	0.073	0.038	0.099	0.044	0.069
Saudi Arabia	0.180	0.141	0.171	0.089	0.064	0.190	0.132	0.131
Syrian Arab Rep.	0.021	0.052	0.012	0.035	0.064	0.191	0.035	0.109
Tunisia	0.125	0.093	0.282	0.361	0.253	0.287	0.237	0.292
United Arab Emirates	0.135	0.215	0.102	0.152	0.123	0.318	0.116	0.228
Yemen, Rep. of	0.003	0.013	0.034	0.052	0.012	0.010	0.018	0.029
MENA	**0.073**	**0.096**	**0.110**	**0.101**	**0.127**	**0.193**	**0.116**	**0.135**
Labor abundant, resource poor	0.096	0.103	0.124	0.178	0.216	0.285	0.165	0.208
Labor abundant, resource rich	0.031	0.073	0.025	0.032	0.058	0.095	0.037	0.062
Labor importing, resource rich	0.083	0.120	0.152	0.096	0.086	0.183	0.122	0.128
Memo items								
Brazil	0.581	0.565	0.483	0.620	0.198	0.436	0.381	0.555
Chile	0.337	0.371	0.048	0.153	0.309	0.449	0.181	0.300
Korea, Rep. of	0.468	0.562	0.483	0.579	0.309	0.544	0.401	0.568
Malaysia	0.416	0.742	0.682	0.649	0.433	0.537	0.588	0.636
Taiwan, China	0.510	0.589	0.605	0.630	0.247	0.420	0.432	0.571

Note: The Intra-Industry Trade Index (IIT) is calculated in the products at the SITC three-digit level as follows: IIT = 1 – SUM_{ij} [|X_{ijk} – Mij_k| / sum (X_{ijk} + M_{ijk})] where X_{ijk} and M_{ijk} represent the exports and imports of products from industry in country (j) to country (k), respectively. The index ranges between zero and one, with larger values indicating a greater level of trade between firms in the same industry. The higher IIT ratios also suggest gains from specialization in different products are being exploited and that the participating country is increasing its integration into the global economy. The classifications of product groups are defined as chemicals (SITC 5), machinery and equipment, and transport equipment.
Source: Staff estimates based on *UN COMTRADE Statistics*.

Except for Morocco, Tunisia, and the UAE, other MENA countries have intraindustry trade ratios of less than 20 percent (Yeats and Ng 2000). The resource-poor countries had the highest levels and a fairly rapid pace of change. But almost all of this was being driven by rapid gains in Jordan and Morocco, while Tunisia stagnated. The levels are far lower than those in Brazil, the Republic of Korea, Malaysia, and Taiwan, China (all above 50 percent) and comparable only to Chile. The lowest levels were evident for the labor-abundant, resource-rich countries, at about 6 percent in 2000, although the trend was rising. For the oil-producing GCC countries, the intraindustry trade index has fallen in machinery and equipment, standing at only about 12 percent in all manufactures. Some countries have seen a large decline in the ratio (Bahrain and Oman), while three others have remained virtually static (Kuwait, Qatar, and Saudi Arabia).

Little Participation in Global Production Sharing

The region as a whole has a large, negative trade balance with OECD countries in trade in parts and components (US$14 billion), with imports accounting for about 15 times the value of exports to these countries. In contrast, China and Malaysia had exports of parts and components to the OECD that are twice as large as their imports. The MENA region thus participates little in global production sharing, exporting primarily low-value finished goods, and importing parts and components for an inefficient and large manufacturing base—typical of inward-looking, import-substitution industrial bases (table 2.8). All three country types show stagnant ratios in exports of parts and components, with some improvement for the GCC countries. In contrast, China's and Malaysia's shares have gone up 4- to 10-fold.

Tourism and Trade in Services

Underperforming in Global Tourism

Tourism, the main service export of the MENA region, fluctuated between 3 and 4 percent of GDP during the 1990s (figure 2.8). Some other regions have done better. The Europe and Central Asia region, a competing destination for tourists from Europe, had a threefold increase in the share of tourism receipts to GDP, overtaking all other regions.

Also, while world tourism trade has expanded fivefold in the past 20 years, MENA's market share has declined from 3.4 percent in 1987 to around 2.6 percent in 2000 (figure 2.9).

TABLE 2.8

The Relative Importance of Parts and Components in MENA Countries

Country	Value of parts and components in OECD trade (US$ million)				Share of parts and components in all manufacture (%)			
	Exports		Imports		Exports		Imports	
	1988	2000	1988	2000	1988	2000	1988	2000
Algeria	6	7	943	994	2.6	2.8	23.5	18.7
Bahrain	39	24	156	208	19.6	6.9	18.1	16.5
Egypt, Arab Rep. of	19	54	1,279	2,142	4.3	3.1	23.5	24.7
Iran, Islamic Rep. of	8	18	941	1,311	1.7	2.2	21.1	25.6
Jordan	25	21	301	276	20.2	8.5	21.0	18.4
Kuwait	42	8	437	505	38.0	3.9	15.4	17.0
Lebanon	3	9	80	242	1.5	3.5	7.6	11.8
Libya	10	6	560	369	3.8	1.6	16.3	21.3
Morocco	33	105	421	1,231	2.1	2.5	14.4	19.2
Oman	22	45	208	330	8.3	14.0	15.2	18.8
Qatar	6	17	115	300	11.1	3.7	16.6	20.4
Saudi Arabia	73	213	1,941	3,298	3.6	7.1	13.5	19.0
Syrian Arab Rep.	1	9	148	338	4.5	2.7	16.2	21.5
Tunisia	72	332	330	859	5.5	7.4	15.8	14.4
United Arab Emirates	31	208	714	2,919	12.2	10.9	16.7	20.8
Yemen, Rep. of	2	1	61	105	47.0	6.7	15.5	19.6
MENA	391	1,078	8,635	15,430	5.2	5.7	17.1	19.9
Labor abundant, resource poor	151	521	2,411	4,751	4.2	4.7	18.6	19.3
Labor abundant, resource rich	17	35	2,094	2,748	2.4	2.5	21.4	21.9
Labor importing, resource rich	171	508	3,133	7,057	6.1	8.4	14.5	19.7
Memo items								
China	379	25,409	2,237	16,091	1.9	11.9	11.1	25.6
Japan	34,212	51,583	5,373	17,268	20.4	20.3	13.5	21.1
Korea, Rep. of	2,841	15,720	5,077	11,128	6.7	18.3	19.4	17.6
Malaysia	452	11,526	1,241	6,959	7.7	22.5	18.8	23.1
Singapore	4,425	9,584	4,492	10,877	32.8	23.4	25.1	22.9
Taiwan, China	5,231	21,369	4,265	11,208	11.5	24.3	17.2	17.1

Note: Parts and components are defined as 62 products in SITC at three- or four-digit level in Revision 2 (see details in Yeats and Ng 2000).
Source: Based on OECD data as reported from *UN COMTRADE Statistics.*

But with favorable endowment of world heritage sites, home to some of the world's key religions and civilizations, the tourism potential of the MENA region remains significant. Regional conflicts may have discouraged tourists from visiting in larger numbers, but infrastructure and marketing efforts have proved successful in some countries, such as Jordan.

Falling World Market Share of Trade in Other Services

The MENA region has also been losing world market shares in exports of nontourism services (figure 2.10). In contrast, comparators in both the East Asia and Pacific and Europe and Central Asia regions have more than doubled their world market shares.

FIGURE 2.8

MENA Tourism Receipts as a Share of GDP

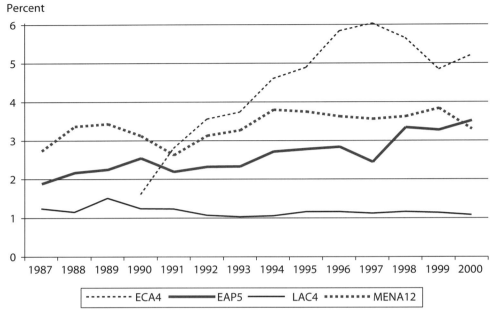

Notes: EAP5 = five countries (China, Indonesia, Malaysia, the Republic of Korea, and Thailand) in the East Asia and Pacific region; ECA4 = four countries (the Czech Republic, Hungary, Poland, and Turkey) in the Europe and Central Asia region; LAC4 = four countries (Argentina, Brazil, Chile, and Mexico) in the Latin America and Caribbean region; MENA12 = 12 countries (Algeria, Bahrain, Egypt, the Islamic Republic of Iran, Jordan, Kuwait, Morocco, Oman, Saudi Arabia, Syria, Tunisia, and the United Arab Emirates).
Source: World Bank 2003.

Labor Migration

While the integration of the MENA region through trade and investment channels has been stagnant or falling during the past two decades, its integration with the global economy through the mobility of workers across national boundaries has been substantial. Labor-abundant countries in the region, whether resource rich or resource poor, have seen an important share of their workers earn their living abroad. Labor migration has contributed to intraregional and interregional integration, creating two broad and distinct patterns of migration.

First, workers from Egypt, Jordan, Lebanon, the Republic of Yemen, Syria, and West Bank and Gaza have migrated to resource-rich GCC countries, predominantly Saudi Arabia.[5] These flows were prompted by the oil booms of the 1970s, which significantly boosted demand for manpower in oil-exporting countries. As a result, the share of foreign population rose significantly in the GCC countries over the 1970s and 1980s (figure 2.11).

FIGURE 2.9

World Market Share in Tourism Receipts

Percent

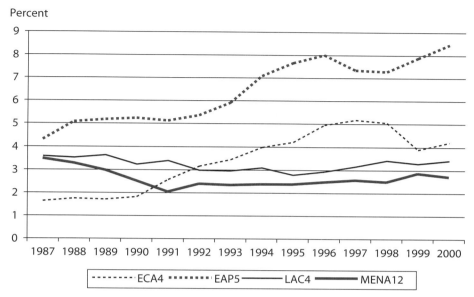

Notes: EAP5 = five countries (China, Indonesia, Malaysia, Republic of Korea, and Thailand) in the East Asia and Pacific region; ECA4 = four countries (Czech Republic, Hungary, Poland, and Turkey) in the Europe and Central Asia region; LAC4 = four countries (Argentina, Brazil, Chile, and Mexico) in the Latin America and Caribbean region; MENA12 = 12 countries (Algeria, Bahrain, Egypt, the Islamic Republic of Iran, Jordan, Kuwait, Morocco, Oman, Saudi Arabia, Syria, Tunisia, and the United Arab Emirates).
Source: World Bank 2003.

FIGURE 2.10

MENA Share of World Exports of Services

Percent

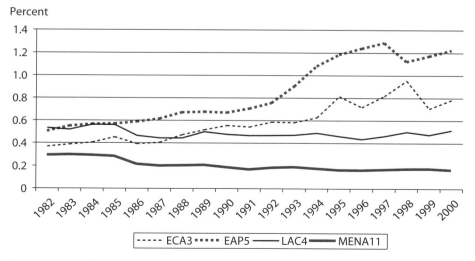

Notes: EAP5 = five countries (China, Indonesia, Malaysia, Republic of Korea, and Thailand) in the East Asia and Pacific region; ECA4 = four countries (Czech Republic, Hungary, Poland, and Turkey) in the Europe and Central Asia region; LAC4 = four countries (Argentina, Brazil, Chile, and Mexico) in the Latin America and Caribbean region; MENA11 = 11 countries (Bahrain, Egypt, the Islamic Republic of Iran, Jordan, Kuwait, Libya, Morocco, Oman, Saudi Arabia, and Tunisia).
Source: IMF, various years.

FIGURE 2.11

Foreign Population as Share of Total, GCC Countries, the EU, and the United States

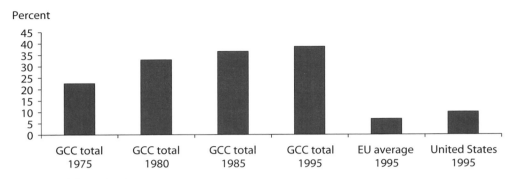

Percent

Source: World Bank data and Girgis 2002.

Second, workers from the Maghreb countries (Algeria, Morocco, and Tunisia) have left the region for Europe. During the industrial boom of the 1960s, several EU countries, such as Belgium, France, and the Netherlands, actively recruited workers from the Maghreb to occupy low-skill jobs in the industrial sector. As economic conditions deteriorated in Europe, immigration restrictions were tightened, but that only led to an increase in illegal migration, especially to southern Europe. Workers from the Maghreb now account for 20 to 40 percent of the foreign-born population in the European recipient countries (table 2.9).

So, where trade flows have been weak, migration has had an important impact on the sending countries—contributing to incomes and foreign exchange earnings from workers' remittances. It has provided an alternative to unfavorable labor market conditions at home. In addition, many migrants have returned home after some time, bringing back skills, experience, and savings for investment, all favoring the local economy (Diwan and others 2003; McGormick and Wahba 1997).

TABLE 2.9

Stock of Foreign Population by Nationality, as a Percentage of Total Foreign Population, Selected EU Countries, Latest Available Year

Country	Belgium	France	Italy	Netherlands	Spain
Algeria	1	17	—	—	—
Morocco	14	16	12	19	18
Tunisia	1	6	4	—	—
Maghreb total	16	39	16	19	18

—Not available.
Source: OECD 2001.

For labor, MENA is one of the world's more integrated regions. Workers' remittances make up a higher share of the economy (as measured by GDP) and of foreign exchange earnings (as measured by exports) in MENA countries than in comparator countries or regions (table 2.10).[6] Net migration rates—the number of immigrants minus emigrants—are also higher than elsewhere.

Despite migration's importance to MENA countries, it is not likely to continue to provide an alternative to trade and investment in the long run. Indeed, it appears to have peaked in the 1980s and leveled off since (figure 2.12). As a share of GDP, MENA remittance inflows peaked at 6 percent in early the 1980s and have since declined to less than 3 percent. Although remittance inflows could be affected by shifting portfolio choices of workers abroad that are influenced by policies of home and host countries, they can serve as an indicator of long-term trends in the migration of temporary workers.

Factor incomes, which includes payments for professional services, also declined sharply over the 1990s (figure 2.13). In Europe, high unemployment rates, pressures from inflows from other regions, and concerns about potential inflows from EU accession countries contributed

TABLE 2.10

Migration in the Economy, MENA and Selected Comparators

Country/region	Share of exports (percent)[a]	Share of GDP (percent)[a]	Net migration rate[b]
Algeria	8.5	2.3	−1.80
Morocco	20.1	6.3	−1.54
Tunisia	9.2	4.1	−0.84
Egypt, Arab Rep. of	23.5	3.8	−1.23
Jordan	52.2	21.8	−0.66
Syrian Arab Rep.	6.9	2.6	−0.16
Yemen, Rep. of	28.5	13.2	0.09
MENA excluding GCC[c]	21.3	7.7	−0.88
GCC[c]	—	—	5.91
Mexico	3.6	1.1	−3.26
Turkey	8.9	2.3	−0.85
Latin America and Caribbean	10.0	3.3	−1.60
Central and Eastern Europe[c]	12.5	2.8	0.12
South Asia [c]	11.7	1.4	−0.47
Sub-Saharan Africa [c]	5.3	0.8	1.58

—Not available.
a. Latest available period 1994–2000.
b. Average annual net migration per 1,000 inhabitants, 1995–2000: negative implies out-migration.
c. Unweighted regional average.
Source: World Bank data, U.N. 2002.

FIGURE 2.12

Workers' Remittances as a Percentage of GDP, Egypt and Morocco, 1970–2000

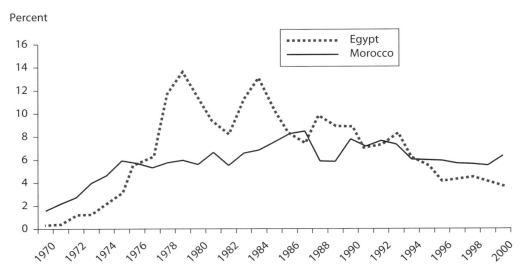

Source: World Bank 2003.

FIGURE 2.13

MENA Share in Factor Incomes

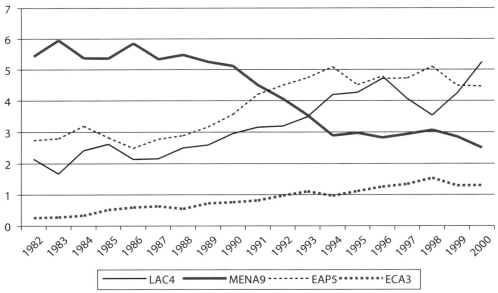

Note: LMIC is an aggregate of data for 63 available lower-middle-income countries.
EAP5 = five countries (China, Indonesia, Malaysia, the Republic of Korea, and Thailand) in the East Asia and Pacific region; ECA3 = three countries (Hungary, Poland, and Turkey) in the Europe and Central Asia region; LAC4 = four countries (Argentina, Brazil, Chile, and Mexico) in the Latin America and Caribbean region; MENA9 = nine countries (Bahrain, Egypt, Israel, Jordan, Kuwait, Morocco, Saudi Arabia, Syria, and Tunisia).
Source: World Bank data.

to a tightening of restrictions in European countries. Falling oil prices and rising unemployment among nationals in the GCC countries, combined with competition from cheaper, unskilled labor from Asian countries, are also limiting the potential for further regional integration through labor flows.

Structural and External Constraints to Trade Expansion in MENA

Explaining the disappointing outcomes described above, trade integration of MENA countries relative to others is determined by a set of complex factors that include structural features (distance from trade partners, size of internal market, natural resource abundance), international political environment (political conflicts in the neighborhood and partner-country trade barriers), and policy variables (protection, macroeconomic policy, and high behind-the-border costs, the latter extending to investment climate). While the role of policy variables in determining trade integration outcomes is discussed at length in the next chapter, here we briefly address the constraints imposed by natural resource abundance and the international political environment.

Resource Abundance and Trade

Natural resource abundance raises the share of nontraded goods and protected sectors, at the cost of the development of competitive traded goods and services sectors, as discussed in chapter 1. Two factors contribute to such a bias against trade. First, natural resources bid up the prices of nontraded goods and services and often result in overvalued exchange rates. Second, rent distribution often favors protection and an aversion to reform. However, there are successful examples of countries, such as Indonesia, Malaysia, and Mexico, which have overcome the disadvantages of natural resource and increased nonnatural resource exports, which shows that policies can effectively overcome a perceived curse. From the MENA region, Tunisia and the UAE may be cited as good examples of countries that achieved fast diversification away from oil, although they both began initially with export sectors dominated largely by natural resources.

Conflicts Impede Trade

Conflict and wars also impede trade (box 2.1). The MENA region has seen an unusually large number of conflicts over the past four decades—

BOX 2.1

Conflicts Impede Trade

Persistent conflict sharply reduces trade openness and growth. Frequent conflicts and militarization are related to the absence of a lasting peace settlement in the region, but also to several interstate and intrastate conflicts. These events raise the risk perceptions and decrease the willingness of both domestic and foreign sources to invest in the region. A recent comparative study of conflict-affected developing countries and a control group of countries not affected (Gupta and others 2002) suggests that the numerous effects include slower GDP growth, falling trade, sharply reduced tourism, rising macroeconomic consequences, large security expenditures, higher fiscal deficits and inflation, and the crowding out of education and health spending. The compounded effects appear to be a sharp slowdown in GDP growth in the preconflict stage (–1 percent GDP growth change) and an even sharper decline during conflict (–2 percent). Given the extent and duration of conflict in the MENA region, the effects are possibly even greater.

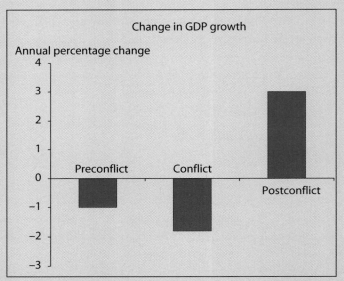

Other research suggests strong, contemporaneous, negative spillover effects of conflict on neighbors, with such effects as high as those of the conflict within a country, with the contiguity or nearness (length of common border) a key factor. These appear to work through general contagion as much as through other channels (such as trade or labor migration or capital flows. When conflict does end, there is a sharp rebound in economic activity (+3 percent GDP change)—signaling the positive effects that end of persistent conflict might have in the MENA region.

Ongoing staff research on the direct effects of conflict on trade in the MENA region is strongly supportive of the above findings: even taking policy, geography, natural resources, and other structural factors into account, conflict has a highly significant and persistent negative impact on trade (and growth). Moreover, there remain strong neighborhood impacts.

Sources: Gupta and others 2002; Ghezali and Lowi 2001; Mesquida and Wiener 2001; Murdoch and Sandler 2002.

some 14 years of civil conflict affecting 8 major countries, and some 15 years of cross-border regional and international conflicts affecting 14 countries (figure 2.14).

Partner-Country Trade Restraints

Even though the region enjoys natural proximity to high-income regions (Europe) and regional and other trade agreements, partner-country restraints impose some significant downsides to trade integration in three areas. The first is international sanctions, which have affected several countries in the region for relatively long duration, isolating them and affecting others in a strong neighborhood effect. The efficacy of sanctions and their costs—not just on the directly affected countries, but on a region as a whole—may need to be reassessed. Second, less than half the population of the MENA region benefits from WTO membership, an even worse level than in Sub-Saharan Africa. As of August 2002, 13 of the 21 MENA countries were members of the WTO, with 5 others in different stages of accession (Algeria, Saudi Arabia, and Lebanon have

FIGURE 2.14

Frequency of Conflict across Regions, 1945–99

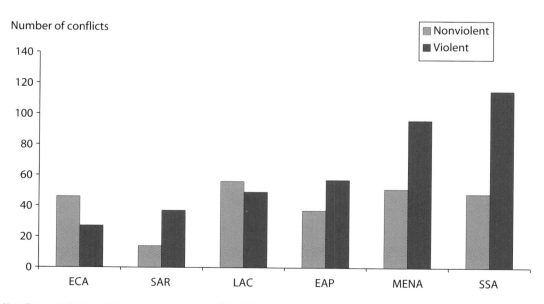

Note: Data available by conflict were mapped to standard World Bank regional classification. EAP = East Asia and Pacific; ECA = Europe and Central Asia; LAC = Latin America and the Caribbean; MENA = Middle East and North Africa; SAR - South Asia; SSA = Sub-Saharan Africa. For definition of violent and nonviolent conflicts refer to http://www.hiik.de/en/index_e.htm.
Source: Heidelberg Institute of International Conflict Research 2003.

working parties established, and Syria and Libya have submitted formal requests). Third, even in the regional trade agreements, exclusions for agriculture, services, and labor and difficult rules and procedures (rules of origin, standards) have often meant that agreements do not produce many results.

Conclusions

The MENA region has considerable diversity in country circumstances. But virtually all have lost ground sharply in global trade and investment integration. Only labor migration has been relatively strong, but even here, recent trends are downward.

Structural and external political factors, such as conflicts, sanctions, and partner-country-imposed constraints, are important in explaining some of the above outcomes. These have imposed significant costs.

But as is shown in the next chapter, policies remain central and can overcome these constraints. Indeed, a full econometric investigation of the interplay of structural, external, and policy factors in explaining cross-country trade performance, including in the MENA countries, suggests that such policies remain central—especially trade and investment climate policies. For example, in two countries sharing the same level of conflict incidence, differences in policies on trade protection and business start-up costs account for a large variation in trade performance. Recent evidence on vibrant export growth (near 20 percent a year growth between 2000 and 2002) in Jordan shows how a country that is heavily weighed down by conflicts or other structural factors in the neighborhood can still benefit from faster trade integration that is policy driven.

Notes

1. West Bank and Gaza would fit in this group, but data limitations have not permitted its inclusion in the analysis.

2. Iraq could be included with this group, but data are limited.

3. Libya would fit in this group too. The United Arab Emirates, a high-income country in World Bank classification, is included as part of the GCC.

4. Long-term evidence from global integration in prices and financial variables, as opposed to trade volumes, also confirms that globalization observed in recent history is actually reglobalization to the prewar

difficult macroeconomic imbalances, and it joined GATT in 1987. A series of wide-ranging reforms were implemented in most key sectors, centered on tariff reductions, exchange rate liberalization, tax reforms, financial sector liberalization, and privatization (Hamdouch 1998). In the 1990s, trade reforms continued with a Euro-Med agreement that it signed in 1996 as an anchor, and it has also implemented some reforms of behind-the-border institutions, including customs. Significant exchange rate overvaluation hurt progress in trade orientation but it has recently improved because of a gradual shift toward more flexible management of the exchange rate.

Jordan also belongs to the category of early, intensive, and steady reformers. Faced with large external shocks related to the collapse in oil prices and hence trade and remittances, Jordan began an early macroeconomic stabilization and structural reform program in the 1984–89 period, including trade, financial sector, and exchange rate reforms. It was resumed in greater depth in the aftermath of the Gulf crisis in 1991–92 when the return of workers from the Gulf and a sharp rise in external debt occasioned another bout of reforms. It has continued since, much stronger since the mid-1990s on trade, privatization, and private sector development. Jordan signed a Euro-Med agreement in 1997 and a free trade agreement with the United States in 2002.

Resource-poor countries have thus generally begun their reforms earlier and more consistently. However, in Egypt and Lebanon the pace has been much slower and the approaches more sporadic. Despite some earlier reform measures going back to the 1970s, **Egypt** began its most recent macroeconomic stabilization and structural reforms after the 1991 Gulf crisis when the limits of state-led development were reached and a major fiscal, debt, and current account crisis coincided. Reforms focused on fiscal and debt reduction and macroeconomic stabilization, along with trade reforms and privatization. In the late 1990s, however, reforms were reversed with significant exchange rate overvaluation coinciding with escalating behind-the-border trade restrictions in customs and standards, resulting in a sharp fall in trade orientation. More recently, reforms have resumed with reductions in tariff rates, the signing of a Euro-Med agreement in 2001, and—more significantly and recently—the floating of the Egyptian pound (in January 2003).

Lebanon too was unable to take advantage of its initially relatively open policies and its resource-poor environment during much of the 1990s. A part of the reason was conflict and its aftermath. Some 15 years of war and civil conflict (1975–90) left a legacy of massive destruction of physical and economic infrastructure and weaker institutions. Reconstruction expenditures and fiscal deficits since then have created large macroeconomic imbalances, which together with pegged exchange rate policies and high interest rates (to finance the growing fiscal deficits), have dramatically reduced the relative trade and investment integration of the country. Since 2000, the government has been attempting to reduce fiscal deficits, address the large debt overhang, reduce trade restrictions, and improve the climate for private investment—but it has a way to go. Lebanon signed a Euro-Med agreement in 2002.

Djibouti is in a special category because of its low income level, proximity to conflict and famine-affected areas, and few resources other than its port (and revenues and assistance related to foreign military facilities). Djibouti has maintained relatively open trade policies, and operates a free port that serves as an entrepot for Horn of Africa trade. However, weak institutions related to low incomes and a legacy of high civil service salaries continue to pose major difficulties in other policy areas, especially fiscal and macroeconomic positions and the investment climate—as do adverse neighborhood effects (such as refugees from conflict).

Later, More Gradual, Sporadic Reformers in Labor-Abundant, Resource-Rich Countries

Similar to the experiences in Egypt and Lebanon, but in some contrast to the more intensive early reformers in the resource-poor countries, are the later reformers in resource-rich Algeria, Islamic Republic of Iran, Republic of Yemen, and Syria. Reforms in these countries have been more gradual and sporadic. **Algeria** was faced with massive shocks in 1986 from the collapse of oil prices, and began some first, limited attempts at trade reform, which were strengthened over 1994–97. It began a large program, focusing on exchange rate adjustment, trade liberalization, domestic price liberalization, public sector reforms and privatization, public finances, social safety nets, and agricultural and housing sector reforms (Nashashibi and others 1998), but reversed itself significantly in 1998 by imposing a 60 percent surcharge on some imports against the backdrop of civil strife and political uncertainties. Mean tariffs hardly changed between the late 1980s and 1990s, according to Oliva (2000). Trade reforms restarted in 2001 and 2002 in the context of efforts to gain WTO membership and to support Algeria's Euro-Med association agreement, which it signed in 2001. Algeria has reduced tariffs, cut maximum tariffs, and simplified structures. The temporary tariffs of 60 percent are being phased out over five years, starting with a 12 percent reduction in 2002. The Euro-Med agreement that Algeria signed in December 2001 envisages a gradual reduction of tariffs on industrial products over 12 years. Private sector investment and participation in housing, water, and energy are also proceeding.

The **Islamic Republic of Iran's** reform efforts began after the end of the 1988 Iran-Iraq war within the framework of its first and second five-year plans—in the areas of foreign exchange, reducing quantitative trade restrictions, relaxing price and quantity controls, and moving toward trade liberalization. However, attempts at exchange rate unification in 1993 failed, and distortions remained strong with the widening of dual rates and restrictions. After a deterioration in economic performance (average growth was less than 2 percent a year during 1995–2000), a severe compression of imports (to make room for external debt repayments as the Islamic Republic of Iran's access to external financing was severely restricted), and effects of economic sanctions since 1996, macroeconomic reform and structural adjustment was again initiated in 1998. Reforms have centered on exchange rate unification, which has since been accomplished, and on extensive trade reforms by replacing nontariff barriers with tariffs, cutting tariffs sharply, removing export restrictions, and replacing overlapping sales taxes with a value added tax (VAT) (Karshenas 1998; World Bank 2001). The Islamic Republic of Iran also significantly adjusted energy prices recently, although subsidies remain high. Banking and regulatory reforms remain largely stalled (World Bank 2003c).

In **Syria**, a significant trade and investment liberalization episode started in 1991 with liberalization of domestic and foreign trade, accompanied by initially encouraging results (augmented by a major oil discovery). The efforts were not sustained, however, because of significant reversals in trade and investment policies, its continued multiple exchange rate system, extensive nontariff barriers, and regulatory and licensing bottlenecks to trade. By 2000, the government had once again resumed attention to trade and private investment climate reforms in the context of concluding bilateral (Euro-Med) and multilateral (WTO application) trade agreements—which included some modest progress toward unification of three exchange rates and some private sector regulatory reforms (World Bank 2002a).

The **Republic of Yemen** has faced major shocks since unification in 1990, including the Gulf war of 1991, the return of 1 million Yemeni migrant workers from the Gulf countries, and renewed civil war in 1994. Since 1995, the economy has recovered but remains highly dependent on oil, which accounted for about a third of GDP (in 2000), 76 percent of revenues, and 90 percent of export earnings. Policies toward trade are relatively open, and exchange rates are supportive, but the investment climate remains quite poor—which is reflected in weak rule of law and property rights, ineffective regulatory frameworks, and problems with security and conflict (World Bank 2002b). The government began to address these issues in 2000 in the context of its poverty reduction strategy.

Reforms in More-Open, GCC Countries

The six GCC economies have long maintained an open trade system, convertible currencies with fixed nominal exchange rates, free movement of capital, and large inflows of skilled and unskilled labor. In addition, their advanced financial systems have been an important catalyst for promoting their integration into the international economy. With the continued erosion of oil prices in the late 1980s, most countries initially implemented adjustment policies involving primarily cuts in expenditure, particularly capital outlays. Despite the expenditure cuts, and given the severity of the decline in oil revenue, aggregate budget deficits increased. This phase was interrupted by the Gulf crisis of 1990–91. The GCC countries emerged from the Gulf crisis in a weaker economic and financial position at a time when the resumption of the adjustment process was further complicated by the continued downward slide in oil prices and a slowdown in global economic activity.

Since 1995 most GCC countries have successfully intensified their adjustment efforts in response to an unfavorable oil market outlook, by introducing medium-term plans incorporating balanced budgets by the year 2000, as well as measures to promote private sector growth and human resource development. A number of GCC countries have encouraged growth in selected areas, such as entrepot trade (the UAE), financial services and tourism (Bahrain and the UAE). It is, however, important to distinguish the relatively greater success in policies to diversify growth among the smaller GCC countries, in comparison with others.

In the largest GCC country of **Saudi Arabia,** reform efforts began much later, in 1999, and have progressed more slowly. Although trade policies are open, production subsidies have been used extensively to protect a large, inefficient, domestic nonoil sector, often publicly owned. The country has begun to consider and in some cases implement a series of structural reform measures to give more responsibility to the private sector, liberalize trade and investment regimes, and generally diversify the economy. The main reform efforts include initiatives to join the WTO (not yet completed), privatize parts of the dominant state sector, improve the FDI climate (including the crucial hydrocarbon sector), and diversify tax revenues away from overreliance on volatile oil prices. In August 1999, the country established a Supreme Economic Council to accelerate reforms..

An accelerated program of customs union among all the members of the GCC has taken effect as of early 2003 with a low common external tariff of 5 percent—unifying tariff rates across the spectrum from the low tariffs of the UAE to the high tariffs of Saudi Arabia. This step has been an important landmark for the GCC, which was established in 1981 to integrate the member countries. Adverse trade-diversion effects are expected to be minimal because trade between GCC countries already attracts no duties, and uniform customs procedures under the customs union would eliminate additional distortionary effects. A currency union is planned for 2010, and the Supreme Economic Council hopes to phase in the membership of the Republic of Yemen, a country with much lower income levels.

Trade Protection and Competitiveness

Of the many factors that affect trade outcomes, price-related ones are usually among the most important (box 3.1). The prices of tradable goods and services are strongly affected by tariff levels and nontariff barriers as well as by real effective exchange rates, which are themselves influenced by macroeconomic policies and conditions. There is compelling evidence that trade protection is high for the developing countries in MENA relative to their income levels. Comparing over regions and over time, we find that MENA trade barriers have been the slowest to come down, and there have been episodes as well of reversals in policy during the 1990s. Exchange rate misalignments, in several countries and over significant periods, have also affected trade performance.

Trends in Tariff and Nontariff Barriers

High protection. Trade protection can be shown by a variety of measures reflecting tariff rates and the tariff equivalents of nontariff barriers. Table 3.1 presents data for MENA and several comparator groups using several different measures whose derivations are described in the notes to the table. All the measures show a similar ranking. Key results include the following:

- Average nontariff barrier protection is higher in the MENA region than in other lower-middle-income countries; indeed, it is higher than in all other regions of the world except for Latin America.

- Average MENA trade protection measured in terms of Anderson-Neary Ideal Measure (Anderson and Neary 1996) is one-quarter above the comparable average for lower-middle-income countries; it is also higher than in all other comparator groups.

- Tunisia and Morocco have among the highest protection rates in the MENA region (and the world) despite several reform episodes since the early 1980s, while Egypt has the highest dispersion of tariff rates.

BOX 3.1

How Do Tariffs and Exchange Rates Affect Export Performance in Egypt?

Egypt's exports as a share of GDP collapsed from 14 percent of GDP in 1990 to about 7 percent in 2000, a staggering loss in trade orientation. A recent study attributes this loss to government trade and tariff policies, and a large exchange rate overvaluation, raising the antiexport bias and destroying any incentive for local firms to export.

The rate of return on investment for producing for heavily protected local markets was twice that for exporting, because trade barriers boosted the profitability of producing for local markets. Rising overvaluation further reduced profitability. Then add to this other costs, such as customs, inspections, taxation regime, and a host of regulatory barriers, and top it off with high port and transport costs. The result is the export outcomes seen in aggregate—with resulting loss of potential jobs approaching millions. Galal and Fawzy (2002) reject the alternative explanation often offered in Egypt (the classic export-pessimism argument): that firms are failing to export because of the inability of Egyptian firms to compete because of outdated technology, management, techniques, and marketing strategies, and therefore that these firms would not respond to better incentives. Instead, they suggest firms can only respond to competitive pressures if trade and tariff reforms are undertaken.

Source: Galal and Fawzy 2002.

- On the positive side, Oman and Saudi Arabia, two oil-rich countries, have lower protection than the average for upper-middle-income comparators.

Slow decline in MENA tariff barriers. Trade protection in MENA developing countries has declined slowly in contrast to the rapid decline observed in other developing country regions (figure 3.1). This kept MENA trade protection the second highest among developing country regions in the late 1990s. Evidence compiled by Dasgupta, Keller, and Srinivasan (2002) also shows little change in average tariff rates (average of six countries: four as above plus Algeria and Bahrain), possibly even some reversals in 1991–95. Using an indirect approach that accounts for the effect of non-tariff barriers, Nash and Andriamananjara (1997), in a sample of eight countries, confirm the finding of reversal for tariff-equivalent of import restrictions for the group of countries they identify as "Trade Adjustment Lending" countries (Algeria, Jordan, Morocco, and Tunisia) in an earlier period, though the restrictions declined in the more recent period, as found in Dasgupta, Keller, and Srinivasan (2002). A cascading incidence of customs, valuations, standards, and other nontariff barriers at the borders have also multiplied high trade barriers (box 3.2).

TABLE 3.1

Trade Protection Indicators for MENA

(most recent year)

Country/region	Simple average	Weighted average	Standard deviation	Nontariff barrier coverage	Anderson-Neary Ideal Measure
Algeria	22.4	15.0	14.3	15.8	20.0
Bahrain	8.8	—	—	—	—
Egypt, Arab Rep. of	20.5	13.8	39.5	28.8	19.0
Iran, Islamic Rep. of	4.9	3.1	4.2	—	—
Jordan	16.2	13.5	15.6	0.0	—
Lebanon	8.3	12.0	11.2	—	22.2
Morocco	32.6	25.4	20.5	5.5	25.9
Oman	4.7	4.5	1.2	13.1	4.4
Saudi Arabia	12.3	10.5	3.1	15.6	11.0
Syrian Arab Rep.	21.0	—	—	—	—
Tunisia	30.1	26.3	12.6	32.8	19.2
MENA	**16.5**	**13.8**	**13.6**	**15.9**	**17.4**
ECA4	**12.9**	**7.2**	**18.3**	**12.4**	**3.5**
LAC4	**12.2**	**12.9**	**6.9**	**48.4**	**13.9**
EAP5	**11.3**	**8.3**	**17.9**	**13.5**	**6.0**
LMIC	**15.3**	**12.5**	**15.0**	**13.4**	**13.2**

—Not available.

Notes: Tariff rates used are most favored nation tariff rates. Nontariff barrier coverage refers to the number of tariff lines that have at least one nontariff barrier. The Anderson and Neary Ideal Measure is the uniform tariff rate that must be applied to the free-trade regime as a compensating variation to return welfare to most recent year of observation (see Anderson and Neary [1996]). The comparators are ECA4 (four countries in the Europe and Central Asia region—Czech Republic, Hungary, Poland, and Turkey), LAC4 (four countries in the Latin America and Caribbean region—Argentina, Brazil, Chile, and Mexico), and EAP5 (five countries in the East Asia and Pacific region—China, Indonesia, Malaysia, Republic of Korea, and Thailand). LMIC refers to lower-middle-income countries (with gross national income [GNI] per capita in the range of US$746–US$2,975). The comparator numbers are simple averages of the data for the respective countries they represent.
Source: Staff estimates based on TRAINS database (UNCTAD, various years).

Nontariff barriers and quantitative restrictions. There has been much improvement in recent years with respect to nontariff barriers in the MENA region. In Tunisia, the earlier extensive quantitative restrictions (affecting some 90 percent of domestic output) have progressively been reduced (textiles, passenger cars, agricultural products), but some items still remain. In Morocco, most quantitative restrictions have been eliminated. In Algeria, quantitative restrictions have been reduced, although temporary reversals occur and prior authorization lists still exist for some items. In Jordan, removal of quantitative restrictions was the main item of trade liberalization in 1988 and reduced coverage from 40 percent to 7 percent of production; most remaining quantitative restrictions have been eliminated since 1995. In Egypt, import licensing was eliminated in 1993, and the scope of quantitative restrictions was progressively reduced. In Lebanon, some import licensing and multiple authorizations remain. Syria has several lists of goods with import eligibility requirements (public sector, private sector, and two negative or banned lists)

FIGURE 3.1

Unweighted Import Tariff Rates

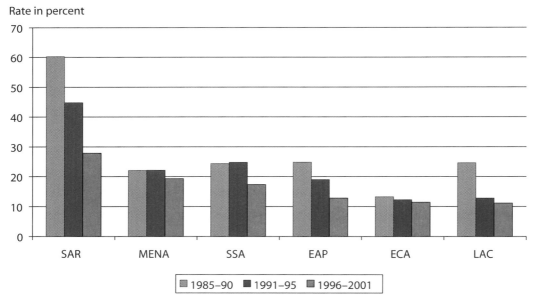

Note: Regional averages are unweighted. MENA average is representative for mainly non-GCC countries, based on nine countries (Algeria, Bahrain, Egypt, the Islamic Republic of Iran, Jordan, Lebanon, Morocco, Syria, and Tunisia). EAP = East Asia and Pacific region; ECA = Europe and Central Asia region; LAC = Latin America and Caribbean region; SAR = South Asia region; SSA = Sub-Saharan Africa.
Source: Staff estimates.

BOX 3.2

Customs, Valuation, and Standards: Progress and Problems

Customs. Jordan has improved its Customs Department by adopting Automated System for Customs Data (ASYCUDA)–based information technology, simplifying procedures, increasing transparency in dealing with the public, speeding duty refunds, and ensuring EU-consistent documents and a green channel for certain imports. Some problems remain, including inconsistent application of rules, tariff rates, testing and inspection, and fines. Accelerated training has played an important role to improve professionalism. (Jordan is now the World Customs Union [WCU]–designated regional representative for MENA.)

Morocco has made progress in customs reform by rationalizing procedures, allowing single goods declaration, customs clearance at the importer's premises, and selective inspection. Other countries also have been improving their services. Lebanon, for example, has also introduced a new information system based on ASYCUDA and other EU-consistent documents and processes. Elsewhere, customs services remain problematic.

In Egypt, enforcement of trade regulations by the Customs Authority requires coordination with a large number of other government agencies, namely the General Orga-

BOX 3.2 (continued)

nization for Import and Export Control (GOIEC), Organization for Standardization, Food Control Department, and others. Although intended as a one-stop inspection, led by Customs, there is no supplementary single-window inspection that harmonizes documentation. The procedure is byzantine and requires 32 signatures for manual filing of documents, while only 6 are needed for electronic filing. However, electronic filing is not easily accessible. Moreover, the Customs Authority is characterized by an aggressive approach to collection rather than trade facilitation, often disputing appropriate classification and value of the cargo, not accepting commercial invoices, and suffering from an overall lack of transparency that creates an environment of great uncertainty. For a regular goods shipment with "clean" documents, the clearance time is about five to seven days, while "unclean" documents take much longer depending on the circumstances. One transport intermediary we interviewed cited that Customs stops every shipment for inspection, and that each shipment is inspected on the basis of a sampling of 10 percent to 100 percent of the goods in the shipment. In the case of containerized goods, virtually all the goods are unstuffed at the port for inspection and are never stuffed again into the container for the inland movement.

In the Republic of Yemen, although services have lately improved, duty drawback mechanisms are still overly restrictive and complicated.

In Tunisia, which is further ahead than most MENA countries in trade services, customs formalities are (surprisingly) viewed as complex and time-consuming and regulations and bureaucratic procedures as nontransparent.

Valuation. The move away from administrative customs valuation remains mixed, as is most evident from the problems noted in Egypt. Morocco has reduced considerably its incidence of administrative practices, but in Algeria, minimum dutiable values were introduced in 1996 and expanded (final consumer goods, food, and textiles). In Syria, the application of customs exchange rates different from import settlement has been another example of administrative valuation, and similar incidences are also found in Tunisia and Lebanon.

Standards. The system of standards has become the most significant nontariff barrier in Egypt. These standards often lack international equivalence, and many were created to enforce quality norms without close relevance to health or safety protection. In addition, testing and certification procedures are lengthy and costly (5 to 90 percent compliance costs for food), and are estimated to have reduced exports by 9 percent. Elsewhere, Jordan's product standards still have to be revised to conform to international standards and inspection procedures need to be simplified. Lebanon still applies a series of standards based on national norms, thereby restricting trade. Progress has, however, been faster in Morocco and Tunisia where most standards (some 80 percent) are now based on international norms. But controls to verify conformity with technical regulations and health norms remain especially problematic in Tunisia.

with a general licensing requirement for all imports (Devlin and Yee 2002; IMF 2002; WTO various years).

Trade Transaction Costs in the MENA Region: An Exporter's Perspective

Zarrouk (2003) reports on a survey of randomly selected import/export companies from nine MENA countries and jurisdictions (Egypt, Jordan, Israel, Lebanon, Saudi Arabia, Syria, Tunisia, the UAE, and West Bank and Gaza). The focus of the survey was the burden of regulations on trade transactions. Some of the answers provided by the respondent sample of 250 companies are as follows:

• Trading costs (excluding customs duties and domestic taxes on imports) average some 10.6 percent of the value of trade. These costs arise from such sources as customs clearance, bribes, certification processes relating to product standards, transshipment regulations, and entry visa requirements. Given that the weighted average tariff for the region is around 14 percent, this means that other sources add a significant layer of additional protection.

• Customs clearance procedures and public sector corruption are recorded as being the two most important contributors to the additional costs of trade (table 3.2).

• Companies spend an average of 95 person-days a year dealing with trade transactions. About 10 percent of respondents have daily contacts with customs and other officials.

TABLE 3. 2

Survey of MENA Exporting Firms: Ranking of Trade Costs

Trade cost	Ranking	Average score[a]	Standard deviation
Customs duties	1	3.0	1.1
Domestic taxes	2	2.6	1.3
Customs clearance	3	2.5	1.1
Public sector corruption	4	2.4	1.4
Inspection, conformity certification	5	2.2	1.3
Transshipment, regulatory measures	6	2.1	1.3
Entry visa restrictions (for business)	7	1.8	1.5

a. Average. Responses were scaled from 1 to 4, where 1 implies the constraint is not costly and 4 means it is prohibitive. Constraints with score equal to or greater than 1.8 are retained.
Source: Zarrouk 2003.

A large number of documents and signatures are required for standard trade transactions (table 3.3). These add significantly to administrative and time costs and create more bribe-taking opportunities.

Exchange Rate Misalignment and Decline in Competitiveness

MENA countries have lost market shares in world nonfuel exports since 1980 (figure 3.2). Moreover, disaggregating by type of export suggests that this loss in market share was pervasive (table 3.4). MENA lost market

TABLE 3.3

Typical Number of Documents and Signatures Required to Process a Trade Transaction in MENA Countries

	Number of documents		Number of signatures	
Transaction	Imports	Exports	Imports	Exports
Air freight	5	5	10–20	8–10
Sea freight	6	5	12–20	0
Road transport	5	5	11–15	11–15

Source: Zarrouk 2003.

FIGURE 3.2

Decline in MENA World Market Share of Nonfuel Exports

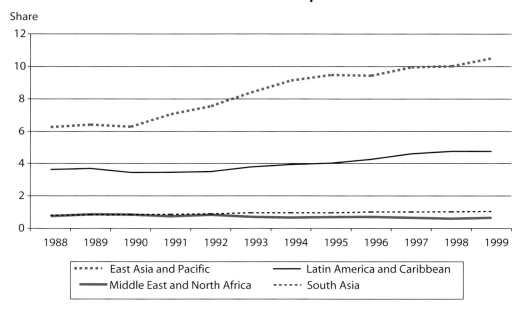

Source: Bank staff estimates based on *WDI* (World Bank 2003b). The Europe and Central Asia and Sub-Saharan Africa regions are not shown because of the lack of data. MENA countries are the geographic region of MENA according to the World Bank definition.

TABLE 3.4

Percentage Share of Regions in Developing Country Export of Manufactures by Category

Region	Total manufactures		Resource intensive		Low technology		Medium technology		High technology	
	1980	1995	1980	1995	1980	1995	1980	1995	1980	1995
East Asia	66.50	75.30	44.60	53.30	76.90	77.30	72.30	73.30	90.10	90.50
South Asia	5.20	3.70	5.00	5.30	8.90	7.30	2.30	1.60	1.20	0.60
Latin America and Caribbean	19.40	15.20	33.80	27.80	10.00	9.40	18.70	20.20	5.80	8.00
MENA	4.90	3.60	10.10	7.50	2.20	4.60	3.10	2.80	0.70	0.60
Sub-Saharan Africa	4.00	2.20	6.60	6.10	2.10	1.50	3.60	2.10	2.20	0.30

Note: Resource intensive includes manufactures such as processed foods and tobacco, simple wood products, refined petroleum products, dyes, leather, precious stones, and organic chemicals (67 SITC three-digit items). Low technology includes manufactures such as textiles, garments, footwear, other leather products, toys, simple metal and plastic products, furniture, and glassware (49 items). Medium technology includes manufactures such as automotive products, industrial chemicals, basic metals, standardized machinery, and simple electrical and electronic products (69 items). High technology includes a fairly small number of research and development–based products such as pharmaceuticals, computers, transistors, and other advanced electronics, complex electrical machinery, aircraft, and precision instruments (20 items).
Source: Lall 1999.

shares in resource-intensive exports, for which it had a relatively large initial share; most of this loss was captured by East Asian countries. In medium-technology industries too, MENA failed to keep its market shares; the relative gainers here were Latin America and East Asia (and now, increasingly, Eastern Europe). In high-technology sectors, MENA shares were in any case low and there was no corresponding improvement. The only sector showing some gain was labor-intensive, low-technology exports, where export shares doubled from a low base. This gain may have resulted from the MFA, which has limited contestability in the world textile and clothing market and rationed trade by quotas.

When losses in market shares are across the board as seen above, there is a strong presumption that competitiveness has been hurt by exchange rate misalignment and overvaluation. Recent assessments of economic policies and performance in developing countries have underlined the crucial issue of the management of the real exchange rate. Though the "real exchange rate" is not a direct policy instrument in the hands of authorities, it can be manipulated in part by actions taken with respect to the nominal exchange rate.[2] In general, countries that avoid real exchange rate overvaluation tend to be more successful in promoting manufactured exports.

The MENA experience with real exchange rate misalignment has been reviewed recently by Nabli and Veganzones-Varoudakis (2002). They show that, during the past three decades, the MENA countries in their sample experienced substantial overvaluation of their real exchange rate—around 29 percent a year from the mid-1970s to the mid-1980s, and 22 percent a year from the mid-1980s to 1999 (table 3.5). In general, the extent of overvaluation did not seem to have significantly decreased during the 1990s—contrary to the experience of Latin American, African, or Asian economies.

Meanwhile, exchange rate volatility has generally been lower in the MENA region (table 3.5), which can surely be explained by the less flexible exchange rate regimes of these countries. This conclusion should be nuanced, however. In particular, during the second subperiod (1985–99), the volatility of the exchange rate in the MENA region is not too different from that in Latin American countries, and is higher than in Asian economies.

The effect of the overvaluation and misalignment of exchange rates on exports is demonstrated more formally through an estimated equation relating exports to a number of variables, including exchange rates for a panel of 53 countries from 1970–80 (depending on the country) to 1999, for both total exports, and manufactured exports (Nabli and Veganzones-Varoudakis 2002).[3] The estimations confirm the negative impact of exchange rate misalignment on both total and manufactured export performance in the countries studied. The elasticity of exchange rate misalignment is rather strong in the case of manufactured exports (–0.72), but smaller but still significant for total exports (–0.10). The weaker elasticity in the latter case can be explained by the fact that total exports of goods and services include products that are less sensitive to exchange rates—such as oil products and other primary goods, which are often owned and managed by governments.

TABLE 3.5

Average Misalignment and Volatility

1975–80/84 (depending on country)	Misalignment (percent per year)	Volatility
MENA	29	7.9
Latin America	20	11.2
Africa (CFA)	61	12.7
Africa (non-CFA)	29	11.3
South Asia	43	13
Southeast Asia	10	5.4
1985–99	**Misalignment**	**Volatility**
MENA	22	12.4
Latin America	10	12.9
Africa (CFA)	28	14.5
Africa (non CFA)	13	16
South Asia	15	8.3
Southeast Asia	5	8.6

Note: CFA refers to French franc zone countries in Africa.
Source: Nabli and Veganzones-Varoudakis 2002.

For the MENA region as a whole, exchange rate policy explains losses in competitiveness and in manufactured exports. Real exchange rate overvaluation has reduced, on average, the ratio of manufactured exports to GDP by 18 percent a year. Manufactured exports, which averaged 4.4 percent of GDP from 1970 to 1999, could have reached 5.2 percent of GDP if no overvaluation had taken place. These losses were more concentrated in the 1970s and 1980s than in the 1990s, because of the higher overvaluation of the currencies during those two subperiods.

Some countries with a more diversified export base, such as Jordan and Morocco (table 3.6), had the highest losses because of misalignment during the 1970s and 1980s. Because of its high level of manufactured exports, Tunisia still incurred a large loss during the 1990s despite a relatively low level of misalignment. In the major oil-exporting countries, the Islamic Republic of Iran and Algeria, the large overvaluation of the currency has certainly contributed to the low diversification of their exports away from oil. But the losses, as measured here, appear small given the low initial level of manufactured exports.

Finally, a significant reason for the persistent misalignment and overvaluation of exchange rates in the MENA region is closely associated with pegged or fixed exchange rate practices. Virtually all MENA countries have followed de facto or formal pegged nominal exchange rates, with only some recent changes toward floating exchange rates (Levy-Yayati, Sturzenegger, and Reggio 2003). This is related to a general fear of floating. While the gains may have been in terms of reduced inflation,

TABLE 3.6

Cost of Misalignment on Manufactured Exports, Selected MENA Countries

Years	Algeria			Egypt, Arab Rep.			Iran, Islamic Rep. of		
	ExpM	Mis	Cost[a]	ExpM	Mis	Cost[a]	ExpM	Mis	Cost[a]
1970–79	3.0	1.79	−1.7	27.0	1.15	−2.9	3.0	1.42	−0.9
1980–89	1.5	1.59	−0.6	19.0	1.22	−3.0	4.0	1.24	−0.7
1990–99	3.3	1.08	−0.2	37.0	1.09	−2.4	7.0	1.84	−4.0
1970–99	2.6	1.49	−0.8	27.6	1.15	−2.7	4.5	1.49	−1.8

Years	Jordan			Morocco			Tunisia		
	ExpM	Mis	Cost[a]	ExpM	Mis	Cost[a]	ExpM	Mis	Cost[a]
1970–79	26.0	1.57	−10.5	16.0	1.49	−5.7	25.0		
1980–89	43.0	1.31	−9.4	39.0	1.08	−2.4	49.0	1.03	−1.0
1990–99	49.0	1.09	−3.1	53.0	1.1	−3.7	75.0	1.16	−8.7
1970–99	39.1	1.25	−7.7	36.1	1.21	−3.9	49.6	1.09	−4.8

a. Cost is the cost of overvaluation as percentage of total exports.
Note: ExpM is the ratio of manufactured exports as a percentage of total exports. Mis is the average misalignment over the period expressed as the percentage rate by which actual real exchange rate exceeds "equilibrium" exchange rate. Positive (negative) values mean overvaluation (undervaluation).
Source: Based on Nabli and Veganzones-Varoudakis 2002.

the tradeoff clearly has been to hurt GDP growth and trade. In developing countries, pegged exchange rates (both short and long) have been significantly and negatively related to per capita output growth (Levy-Yayati, Sturzenegger, and Reggio 2003).

Behind-the-Border Constraints

Integration is not only a function of trade barriers and macroeconomic policy. The process of integration involves a prior phase of investment supply response that is influenced not only by border price signals but also by a host of behind-the-border investment climate factors that affect the domestic costs of production (box 3.3). One important class of such constraints includes barriers to entry imposed by regulatory policies and institutional practices.

Barriers to the Entry of Firms

Business dynamism is affected strongly by how easy it is to go into or out of business.[4] The more difficult it is to set up a business, the less likely it is that potential entrepreneurs will make the necessary investment of time and effort. In particular, high costs of entry are likely to deter the setting up of small and medium enterprises, which are usually a significant source of new employment. It has also been found that business entry costs and regulations are a critical determinant of the export of manufactures (Tybout 1997), probably because such exports are often initially undertaken by small and medium enterprises.

Some recent evidence shows also that high entry costs are a significant deterrent to FDI, and thus to trade (World Bank 2003a). The higher the entry costs, the lower the inflows of FDI (figure 3.3). It may be surmised that high entry costs deter domestic investment as well, especially that forthcoming from small and medium enterprises.

How high are the barriers to entry in the MENA region? Some indicative data on the costs of setting up a new business have recently been compiled for a large sample of countries, including 11 MENA countries. These data show the following (table 3.7):

- In terms of number of procedures, MENA countries are on par with LAC4 and have a greater number of procedures compared with EAP5 and ECA4.

- Though the duration of procedures in MENA is at the lower end, markedly lower than EAP5, MENA entrepreneurs lose out in bearing a distinctly higher cost.

FIGURE 3.3

High Entry Costs Inhibit Foreign Direct Investment Inflows

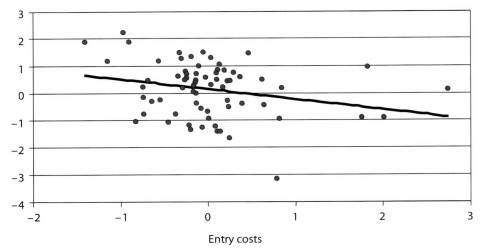

Partial correlations controlling for
market size, human capital,
and macroeconomic stability

Entry costs

Note: The entry cost measure used in the figure refers to the costs of obtaining the necessary permits and licenses and other procedures required to set up a new establishment. See Djankov and others (2001)
Source: World Bank staff.

- Four of the 11 MENA countries (Egypt, Lebanon, the Republic of Yemen, and Saudi Arabia) are in the costliest 20 percent among the 110 countries for which survey results were available).[5]

Significant barriers to entry are also often imposed on cross-border investment flows. A recent survey (Zarrouk 2003) found the typical impediments to intraregional investments in MENA (table 3.8) as ranked by potential investors.

Trade also is affected by the costs and reliability of logistical services provided by ports, customs authorities, and transporters. Box 3.4 describes how the activities of one garment exporter in Jordan are affected by various logistics issues. More generally, logistics in MENA have the following characteristics that bear on the region's competitiveness in world trade and investment.

- *Freight costs (inclusive of insurance).* These costs in MENA countries are the second highest among world regions, higher than in South Asia, East Asia, Latin America, and middle-income European regions. For example, freight costs place a 19 percent cost handicap on MENA exporters compared with their middle-income European competitors.

TABLE 3.7

Cost of Complying with Official Requirements to Set Up New Businesses

Country/region	Number of procedures	Duration (days)	Cost (percentage of GNI per capita)	Percentile rank of cost
Algeria	18	29	35.7	0.605
Egypt, Arab Rep.	13	52	76.3	0.816
Iran, Islamic Rep. of	9	69	10.9	0.201
Jordan	14	89	48.0	0.706
Lebanon	6	46	116.0	0.871
Morocco	13	62	18.6	0.431
Saudi Arabia	13	99	152.9	0.899
Syrian Arab Rep.	10	42	16.9	0.366
Tunisia	9	47	21.3	0.495
United Arab Emirates	10	29	24.4	0.559
Yemen, Rep. of	13	95	316.6	0.972
MENA	**12**	**60**	**76.1**	
EAP5	**10**	**72**	**16.1**	
ECA4	**10**	**66**	**34.0**	
LAC4	**12**	**59**	**14.2**	

Notes: LAC4 = four countries in the Latin American and Caribbean region—Argentina, Brazil, Chile, and Mexico; EAP5 = five countries in the East Asia and Pacific region—China, Indonesia, Malaysia, Republic of Korea, and Thailand; ECA4 = four countries in the Europe and Central Asia region—Czech Republic, Hungary, Poland, and Turkey.
Source: World Bank staff estimates based on surveys available at http://rru.worldbank.org/doing business/default.aspx; World Bank 2003d.

BOX 3.3

Investment Climate in Morocco

A recent World Bank Firm Analysis and Competitiveness Survey of Morocco (covering 859 enterprises) and its comparison to similar surveys in China, India, and Thailand provides a perspective on underlying causes of the region's weak investment climate.

Specific weaknesses in the investment climate in Morocco include:

- *Limited entry.* In Morocco it takes 13 permits to open a business, relative to 10 in India, 6 in China, and 3 in Thailand. The median number of days required in this process is 30 in China and Thailand, compared with 57 in Morocco.

- *High labor costs.* Relative to China and India, wage rates in Moroccan manufacturing plants are twice as high while labor productivity is roughly comparable with China and slightly higher than India. This is further underscored by a real exchange rate appreciation of 42 percent relative to China and 64 percent relative to India over the past decade. For skilled and unskilled production workers, Moroccan employees have less education on average than similar employees in Thailand or India. In addition,

(Box continues on the following page.)

BOX 3.3 (continued)

there is much less training available in Moroccan firms, relative to other emerging market economies. In the industries surveyed, about 40 percent of Korean firms have formal training programs, and 30 percent of Thai and Indian firms have training programs, but only about 15 percent of Moroccan firms have such programs.

- *Low-quality, costly infrastructure services—particularly telecommunications and transport.* Telephone lines per 1,000 people in the largest city in China are roughly three times more costly than in Morocco (although recent reforms as a result of telecommunications liberalization have led to a large increase in mobile phones) and the cost of shipping a container of textiles from Morocco to the United States is twice the level in China. Moroccan firms also pay about twice as much for energy as firms in Thailand or China.

- *Limited access to finance.* Moroccan manufacturing firms are financed overwhelmingly from owner equity and retained earnings. For the typical balance sheet, only 20 percent of financing comes from the banking sector, relative to India (36 percent) and Thailand (47 percent). Interest rates are also high in Morocco, 13.3 percent, in comparison with 5.9 percent in China, and 7.8 percent in Thailand. Not surprisingly, investment rates in Indian and Chinese firms have been considerably above investment rates in Moroccan firms.

- *Low levels of innovation.* Morocco lags far behind China in research and development spending by firms. Only 5 percent of the firms sampled in Morocco report any research and development spending. Only 9 percent of firms have an ISO (International Standards Organization) 9000 certification or are in the process of obtaining one (the ISO certification ensures that a firm is meeting international technical standards in its production process). Firms in Thailand spend about 6 percent of sales on research and development, and those in China spend 2 percent.

TABLE 3.8

Rankings of Constraints to Intraregional Investment in MENA

Constraint	Rank
Legal system enforcement	1
Agency law restricting business to nationals	2
Prohibited foreign ownership of real estate	3
Limitation on foreign ownership	4
Government corruption and red tape	5
Tax system and fees	6

Source: Zarrouk 2003.

The cost of insurance and freight (CIF) and free-on-board (FOB) shipments, as a measure of shipping costs, for MENA countries (Bahrain, Djibouti, Egypt, the Islamic Republic of Iran, Jordan, Kuwait, Libya, Malta, Oman, Qatar, and Republic of Yemen) ranges from about 11 to 15 percent, compared with 5 to 10 percent in other developing countries (Argentina, Bolivia, Brazil, Chile, China, Colombia, Mexico, the Philippines, the Republic of Korea, South Africa, Turkey, and Uruguay).

- *Customs clearance time.* Median customs clearance time in the MENA region averages 5.5 days and is 2 days longer than the developed country benchmark and significantly greater than in such comparators as Chile (3 days), Mexico (4 days), and Thailand (4 days).

BOX 3.4

Jordanian Garment Exporter Faces Difficult Cross-Border Procedures

A case study of logistics for this report focused on the problems of a Jordanian garment exporter. This is a major exporter in Jordan with two facilities located in Jordan's qualifying industrial zones (QIZs), in Amman and Irbid. The company also has a sister company that produces yarn for the garment market and provides its raw materials. Clients are based in the United States and Europe, including Target and K Mart. The transaction studied was a consignment of 90,000 pieces of cotton shirts ordered by a U.S. buyer. The company prefers to do business on letter-of-credit (LC) terms for established as well as new customers, and so a contract of sale is drawn up using this mechanism. The order is processed once the LC is accepted, followed by planning and organizing the production logistics. Samples are produced and tested to ensure quality compliance and control given the different colors and sizes specified in the order. The activity takes about 4 weeks to complete; by the time it is completed 28 days have elapsed.

Raw material inputs are largely sourced from a sister company through raw cotton from Egypt and Syria that is transported by ship to Aqaba and trucked inland. This textile company therefore keeps no inventory of yarn, and purchases the material on the basis of production demand. However, accessories such as buttons, sewing threads, price stickers, name labels, size labels, polyethylene bags, and so forth, are sourced from abroad as per the contract. Accessories are flown in on a just-in-time basis from Hong Kong, China, at a cost of US$2 per kilogram, and sometimes by courier at a cost of US$10 per kilogram inclusive of customs clearance service. Given the size of the order (90,000 pieces of shirts), the airfreight cost is US$19,000. Production times for this order require 30 days of knitting, dyeing, cutting, inspecting, sewing, ironing, inspecting, pack-

(Box continues on the following page.)

BOX 3.4 (continued)

ing, and re-inspecting. Typical production rates are 3,000 shirts a day. Shortly before completion, preshipment preparation begins by coordinating shipping logistics with the buyer, who is taking delivery of the order at the Port of Haifa. The company contacts the buyer to finalize shipping arrangements and instructions are given to the buyer's nominated freight forwarder who in turn coordinates with the shipping line to release the empty forty-foot equivalent unit (FEU) container.

Why Haifa? Jordanian exporters are increasingly being requested by buyers to place shipments at Haifa for transfer of cargo ownership and shipping. Two exporters interviewed for this study indicated that their orders are shipped through Haifa rather than Aqaba, a practice adopted because of better service frequency even though the liner rate is more expensive than that of Aqaba. This routing also involves a land-border crossing to Israeli territory and the attendant problems of border inspections. Jordanian and Israeli customs procedures combined require additional documentation. The company prepares the documents for export, such as commercial invoice, certificate of origin, packing list, export declaration, and additional documents required for transit through Israel. Importantly, each container is to be treated as a single shipment, and so four separate sets of documents are generated, as required by Israeli customs. Once the freight forwarder notifies the truck operator to pick up the empty containers from the shipping line's container yard in Amman, and delivers them to the plant, the cartons of shirts are packed. Documents are also handed over to the nominated freight forwarder who will facilitate the transit through Israeli territory.

Cross-border formalities begin once the container is trucked to the border at the bridge. The trucking time is short, taking only one hour, with a total charge of US$1,120, or US$280 per container. At the bridge, the nominated freight forwarder (or his clearing agent) hands over the export declaration form together with other documents to Jordanian Customs officials. Once approved, the documents are handed back to the clearing agent, and the truck moves to the Israeli side of the border to meet up with Israeli Customs officials. At the Israeli Customs station, the set of documents is handed over for inspection, and the container is transferred from a Jordanian truck to an Israeli truck. Since the Israeli side of the border only processes 15 trucks a day, a consignment of 4 containers may be caught by the processing limit if it reaches the bridge during the latter part of the day. In this case, the full consignment is processed the next day.

A journey to Haifa takes only 1.5 hours, because the distance is short, and the convoy of trucks travels in bond until it reaches the container terminal. Costs of haulage from the bridge to the Port of Haifa are nearly US$1,000 per container, and so the total cost for the four containers is about US$4,000. The containers stay in the terminal for two days before they are loaded onto the container ship, with terminal charges of US$180 per FEU. After 23 days, the container vessel arrives in New York with total ocean

BOX 3.4 (continued)

charges for the four containers at US$9,200, or US$2,300 per FEU. The transaction is completed when the containers are unloaded and cleared through the New York terminal and transported to the buyer's distribution center.

This logistics chain is relatively trouble free with the exception of the cross-border procedures required to export through the Port of Haifa. Air freight for just-in-time delivery of accessories is the most costly link in the logistics chain, although total logistics cost are only 6.7 percent of the landed product price.

Source: Devlin and Yee 2002.

Political Economy of Trade and Investment Climate Reform

Why have trade policy, and investment climate, reforms been slow and not shown much progress in many countries in the region despite relatively long-standing, known benefits of such reforms? The fundamental reasons are to be found in political economy factors.

Past Winners and Losers in the Political Economy of Reform

A coalition of relatively powerful constituents has stood to lose from trade and investment climate reforms to open the economies in the region. These constitute primarily powerful public sector agencies that often control the trade and investment gateway points (customs, taxation, standards, and certification), public sector enterprises (manufacturing and services providers in telecommunications; ports; stevedoring; road, sea, and air transport; banking; and utilities) and their workers and unions, and private sectors in protected import-substitution activities. State-owned enterprises still represent on average about one-third of GDP in the region (Petri 1997). At the same time, agriculture too is heavily protected, and the rural sector, both large and small farmers, constitutes another strong element of support for the status quo. There is no strong incentive for the political leadership to trade reform in the presence of such strong, vested interests in the status quo. The current system of distribution of rents from oil and aid flows has seemingly been sufficient to keep this coalition in place.

At the same time, a large section of civil society, media, and intellectuals, usually representing the better educated, have also shared in strong protectionist and nationalistic tendencies. This is consistent with the findings of political economy studies elsewhere (Mayda and Rodrik

2001), which suggest that in poorer countries, the social views of the better educated can often lead to an identity of interests with business and bureaucratic elites despite the fact that the educated elite stand to gain from more open and competitive economies. This is the opposite, for example, of the case in richer countries where the relatively skilled and educated tend to be strong supporters of trade and investment reforms and the relatively unskilled oppose such reform.

The potential winners from reform tend to be poorly organized and have little political clout—unemployed workers, new entrants to the labor force, educated youth, and small existing or new manufacturers in new export-oriented industries and services.

The incentives to trade liberalization have thus been weak economically and politically. The static losses to powerful current interests have been perceived to be larger than the prospective dynamic gains to future generations; and current conditions may not provide sufficient gains from integration without deeper reforms. And even if the economic incentives are strong, the political incentives have been weak—in the absence of a crisis (Galal 2000).

Some Empirical Evidence

In MENA countries, the measured evidence suggests high pressure of import substitution lobbyists, and a weak base of support for trade liberalization (such as exporters).

The first generation of theoretical and empirical models in the literature has focused on structural reasons. These have generally argued that trade is restricted because politically influential groups seek such interventions to improve their welfare. Mayda and Rodrik (2001) also advance other reasons why trade restrictions may be favored: as a means of reducing costly redistribution and as informationally efficient. Cross-country studies of political economy barriers to trade reform are, however, few. Nabli (1990) in a study of 51 liberalization episodes in 1950–80 identifies five factors that are critical in the process of trade liberalization: the power of import-substitution industries, the strength of export-oriented industries lobbies, the time lapsed since the beginning of the import-substitution regime, the size of the country, and leadership commitment and role.

To find empirical support for the influence of competing lobbies, import-substitution industries, and export-oriented industries, we examined evidence from the recently available trade and production database from Nicita and Olarreaga (2001). This allows the construction of more accurate measures of power of lobbies than was possible before. This advantage comes from the concordance of international standard industrial classification (ISIC)–based industrial production with SITC-based tariff and trade data. Based on a sample of 24 developing countries for which full datasets are available, we test the association between the power of the import-substitution industries and the export-oriented industries lobby in the early 1990s with the level of trade protection in late 1990s. The power of the import-substitution industries lobby is measured by the share of value added in industries (three-digit ISIC) that enjoy an import tariff rate of 15 percent and greater, but export less than 20 percent of output. The power of the export-oriented industries lobby is measured by the share of value added in industries with at least 20 percent production that is exported.

That the power of the import-substitution industries lobby is associated with higher degrees of protection is evident from figure 3.4. The positive association between the size of the export-oriented industries lobby and lower levels of trade protection are seen in figure 3.5. Contrasting the power of the demand and supply of pressure for endogenous determination of reforms, figure 3.6 points to the fact that greater trade liberalization is associated with a weaker import-substitution industries lobby and a stronger export-oriented industries lobby. The two MENA countries included in these charts, Egypt and Morocco, display high pressure from the import-substitution industries lobby and weak liberalization lobby pressures.

FIGURE 3.4

Import-Substitution Industries Lobby Keeps Protection Rates Higher in Egypt and Morocco

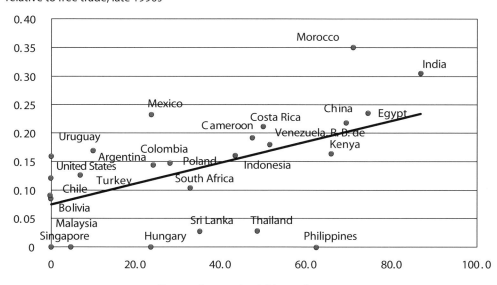

Source: Staff estimates based on Anderson-Neary Ideal Measure and Trade and Production database.

FIGURE 3.5

Export-Oriented Industries Lobby Helps in Lowering Protection

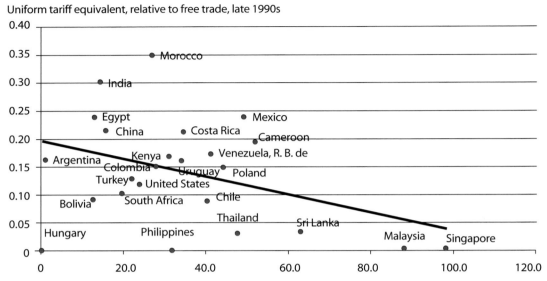

Uniform tariff equivalent, relative to free trade, late 1990s

Source: Staff estimates based on Anderson-Neary Ideal Measure and Trade and Production database.

FIGURE 3.6

Endogenous Determination of Protection Determined by Import-Substitution Industries and Export-Oriented Industries Lobbies

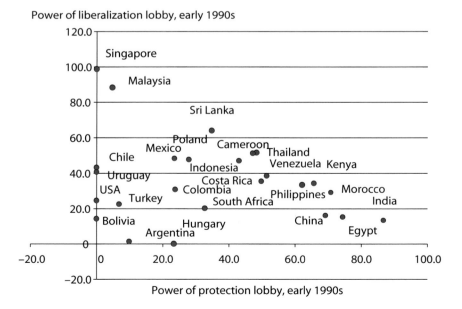

Power of liberalization lobby, early 1990s

Power of protection lobby, early 1990s

Note: The circles represent the trade liberalization index (Anderson-Neary Ideal Measure).
Source: Staff estimates based on Anderson-Neary Ideal Measure and Trade and Production database.

dards and inspections, reform customs, and deregulate services and domestic and foreign investment. Implementing the package will take time, possibly a decade or more in most countries. That time frame will allow countries to progressively break down the natural constituencies of support for the status quo and to deal with sectorwide reforms. The process will require political leadership, technical capacity, public support, management of transition costs, and support from external partners.

- Some of the resource-rich countries in the Gulf region are showing the way in trade and structural reforms. They have a US$355 billion GCC customs union; are liberalizing private entry in power, water, real estate, and other previously protected sectors; and are reforming banking and financial regulations. These countries have sector-specific strategies for such niche areas as tourism, information technology, entrepot trade, and media, and they are strengthening their macroeconomic policies. For the future, the main challenges are to make the customs union work, implement privatization and financial sector regulation, and reform labor markets.

- Gradualism may be appropriate in some sectors. Sectors with possibly large job losses—especially in the public sector and in agriculture—will require careful management throughout the region.

The Broader Reform Agenda

Faster growth of output, productivity, and jobs will result if MENA countries tackle deep-seated barriers to trade and investment. Reforms need to go beyond shallow and limited trade policy reforms at the border and numerous trade agreements, which were the staple of the 1990s, to much deeper domestic policy reforms. Liberalizing trade in goods as well as liberalizing services might yield much bigger gains in welfare. It also is critical to accelerate tariff and nontariff reforms, move to appropriate exchange rate regimes, and improve the investment climate.

But a broader agenda of reforms, elaborated in the three companion volumes to this report, will need to complement the following reforms:

- Improving governance to increase the voice of citizens and the accountability of government.

- Putting gender issues at the center of development.

- Producing a skilled labor force for knowledge-based manufacturing and services.

The Future: Specialization and Exports

In manufacturing, international trade is cutting up the production chain and permitting finer gradations of specialization within that chain among skills and labor costs and productivity. Small, resource-poor countries in the region stand to benefit from such production chains—and given their size, the prospects are virtually unlimited in world markets. Larger countries will also benefit from such specialization. Their larger domestic markets, and proximity to major international markets, will drive a much larger range and scale of domestic manufacturing possibilities.

The prospects for specialization in manufacturing will thus remain immense and undiluted in all MENA countries. The manufacturing sectors of most MENA countries are small by international standards—almost half the typical levels in other lower-middle-income countries. The prospective gains from more open trade and dwindling mining sectors over time are large (table 4.1).

Services are dominated by large public sectors, with central government wages and salaries at 12 percent of GDP, more than twice the 5 percent in other countries. Low-value, low-productivity private services are probably overserved. With more openness and trade, a shift is likely to more productive private services, with a corresponding reduction in low-productivity and overstaffed public and private services. Tourism, transport, finance, and telecommunications are sectors with rapid growth potential.

Agriculture's share in the production structure is likely to remain about the same or decline—given the limited cultivable land and water resources in the region. Opening trade and reducing subsidies will hasten the shift away from agriculture. Given the high employment in agriculture, often on poor, marginal lands, the transition issues will be significant and will thus need careful management (chapter 6). Even so, the opportunities for faster growth in less water-intensive crops remain good.

Making Trade Reforms Successful

The objectives of trade reform are always to accelerate growth, diversify economies, and generate faster growth in productive employment opportunities and living standards. The distinguishing characteristics of effective trade reform rest on three overriding factors: (1) eliciting an adequate supply of private investment response, whether from domestic or foreign investors or both; (2) inducing technological or productivity gains from a more open economic system; and (3) minimizing output

TABLE 4.1

Structure of Production, 2000

Category	Algeria	Tunisia	Egypt, Arab Rep. of	MENA	Lower-middle-income developing country comparators
Per capita income (PPP$)	5,040	6,070	3,670	5,270	4,600
Production structure (percent)					
Agriculture	9	12	17	14	14
Manufacturing	8	18	19	14	27
Mining and utilities	52	11	15	23	14
Services	31	59	49	48	45

Note: PPP = purchasing power parity.
Source: World Bank 2003.

and job losses in the transition. The content, pace, and sequencing of trade policy reforms, when tailored to elicit these outcomes in specific settings, make reforms effective. Indeed, many relatively successful countries (for example, China, India, or Vietnam) have often undertaken what look at first sight to be incomplete or nonorthodox approaches to liberalizing trade and investment. But they have produced outcomes that are often better than in many other cases where reforms have been much more orthodox and complete (as in Brazil or Argentina). That is why design of policies has to be tailored to the circumstances.

Sequencing and the Speed of Reforms

The debate on sequencing and speed of reforms, intense in the 1980s for Latin America, gained even more attention for the transition countries of Eastern Europe in the 1990s, if for a much wider array of economy-wide policies. Even so, there is support for the notion that optimal sequencing might often favor a more incremental "gradualist" approach than a program of comprehensive and immediate reforms ("big-bang" approach) in the context of a crisis. The reasons range from allowing the costs of reform to be spread over time (avoiding the danger of reversals), to institutional arguments for creating adequate capacity and learning, and to political economy arguments of building support for reforms. The counterarguments for faster change are to gain credibility, ensure complementarity among different parts of the reforms, reduce uncertainty, and capture opportunity.

What does international experience suggest about the optimal sequencing of trade policy reforms? The consensus is clear on the relationship to macroeconomic policies. First, macroeconomic stabilization must precede trade reform. Stabilization is a precondition because instability distorts the signals transmitted by changes in relative prices brought about by trade reforms. Second, successful trade reforms generally must be preceded by a depreciation of the real exchange rate—to ensure the sustainability of the liberalization process by dampening the excess demand for importables (Agenor and Montiel 2001). The real exchange rate can be influenced either by nominal devaluation or restrictive demand policies. A depreciation of the real exchange rate prior to trade reforms offsets the adverse effects—for the balance of payments and for domestic producers—of cuts in tariff protection, while stimulating exports.

Exchange rate flexibility is critical to successful trade reform (Bannister and Thugge 2001). Cross-country studies suggest that once this initial condition is met, there is little to be gained from further depreciation. The lower tax revenues from tariff cuts may constrain the government's ability to maintain fiscal balance and thus the pace of tariff reductions. But trade reform compensates for this automatically by raising the tax base through higher imports. It is also a disincentive to smuggling, underinvoicing, and rent seeking, again raising tax revenues. It is suggested that there is no significant relationship between trade reform and the revenue collected from external trade taxes. But when there is concern over the fiscal impact, tariff cuts can proceed in steps—gradually reducing the level and structure of tariffs and expanding the domestic revenue base, including a VAT. Of nine countries that undertook 35 trade-oriented adjustment programs in the 1980s, five improved their revenues, and only three experienced declines—and as a group the trade taxes as a share of GDP rose modestly after reform (Tarr and Matusz 1999). Quota reformers also raise more revenues (Thomas, Nash, and Edwards 1991; figure 4.1).

For example, in Morocco, customs duties are an important source of revenues for the national budget, and accounted for 4.2 percent of GDP in 1995—just before tariffs started to be dismantled under the association agreement with the EU. In 1996–2000, revenues from customs duties fell to 3.3 percent of GDP, a significant and large loss. But revenues from a new VAT on imports rose in the same period to 3.3 percent of GDP, more than compensating for the losses from customs duties. Moreover, most of the decline in import tariffs was compensated by a nearly 25 percent rise in imports, so that customs duties also continued to generate higher revenues.

What about the sequence and pace of trade reforms themselves? By now, the evidence is relatively clear from liberalization episodes around the world that:

- First, to build momentum, programs must start boldly and then follow through with further measures. This proves more durable than an

FIGURE 4.1

Import Taxes before and after Reform
(percentage of GDP)

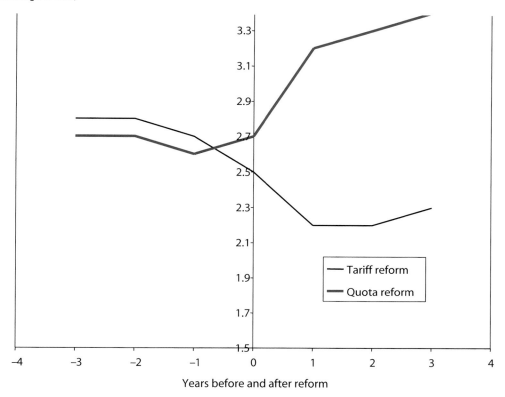

Years before and after reform

initially hesitant approach, which creates doubts about the credibility of the program. So, trade reform must encompass broad-based liberalization and widen its domain successively and quickly—so that more individual sectors or groups are able to perceive the benefits.

- Second, programs that decisively reduce import quotas or import licensing monopolies succeed more than those that retain such privileges. That step sends a clear signal that no rent-seeking, special enclaves deserve more protection than others—and that such actions provide widespread benefits to consumers and others through lower prices and higher-quality goods.

- Third, tariff reform must make across-the-board cuts in tariffs, setting as little administrative discretion as possible, and progressively lower ceilings within a time-bound program. Indeed, lowering all tariffs to as uniform a rate as possible is the best way to do away with a discretionary and administrative approach, which fosters deeper lobbying and rent seeking that can derail the credibility of the program.

- Fourth, reforms must go well beyond at-the-border trade policies to eliminate behind-the-border impediments in customs, standards, ports, and other barriers. Indeed, trade reform cannot work without such complementary reforms.

- Fifth, trade reforms must be accompanied by consistent and bold investment deregulation to free up new entry and allow private investment to respond. That investment response is probably the most decisive element in the success or failure of the entire program.

- Sixth, the financial sector needs to allow the shift in resources from previously protected and unproductive, state enterprise–dominated sectors to the new exportable sectors.

- Seventh, a case for gradualism can nevertheless be made for sectors in which job losses are likely to be significant.

Managing Transition Costs and Job Losses

Even though benefits in the medium to longer term are clear, policymakers and politicians still fear short-run adjustment costs. A review of studies concludes that adjustment costs are usually small compared with the benefits of trade liberalization. Studies that focused on manufacturing employment find that it typically increased within a year after liberalization. Adjustment costs are therefore usually short term, ending when workers find alternative jobs. Estimates of the duration of unemployment in most industries are not high. In many industries, normal labor turnover exceeds dislocation from trade liberalization, making downsizing relatively easy. Interindustry shifts minimize the dislocation of employment, with labor-intensive industries often growing faster, and the biggest gains to employment coming from new firms, typically small ones.

A case can be made for gradualism in some sectors because trade liberalization might affect income groups and some sectors and industries quite differently, with winners and losers. Reforms may also have a large output cost in some sectors and industries in the short term because reallocating capital takes time and is limited by the inflexibility of labor. A large increase in unemployment might also weaken support for the reforms. So the pace of across-the-board reforms should take into account sectors in which the costs of adjustment are likely to be large. For example, NAFTA delayed the liberalization of trade in maize for 10 years, phasing it in to allow for adjustment by rural subsistence farmers in Mexico (Hufbauer and

Schott 1993). The long adjustment period was considered necessary because of the price difference between long-protected Mexican domestic maize production and U.S. maize exports.

Similarly, a slower pace of attrition in long-protected public sector enterprises may well be needed in state enterprise–dominated transition countries, where the cost of large labor downsizing may be politically difficult, threatening the trade reform program. But where there are no compelling grounds for such actions—no major industries or public sectors with large labor forces threatened by trade liberalization—there is little to be gained from gradualism.

In many MENA countries, some sectors will likely suffer significant job losses—such as capital-intensive manufacturing, public enterprises, and agriculture. Business expansion takes time, and in some cases the investment climate may not be sufficiently attractive—leaving restructured and export-oriented companies without incentives to expand and to absorb labor released by the shrinking sectors. So job destruction may outpace job creation because lowering trade barriers may initially hurt sheltered domestic producers and displace unskilled workers in import-competing industries (Rama 2001).

Although import-competing industries are usually capital intensive, MENA industries—like those in many middle-income countries—are intensive in unskilled labor. They are also often protected disproportionately because they face potentially stiff competition from lower-cost producers (Wood 1997). Before the trade liberalization in Morocco, the nominal tariff and import license coverage in apparel and footwear was among the highest in manufacturing (Currie and Harrison 1997). And in 1995 in Egypt, import-weighted tariffs on textiles were about three times higher than average tariffs for the economy (Dessus and Suwa-Eisenmann 1998).

Whether there would be significant job losses in particular sectors depends on four issues:

- The underlying aggregate growth in the economy, with higher aggregate growth offsetting the downward pressure on these sectors.

- The ability of the trade liberalization program to insulate some sectors from overall trade liberalization measures, by providing partial time-bound protection.

- The compensatory measures to allow enterprises to manage the transition more smoothly—such as providing enterprises with funds to restructure operations, such as in the Tunisia *mise à niveau* program and similar programs in Morocco and Egypt.

- The ability to restrain job losses in state-owned enterprises without derailing the objectives of reform (allowing losses to mount temporarily in state-owned enterprises while downsizing operations as an implicit compensation measure).

The investment response of new firms and new entry into new sectors are also critical—with quick payoffs in new activities. Mexico jump-started the *maquiladora* border investments to generate new jobs—while negotiating longer phase-ins of trade liberalization for employment-heavy sectors, such as automobiles, agriculture, and pharmaceuticals, and leaving the state banking and oil sectors relatively untouched.

Small and medium-size development and new entry is likely to be especially critical, highlighting the critical need for investment climate improvements and for reducing the costs of new entries and start-ups of new businesses. In experiences around the world, such new entry has often been the driving force of gains in employment.

Successful transitions rely on many new businesses, buoyant growth, and compensatory mechanisms. In Tunisia and Morocco in the late 1980s, net job losses in heavily protected manufacturing sectors were quite small, and aggregate employment remained buoyant even in the transition. But job destruction has been particularly dramatic when trade policy reform has been associated with large-scale downsizing of state-owned enterprises and the absence of structural reforms to induce new private sector entry. In the transition economies in Eastern Europe, millions of workers were made redundant so that the restructured enterprises could become profitable as private firms. In Algeria in the early 1990s, trade liberalization coincided with a sharp macroeconomic downturn and fiscal retrenchment, with fairly massive job losses in previously heavily protected sectors. An estimated 500,000 workers—about 10 percent of the labor force—lost their jobs from 1991 to 1998 as a result of (still partial) restructuring of nonviable state-owned enterprises, contributing to the eventual failure of the program.

All this highlights the need for careful design in the pace and sequencing of trade and investment climate reforms—and for close monitoring and early corrections, but without backtracking, which can be costly for the credibility of the program. In China, India, Indonesia, Mexico, Vietnam, and elsewhere, transition issues have generally been handled well through:

- Liberalizing early in key areas and inputs, and addressing key bottlenecks (such as customs or inspections) to jump-start new export-oriented activities.

- Embarking on large-scale and upfront domestic investment deregulation to foster new entry and job growth.

- Delaying state enterprise downsizing and job losses, but exposing them to competition and reducing the scale of their operations so that losses are held in check by hard budget constraints.

- Instituting compensatory mechanisms for firms that can restructure.

- Maintaining competitive exchange rates.

- Phasing reforms in with the macroeconomic cycle.

A similar strategy is possible for all countries in the MENA region, so the political and economic fear of large job losses should not be a significant reason for deferring the reform agenda.

In agriculture it is even more likely that trade liberalization needs to calibrated carefully, with adequate pace and sequencing to avoid risks of large job losses. Because of high protection levels enjoyed by the field crops and livestock, eliminating or significantly reducing tariffs in these sectors will pose serious challenges (Chaherli 2002). In higher potential agro-ecological zones and in irrigated areas, adapting to trade liberalization will be easier.

Most studies indicate that the typically subsidized, low-productivity rainfed cereal production in drier agro-ecological zones, with small producers, will bear the brunt of trade liberalization. The implicit labor displacement would be significant. So labor transfers within and from the agricultural and agro-industrial sectors will be critical in managing the transition. At the same time, the huge trade and pricing distortions in agriculture raise prices for industrial users and urban consumers—and misallocate the scarce water resources. A carefully phased plan for reducing the trade and pricing distortions, while putting in place compensation for marginal farmers to switch to alternative activities, will thus be essential (chapter 6).

Export Processing Zones

Export processing zones and other special economic zones have been proposed to jump-start export and private investment activities and avoid the coordination and transition problems associated with economywide opening and liberalization. Jordan has QIZs and the Aqaba free trade zone. In Morocco there is heavy emphasis on the free port of Tangiers and in Dubai on Jebel Ali. Tunisia offers generous tax advantages to offshore sectors. Egypt has a number of special and free trade area zones.

Experiences with export processing zones are mixed. When they work, there can be positive spillovers for the rest of the economy. But growth can come at a high cost, as in Tunisia. And unless the gains translate into economywide productivity and competitiveness, small changes in the world environment may push foreign firms to other shores. In larger, resource-rich countries, export processing zones may result in short-term gains in investment, exports, and employment, but these gains diminish over time and divert attention from more fundamental problems. Special economic zones present similar problems. They work only in special circumstances (China, with its proximity to Hong Kong, China) and can be costly to build and operate. In Iran free trade zones have failed to achieve their primary goals of increasing exports and attracting foreign investment.

The biggest single reason for new entry into such offshore platforms is to avoid the cumbersome customs and administrative formalities that afflict domestic markets and discourage spillovers of openness and trade. Offshore programs have helped to correct strong antiexport biases. However, the future of such special areas is in question. They are attempts to apply a trade policy instrument in limited locations and applicability to compensate for broader failures in investment climate throughout the entire economies. Reforming the investment climate directly would yield far more of the potential gains from trade integration.

Anchoring Reforms in Regional Integration Agreements

An important part of the trade and broader economic reform strategy in MENA countries will be revitalized regional trade agreements. There are several ways to make these trade agreements work better.

First, trade with Europe, the natural geographic trade partner of the MENA region, falls far short of its potential (Nugent 2002). With new members expanding the size and scale of the EU market, the potential gains for a number of MENA countries are expanding as well. The Euro-Med agreements and the Barcelona Process could be strengthened by accelerated commitments by MENA countries to reduce trade barriers, liberalize services, and phase in domestic agricultural reforms. The EU could offer immediate expanded access to its markets for agriculture, as well as increased temporary migration, funds for managing transition costs, and more efficient rules of origin (chapter 7).

Second, as trade and investment barriers to the rest of the world are reduced the biggest beneficiary will be intraregional trade because of the countries' proximity, language, and other ties. The Maghreb countries will continue to be pulled more toward the EU because of the greater similarity of economic structures and the much bigger EU markets. But accelerating intraregional trade will be as important for Mashrek and GCC countries, with the GCC customs union creating a large common market for the other Mashrek countries. Substantial expansion in regional trade is possible if the barriers to trade and investment that apply to all countries are progressively eliminated for countries in the region. Intraregional trade agreements could be strengthened by mutual agreements to reduce product exclusions in agriculture and services and to harmonize customs and regulatory processes (standards, investment and other licensing processes, visa restrictions).

Third, MENA countries would do well to maintain open access to world markets, anchoring their trade and investment reforms in a multilateral framework such as the WTO, to give them greater credibility. But first more countries in the region will have to become full members of the WTO (box 4.1).

BOX 4.1

Why Are So Few MENA Countries Members of the WTO?

Less than half the population of MENA region lives in a WTO member country—the lowest share of all developing regions. As of August 2002, 13 of the 21 MENA countries were WTO members and 5 were in various stages of accession (Algeria, Lebanon, and Saudi Arabia have established working parties, and Libya and Syria have submitted formal requests). Algeria established a working party as long ago as 1987, and Saudi Arabia in 1993, yet the Islamic Republic of Iran, Iraq, and West Bank and Gaza have not yet requested membership. In 2002, the WTO established a special unit to attend to the MENA region's needs.

Why such reluctance by MENA countries to join the WTO? First, the trust in rule-based international trading is slow to build in a region with a disproportionate share of countries under trade and foreign investment sanctions: the Islamic Republic of Iran, Iraq, and Libya. Second, for the Mediterranean MENA countries, preferential trading arrangements with the EU have immediate appeal because of geographic proximity and EU financial and technical support. Third, primary oil exporters with little other trade are wary of the perceived ambivalence toward bringing oil trade under the WTO. When oil prices are rising there is a threat of "disciplining" the oil cartel for production quotas deemed in violation of Article X of the WTO. However, when oil prices are falling, countries are reluctant to reduce oil import tariffs.

The case for speeding up the WTO accession process and beginning active participation in the Doha agenda is compelling (Hoekman and Roy 2000). WTO rules on national treatment, most favored nation treatment, and the primacy of tariffs as a trade policy instrument ensure more efficient resource allocation; WTO-consistent laws and regulations establish good practices, policies, and institutions; nondiscriminatory market access is guaranteed for all WTO members; and the enhanced credibility of government policies that are bound as commitments to the WTO gives investors greater confidence in the permanence of reforms.

Reforms in Resource-Poor Countries: the Arab Republic of Egypt, Jordan, Lebanon, Morocco, and Tunisia

Trade policy reforms in the resource-poor countries have been under way for more than a decade. While their reforms are relatively advanced for the region, they lag behind the rest of the world, especially successful reformers, on virtually every trade protection indicator (see chapter 3). At 36 percent, Morocco's unweighted average tariff is the highest among comparable countries (the average is 15 percent for lower-middle-income countries). And in Tunisia, with the longest history of trade reform, the average rate is still 30 percent and nontariff barriers remain extensive, some 33 percent of all tariff lines—among the highest coverage in the world. Jordan, more advanced in its reforms than the other countries, needs to sustain its progress, which is made difficult by the exogenous drag on its integration of its conflict-ridden neighborhood (World Bank 2002a).

Countries need to move on to a new round of decisive and credible trade liberalization. There is little reason for gradualism. After more than a decade of adjustment time for domestic industry, enormous pressures in domestic labor markets for new jobs, and huge potential benefits of accelerated reform, gradual trade reforms for certain categories of imports have simply encouraged firms to invest in highly protected sectors, maintaining high antitrade bias.

The underlying political economy of protection remains deeply entrenched, even though it benefits few segments of the population. The import-substitution industries lobby keeps protection high in these resource-poor economies, with benefits going to a few large industrialists and officials, while the voice of exporters, especially small firms, is diffused and weak. So, high protection remains in force. A decisive break is needed if these countries are to benefit fully from the opportunities of faster integration. There is no reason why these countries cannot rapidly increase trade integration and job creation in the next few years, given their favorable size, endowments, and proximity to major industrial country markets. Immediate neighborhood effects will continue to diminish prospects in Jordan, but even there, nonoil exports have been growing dramatically in the past three years (more than 20 percent a year), and thousands of new jobs have been created, although concerns about employment of foreign nationals point to labor market issues and the skills and competitiveness of local employees, which have to be addressed. For Egypt, the needed reforms are more complex, given its large size and strongly protected national markets and because it shares some of the characteristics of resource-abundant countries (see below).

Tariffs and Nontariff Barriers

Countries need to accelerate tariff reductions and apply them across the board. That step includes avoiding any trade diversion effects of regional trade agreements by providing only marginal tariff advantages—if any— to regional trade partners. Any revenue losses can be recouped through domestic taxes, such as a VAT. Tariff peaks need to be drastically reduced, as in food products and light manufactures.

Nontariff barriers need to be replaced by tariffs. Tunisia replaced import licensing with administrative barriers, such as *cahiers de charge*, which still impede trade. Egypt reduced nontariff barriers and eliminated import licensing in 1993, but some product groups (textiles and clothing) still face large nontariff barriers. Replacement of nontariff barriers with their tariff equivalents would create transparency and competition.

Domestic standards and inspections often lack any international equivalence, and many countries enforce quality norms that provide little health or safety protection. Testing and certification procedures are lengthy and costly. In Egypt, standards application has become the most significant trade barrier. Standards and inspections ought to be aligned with WTO principles.

Euro-Med Agreement

Instead of the Euro-Med agreement of scheduled tariff reductions, which is too slow, negotiations should focus on achieving greater benefits from trade partners in return for offers of accelerated trade reform. For example, Tunisia's trade liberalization has focused on the association agreement, yielding significant gains in protection for Group 1 and 2 products (capital goods and intermediates). However, Group 3 and 4 products (consumer goods and close substitutes to domestic production) received long-term exemptions. As a result, effective protection remains high, at more than 60 percent. In more heavily protected manufacturing, such as food and metal products, effective protection has increased dramatically to more than 200 percent.

Exchange Rate Policies

Exchange rate polices need to be supportive of an accelerated round of trade reform. Significant adjustments of real exchange rates, through nominal rate adjustments or domestic demand measures, need to precede trade reforms. Tunisia has a managed float, with a real exchange rate target. Morocco and Jordan have pegged exchange rate polices. Morocco's persistent overvaluation contributed significantly to its poor export performance during the 1990s, but more recently, it has been moving gradually to more flexible exchange rates. Egypt's recent depreciation and shift to a floating exchange rate offers the opportunity to slash tariff protection across the board from an average of 28 percent to 10 to 15 percent, because the depreciation will protect import industries. In Lebanon, macroeconomic reforms are needed before the country can reap any benefits from trade reforms.

Customs Reforms

Customs reforms are proceeding well in Morocco (box 4.2) and Jordan, but need to be accelerated in Egypt and Tunisia. Customs procedures remain complex and time consuming. In recent surveys Tunisian firms report that it can take three weeks or more to comply with administrative bottlenecks. The costs are especially high for small firms. In Egypt, enforcement of trade regulations by customs requires coordination with multiple government authorities, with complex procedures and little transparency. Customs frequently inspects every shipment, even opening containerized cargo, with extremely high transaction costs.

BOX 4.2

Best Practices in Customs Reform: Lessons from Morocco

Morocco has been implementing customs reforms by following principles suggested by the World Customs Organization and through technical assistance from other partners. A small but effective unit was established, and new performance-based bonuses for customs officers were implemented and stemmed corruption. With active private partnership, four main elements of the program have included (1) simplified procedures and selective controls—replacing sheaves of forms, setting up approved clearing centers in approved companies and warehouses outside the customs perimeter to decongest ports, creating a national clearing credit system empowering customs staff to clear goods at premises of approved importers, and implementing selective controls through red and green channels, with 85 percent processed under no-inspection-required green channel by 2001; (2) increased use of information technology—by the end of 2000, the Customs Administration had computerized its operations and extended selective services to approved companies; (3) improved management of special customs procedures—new procedures have simplified special imports arrangements particularly for temporary imports, exports, and bonded warehouses; and (4) enhanced private partnerships—extensive consultations, easy-to-use websites to track clearing operations, and easier customs guarantees to simplify procedures.

Services and New Businesses

Critical service sectors need to be opened up to competition, especially in telecommunications, financial services, transport, education, and health. Commitments to market access require reexamination, especially in Jordan and Tunisia. In Jordan and Morocco, port and road transport deregulation is critical in view of the high transport costs. Privatization and regulatory reform in air transport are also urgent, especially in air-freight services. Tunisia requires further telecommunications liberalization. Egypt, Jordan, and Tunisia may need to actively encourage competition from foreign banks, by opening up their banking sectors.

Deregulation to reduce bureaucratic procedures and transaction costs for new firms is needed in all three countries. The great number of steps required to open a business is extremely costly and exceeds most standards.

Reforms in Labor-Abundant, Resource-Rich Countries: Algeria, the Islamic Republic of Iran, Syria, and the Republic of Yemen

The natural resource–rich countries have a more complicated task in shifting from state-dominated and protectionist economic systems to open, market-led systems. Much of the core support for reform has to come from the very sectors that stand to lose initially from trade policy reforms—the dominant, protected public enterprises and private sectors. Influential elements of the broader civil society retain a distinct bias toward the status quo because of the rents that accrue to the educated middle class in these closed systems. The private sectors have often been driven underground and are weak. Oil resources and rents have influenced the highly centralized decisionmaking process and the growth of vast public sectors. Not surprising, then, that reforms are episodic: when oil prices fall and macroeconomic stability is threatened, momentum gathers on the need for reform. Reform is then reversed or stalled when prices recover.

Yet the current situation is inherently unstable, and there are significant pressures for more credible and consistent change. The biggest pressure comes from labor markets. The current system is unable to generate enough jobs for a young, educated, and rapidly growing labor force. Unemployment rates are among the highest in the world, and real wages are falling. Falling per capita oil rents compound the problems. And even the most protected domestic industries are increasingly threatened by accelerating competition in world markets. At some point reform becomes inevitable. The political leadership realizes that and is more responsive to reforms in a process that they can manage, while yielding benefits for a greater number and limiting the costs of the transition. Fundamental changes in governance and institutions must accompany trade policy reform to encourage competitive entry of private investment, especially in low-income countries such as the Republic of Yemen (box 4.3).

What, then, is needed for successful trade and investment climate reform? Successful experiences around the world, such as in India (box 4.4), China, Malaysia, Mexico, the transition economies in Europe (box

---

BOX 4.3

Yemen: The Importance of Investment Climate and Governance in Low-Income Settings

For thousands of years, the Republic of Yemen was at the center of Arab intraregional trade, generating prosperity. With the collapse of Ottoman rule in 1919, the traditional local rulers who took over in the north shut the country off from the rest of the world for decades, drastically reducing living standards. In the south, British colonial rule was concentrated in Aden, while the other provinces were governed under traditional feudal rule. Since unification in 1990, modern elections and governance systems have begun to build new systems and faster growth and development, helped by oil revenues.

Accelerated trade integration depends on further improvements in investment climate and governance. The Republic of Yemen now enjoys greater macroeconomic stability and a supportive exchange rate following large, real effective depreciation. In the past few years, nonoil exports have expanded, but performance remains well below potential: some US$23 million annually today, versus an estimated potential of US$860 million (Someya 2001; World Bank 2002b). The Republic of Yemen also has relatively strong business traditions, with successful multinational enterprises operated by traders.

Fundamental investment climate changes are essential, however. Insecurity, violence, and weak property rights are long-standing issues. A survey of Yemeni firms in 2001 suggests that poor governance manifests itself in several ways: corruption and inefficiency in interactions with officials, ineffective or absent institutions for enforcement of contracts and land rights, and weak performance of public services (high entry costs to establish a new business). These problems create massive bottlenecks for private investment, especially for small and medium-size firms.

Systemic improvements in governance will require high-level support, consensus, and careful implementation within a rules-based system. In the meantime, ring-fencing within special areas, such as in the Aden free port area, is being tried. At the local level, greater responsibility, accountability, and competition among governorates and urban areas is helping to create stronger incentives for achieving results, complementing efforts at the national level.

4.5), and Tunisia, Jordan, and the United Arab Emirates in the MENA region, highlight five critical factors:

- Strong political leadership at the highest levels, determined to implement fundamental reforms and to overcome resistance from those who stand to lose initially. Some kind of crisis is probably needed to provoke such firm commitment.

- Strong technical capacity in a high-profile interministerial team to design and implement the most urgent reforms with high payoffs and

---

BOX 4.4

What Prompted India's Trade Reforms?

For most of its postindependence history, India pursued import-substitution industrialization, emphasizing central planning and a large role for the public sector. The balance of payments crisis brought on by the Gulf war led to reforms in trade policy and investment deregulation in 1991. Policies to open up the economy continued even after the balance of payments crisis ended, despite significant domestic opposition. Why? The challenges of external globalization played a part, as did the challenges of the labor market. One researcher has suggested, however, that a strategic rivalry with China also prompted the reforms (Alamgir 1999).

China, starting from a lower base (1960 per capita income of US$75 to India's US$206), has outpaced India by most accounts. By 1995, China's reported per capita GDP had surpassed India's, with trade and foreign investment as engines. Alamgir reports that successive Economic Surveys, the annual stock-taking by the Indian Finance Ministry, reported on the much more dynamic performance of China and East Asia as core lessons for sustaining and accelerating trade policy reforms. Before liberalization started in 1991, India's peak tariff was 300 percent, the highest in the world, and China's was 150 percent. Beginning in July 1991, India matched China's reductions in peak tariffs and then in other tariffs. In January 1992, China reduced tariffs on 225 items and adopted a harmonized classification system. India followed suit in April, lowering peak tariffs to 110 percent and also adopting a harmonized system. By the end of 1997 China and India had both competitively lowered their average tariffs to 20.1 percent and 20.3 percent, respectively. Alamgir argues that this was not mere coincidence. Indian policymakers consistently lowered tariffs despite domestic outcries, under both strong majority and shaky coalition governments, "remarkable in a country as politicized and fragmented as India."

In the core MENA region, examples are fewer, and the emulation of better performance weaker still. Yet in the smaller Gulf states, close watching of one another's performances and rapid adoption of best practices seems to explain better performance in a wide array of policies.

consistent and credible changes over time. Reforms need to suit specific country contexts.

- Strong consensus and support from the private investment community, civil society, media, think tanks, and others that reforms are urgent and needed. Building that consensus in advance is a key.

- Managing transition costs carefully so that losses in jobs and output are kept to tolerable levels, while maintaining a consistent pace and sequence of reforms that produce positive and visible gains—with no backtracking

---

BOX 4.5

Lessons from Integration and Transition Experiences in Eastern Europe

The success of integration in Central and Eastern Europe offers several lessons (World Bank 2000):

- Integration agreements recognized the associated countries' ultimate objective of full accession to the EU and went beyond the narrowly conceived issues of market access to include realignment of economic systems.

- Differences in initial conditions and the speed of reforms help explain differences in performance. For example, Hungary, Poland, and Slovenia were more open to begin with than were Bulgaria and Romania, while the Baltic states did not introduce market reforms until they became independent in 1991.

- The depth of macroeconomic and structural reforms was also crucial in explaining why some countries did better than others—with the boldest reformers achieving the best transition results.

- Once macroeconomic stabilization was under way, structural reforms made a greater contribution. External trade liberalization, price liberalization, privatization, banking reforms, and enterprise restructuring and privatization have often played a key role.

- New activities have been the main drivers of private sector growth, and countries with the most FDI have performed best.

- Hard budget constraints for state enterprises and banking sector reforms were important in most cases.

- Political change was a powerful imperative for success. Countries that undertook bolder and more substantial reforms did better. The Czech Republic, Estonia, Hungary, and Poland led in this area.

- Consistent support from external partners that does not dilute incentives to reform. External partners need to support the best examples to allow spillover effects of learning on the rest of the countries (see box 4.5).

Preconditions for Reform

Taking into account these factors, what should the countries in the group of larger, resource-rich countries do to initiate and sustain effective trade reform?

Countries first need to achieve macroeconomic stability—as most have—at a reasonable level of oil prices. But they also need to deal with the massive distortionary effects of oil rents on traded goods and services. This means managing the booms and busts better, avoiding the stop-go cycles of structural reform and backtracking, to progressively reduce the rent-seeking effects of oil. For example, during the 1979–81 boom, more than 40 percent of Indonesia's oil windfall was saved abroad, and supporting exchange rate policies allowed the nonoil sectors to grow despite the oil boom.

Specifically, countries might need to:

- Establish fiscal rules that insulate government spending from windfalls and downturns, by setting up explicit rules-based mechanisms for saving or drawing down temporary oil funds.

- Set aside an increasing proportion of oil revenues as longer-term surpluses for future generations (as a provident fund for old-age pensions for the current generation or for social safety nets for job losses in the transition).

- Establish a more realistic, longer-term equilibrium real exchange rate.

To be credible these measures need to be backed by constitutional-type reforms so that the rules cannot be easily changed. Many of these countries distribute a significant part of the oil rents as production subsidies or low energy prices to consumers, with the same distortionary macroeconomic effects as public spending. Energy prices need to be raised progressively to world levels. Diversification and growth of nonoil traded goods and services will be impossible without some combination of these measures.

In less well-endowed countries, such as Syria, floating market–determined exchange rates may be needed to move exchange rates to more realistic levels.

Domestic pricing deregulation for key traded goods and services is another precondition to effective trade reform. Price controls, regulations, and subsidies, so pervasive in these economies, muffle the price signals through which trade policy reforms work.

Trade Policy Reforms

Having achieved these basic preconditions, governments can move on to trade policy reforms. Across-the-board cuts in tariffs spread the costs of reform across all sectors, increasing the benefits and reducing resistance. The goal should be a uniform tariff rate of about 10 percent (a target lower than in resource-poor countries because offsetting oil revenues should permit lower trade taxes). Algeria's tariff reduction program is progressing and a five-year program to eliminate the additional 60 percent duty is being implemented. But the mean tariff is high at 22 percent, and administrative procedures tend to be unpredictable, discouraging investment. Syria's effective tariff rates are low at 8 to 10 percent of CIF value, implying simple average tariff rates of about 21 percent, but the structure of tariffs favors capital goods and penalizes consumption goods (Lucke 2001). Lowering all tariffs and reducing dispersion would bring large benefits to consumers (2 percent increase in consumption) with little effect on domestic production. The Islamic Republic of Iran's unweighted tariff equivalent of tariff and nontariff barriers is about 30 percent. An across-the-board cut in protection would have large beneficial effects (World Bank 2001).

Import duties can be replaced by a stronger nonoil tax base, boosting overall government revenue. In Algeria, for example, the complexity of the VAT and other taxes and high rates of evasion result in low yields. The Islamic Republic of Iran's import licensing is governed by three overlapping classifications of goods administered by the Ministry of Commerce, a second list of permissible imports with foreign exchange earned from nonoil exports, and a third positive list of exempt items. Free trade zones provide loopholes for import licensing, a rich source of rent seeking and tax avoidance. In Syria, coverage of nontariff barriers is extensive and administratively complex. Export restrictions and bans are also in place in various countries, and quality control checks and technical standards are also major impediments to trade.

Customs reforms are also needed. Customs frequently inspects every shipment, including containerized cargo, leading to high transaction costs.

All countries would benefit from deregulation of services and the introduction of competition to state-owned and -operated activities—in ports, transport, telecommunications, and finance. The waiting time for a fixed telephone line is 10 years in Syria and 6 years in Algeria. Algeria, the Islamic Republic of Iran, and Syria limit foreign bank activity, with state-owned banks dominating (up to 95 percent of assets). The result is poor services, high costs, extensive lending to state enterprises, shaky balance sheets, and weak financing of new activities and trade. Financial sector reform ranks high on the agenda of services requiring critical attention.

Finally deregulation of domestic and foreign investment is also critical for export and trade activities. Attracting more FDI will require deepseated reforms and improvements in the business climate and the environment for private sector activity.

The required trade policy reforms are quite different from those of the labor-abundant, resource-poor countries (box 4.6). A consistent and credible package of reforms needs to be systematically implemented over a 10-year or so period in most of these countries, with strong political leadership and strong technical capacity in an interministerial team with the

---

BOX 4.6

How Does the Policy Package Differ for Labor-Abundant, Resource-Rich Countries and for Resource-Poor Countries?

The recommended policy mix for both groups appears similar: reduction of tariffs and nontariff barriers and behind-the-border customs and services deregulation. But there are major differences. First, the package of reforms in larger, resource-rich countries must include prior macroeconomic and microeconomic reforms for dealing with the oil-rent distribution problem. Without that, these countries cannot begin to create the necessary institutional improvements and exchange rate changes that will allow greater trade in goods and services. Second, larger, resource-rich countries must address domestic price deregulation if there is to be a significant supply response. Domestic sectorwide reforms carry much greater weight than in resource-poor countries.

Third, financial sector reform is more urgent in resource-rich settings, because it is essential for enabling shifts in resource allocation and supply response gains from trade reforms. FDI can play a larger role in resource-poor countries. Fourth, trade and domestic price deregulation in resource-rich countries will need to be more carefully differentiated to avoid large negative impacts on jobs in public sectors that act as implicit employment safety nets—for example, by targeting a progressive attrition of workers rather than massive layoffs (as in China, India, Indonesia, Mexico, or Vietnam). Finally, a major difference between the two cases is a much longer proposed phasing of reforms in large, resource-rich countries (up to 10 years) than in resource-poor countries (2 to 3 years).

How do the suggested reforms differentiate from standard reform recommendations? Here too, there are significant differences. First, no one-size-fits-all policies make sense: the packages recommended here seek to recognize country specificities more carefully, especially in terms of size, oil-rent resource effects, and institutional-cum-political economy effects, as indicated above. Second, they recommend more careful consideration of potential transition and adjustment costs, in sectors such as public sector job losses and those affecting agriculture. Third, the timing of reforms is more gradual and systematic.

power to address the most critical bottlenecks. Indonesia implemented successive annual trade deregulation packages during 1986–94. A strong team successively handled tariff reductions, removal of nontariff barriers, customs services, and complementary reforms over a range of increasingly difficult areas. Rent-seeking constituencies were prevented from obstructing the dismantling of import protection built up since independence (Bhattacharya and Pangestu 1993). Nonoil exports rose from 25 percent to 75 percent of total export earnings, and nonoil taxes and GDP rose by equally impressive magnitudes (Dasgupta, Hulu, and Das Gupta 2002).

Public sector enterprises in manufacturing and service sectors, which employ large sections of the labor force, are the greatest obstacle to effective trade reform in many of these countries. These enterprises are threatened by many of the trade measures, and by the change to a private sector–led economy. They also form a natural coalition with others who stand to lose from trade reforms, especially a smaller group of rent-seeking constituencies that directly benefit from many of the current trade restrictions.

Trade policy reformers will need to isolate and break up these natural constituencies of support for the status quo. One way is to increasingly isolate them by removing the main sources of their rents in trade, typically by removing administrative discretion, setting tariff rules, and eliminating licensing and quota barriers. That would release large and visible benefits to consumers, through lower prices and greater availability of consumer goods, raising aggregate consumption by as much as 3 to 5 percent. It would be important to deal carefully with state enterprises and potential job losses, by allowing some state enterprises to remain in operation with harder budget constraints. A progressive reduction in the size of state enterprises could avoid large job losses (as in Indonesia).

Investment deregulation and reforms in key sectors would also be needed in ports, transport, telecommunications, customs, standards and inspections, banking, and finance. A recent study by the McKinsey Global Institute suggests that sector-specific regulatory issues are the most important impediment to faster growth in every country in the world (box 4.7).

Reforms in Labor-Importing, Resource-Rich Countries: The GCC States

The resource-rich GCC countries face two main challenges: accelerating nonoil growth to generate adequate employment opportunities for the 70 percent of the population who is under 30 years old and a rapidly growing population (while it is moderating, the level is still high at 3 percent), and reducing vulnerability to oil price fluctuations. On both ac-

---

BOX 4.7

The Importance of Competition Issues and Sector Reforms: Labeling Requirements in Egyptian Textiles

Sector-specific issues include competition policies, restrictive practices, state ownership, and pricing reforms. Consider the textiles industry, an important export sector in much of the MENA region, with high levels of employment. In Egypt the textile sector employs some half a million workers and accounts for 40 percent of exports earnings. Trade channels are highly restricted. Capacity utilization varies from 40 percent to 85 percent, and problems abound, from the unavailability of inputs to poor maintenance. By the late 1990s, the accumulated debt of public companies was substantially higher than their fixed assets, suggesting insolvency. Protection rates are high, with tariffs alone at more than 70 percent. When the ban on imports was lifted, the Ministry of Supply and Foreign Trade required that all imported fabrics have the importer's name woven into the label, effectively stopping all imports. This measure was designed to protect state-owned fabric producers at the expense of privately owned garment manufacturing firms, which had increasingly turned to imported cloth.

---

counts, the smaller GCC countries have done well. They have maintained open policies on the movement of goods, labor, and capital within member states and relatively open policies with respect to the rest of the world, which has helped to diversify exports. They have also responded well to oil price volatility by using their oil resources to modernize their infrastructures, provide employment, expand education, and improve social indicators. But challenges remain. Per capita incomes in Saudi Arabia have fallen (in nominal terms) from a high of about US$26,000 in the early 1980s to about US$6,000, an almost unprecedented drop.

The GCC countries have embarked on even deeper reforms that promise to sustain these basic policy directions and accelerate their integration with the global economy. They have established a US$335 billion customs union, which will allow them to forge a larger common market with lower trade barriers to the rest of the world, with a standard 5 percent external customs tariff. The goal is to form a homogeneous unit to facilitate intragroup trade and collective negotiations with the WTO and to attract foreign investment. The agreement contains clauses on the establishment of a monetary union and the launching of a common currency by 2010 to reduce the transaction costs and uncertainty of bilateral exchange rates and deepen integration. Convergence of unilateral monetary and exchange rate policies will require attention (Jadresic 2002). The customs union also sets up a new independent Gulf authority for enhanced coordination across states.

Good progress is being achieved in opening up private and foreign investment in restricted areas. Independent power projects are being enhanced in Abu Dhabi, Dubai, Oman, and elsewhere. Water sectors are also being opened to foreign and domestic investment. Corporatization and privatization measures are also being advanced, along with pricing reforms. Abu Dhabi raised electricity and water charges for expatriates by 80 percent (above cost for the first time). Foreign ownership of real estate has also been opened up in Bahrain, and offshore-type real estate liberalization is proceeding well in Dubai. Kuwait recently adopted measures to open up to foreign investment. Regulatory improvements are being introduced in the banking and financial sectors. High standards of technical excellence are being established in infrastructure services, matching global best standards.

Sector-specific strategies are also being pursued, with private investment and partnerships to develop special niches. These include development of subregional hubs for information and telecommunications, which are attracting international investors.

Personnel and income policies to facilitate productive employment opportunities are ongoing. And the pullback from state involvement in productive activities has been accompanied by tax and expenditure reforms to strengthen public finances and reduce oil price volatility.

Challenges in trade integration lie mainly in four interlinked areas. First, labor markets suffer from wage rigidities, skills mismatches, and institutional factors. Some GCC countries are replacing foreign workers with nationals by setting quotas on expatriate workers and raising employment costs for expatriates. These policies could be counterproductive in the longer term because wage flexibility and skilled workers are needed for growth of the nonoil sectors. Mandatory systems are not a good substitute for wage flexibility. Education and skills training improvements are also critical.

Second, the government wage bill, defense and security spending, and subsidies and entitlements are straining government budgets. The traditional role of the government as dominant employer and wage policy setter needs reconsideration, as do subsidies for food, health, education, and basic industries. Explicit subsidies are small by international standards (2 to 3 percent of GDP), but implicit subsidies through low energy prices and long-term loans are significantly larger. Revenue policies will also need attention, especially fees for utility services and the introduction of broad-based consumption taxes.

Third, structural policies to diversify economies will need continued attention, especially privatization since most of the larger, nonoil industries remain in public hands. New regulatory standards are needed for financial markets and to spur development of local equity markets. Finally,

FIGURE 5.1

Static Welfare Gains from Service Liberalization
(in 1997 US$ billions, for 2015)

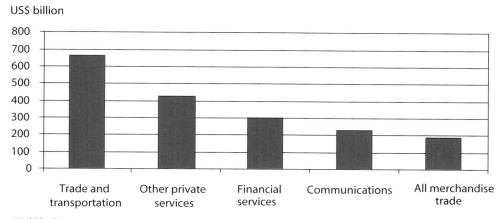

US$ billion

Source: World Bank 2002a.

The recent experience of countries in Central and Eastern Europe—where privatization and trade liberalization went in tandem with service sector reform—shows the potential for generating a large increase in service employment. Case studies also point to significant potential employment gains. For Tunisia, in a high-case scenario, ICT development—spurred by opening up telecommunications markets to competition and exports of software and information technology (IT)–enabled services—could boost GDP by as much as 4.4 percent and raise total employment by about 2.6 percent in the medium term (World Bank 2001c).[2]

Service Reform and Export Niches in Information Technology

Liberalizing key services, such as transport and telecommunications, greatly facilitates the development of export capacity in other services, especially in tourism and ICT. The importance of promoting sustainable tourism development in MENA countries can hardly be overstated, given the potential for job creation and export revenues. But the potential is also good for exports of ICT services. Good examples of developing country success stories are the booming Indian exports of ICT business services and software, while Malaysia has become an international hub for business-to-business (B2B) trade in ICT products and especially semiconductors. Indian software exports grew from US$225 million in 1992–93 to US$1.8 billion in 1997–98. By 2008 the Indian ICT sector could provide about 2.2 million jobs, generate 35 percent of India's export earnings, and attract US$5 billion of FDI (World Bank 2001b).

MENA has yet to become a hub for export-oriented ICT services, although a number of countries have the human resources and capabilities for doing so. Software development and related activities are starting to create export niches. In Egypt, the good capabilities in software are evident in the high quality of some software packages produced locally and exported to the Gulf states—and in the growing market for offshore software development. Software exports have also increased in Tunisia, although that has been driven by the activities of a handful of high-flyer firms (World Bank 2001c; University of Napoli Federico II 2001). Still, software development remains limited in most MENA countries, because firms tend to be small, lacking critical technologies and project management know-how. They also concentrate on the small and cost-sensitive domestic markets, which tend to be dominated by government procurement because of the low computer penetration. The software and computing services industry is also impeded by widespread software piracy, which must be addressed by better enforcement of laws on intellectual property rights.[3]

The global market for ICT-enabled services is also booming, and is expected to exceed US$140 billion by 2008, a dramatic increase from the US$10 billion estimated in 1998 (box 5.1). The development of the offshore ICT-enabled services industry is driven by the need for multinational companies to reduce business and transactions costs that is being facilitated by falling telecommunications costs.

In the MENA region the provision of ICT-enabled services remains at the very beginning stages of development. Several Jordanian firms are engaged in a variety of data-conversion tasks for export markets. Call centers have been a significant growth opportunity in Morocco since 2000, resulting in large part from telecommunications deregulation. Egypt has a few companies engaged in offshore engineering and design, as well as remote education activities.

Status of MENA Countries' WTO Commitments in Services

The WTO General Agreement on Trade in Services (GATS) commits member governments to undertake negotiations on specific issues and to enter successive rounds of negotiations to progressively liberalize their trade in services. The first round of service negotiations started officially in early 2000 under the Council for Trade in Services. The Doha Declaration endorsed the work already done, reaffirmed the negotiating guidelines and procedures, and established a deadline for the conclusion of the negotiations as part of a single undertaking (WTO 2001). Participating in the multilateral process of trade liberalization in services is

BOX 5.1

The Global Market for ICT-Enabled Services Provided in Offshore Locations

ICT-enabled services encompass a broad range of activities made possible by advances in telecommunications and computing power and the spread of the Internet. Faced with skill, staffing, and time constraints, firms in industrial countries turn to ICT professionals in developing countries for a variety of administrative, back-office, and professional services.

International companies can realize cost savings estimated at 40 to 50 percent from outsourcing noncore, back-office processes to lower-cost locations. Even larger savings are possible in more sophisticated white-collar work, given significant wage differences for such workers between high-income and developing countries. Unlike software development, which is sensitive to cyclical trends, companies are always under pressure to reduce back-office operating costs.

ICT-enabled services provided in offshore locations in emerging markets include:

- Data conversion, comprising operations that convert data or graphics into an electronic format, a labor-intensive process. Examples include simple data entry, digitization, medical transcription, and deposition summaries.
- Voice center operations, relatively low-end activities, which include offshore reservation centers, insurance claims processing, call centers, and telemarketing.

Projected Global Market for ICT-Enabled Services (US$ billion)

Segment	1998	2008
Customer services	6.5	33.0
Finance and accounting	1.5	15.0
Translation and transcription	1.3	20.0
Engineering and design	0.3	1.2
Human resource services	0.4	5.0
Data search, integration, and management	0.2	44.0
Remote education	—	18.0
Consulting	—	15.0
Web site services	—	5.0
Market research	—	3.0
Total	10.0	142.0

— Not available.

- Outsourcing back-office and professional and administrative services, such as human resource management. India is an example of a country that benefits from outsourcing of noncore processes to third parties by multinational companies.

Given the lack of a consistent definition of the ICT-enabled services industry and the dynamic impacts of technological innovation, it is hard to develop an accurate indication of overall market size. But recent studies indicate an enormous and rapidly growing market, perhaps larger than the entire global software industry.

particularly important for developing countries. Because many domestic providers of services in developing countries operate below international efficiency standards, securing effective competition in domestic markets has to go in tandem with lowering trade barriers in services and making room for foreign entry into domestic markets.

Contrary to steps taken by other developing countries, and despite recent initiatives, the MENA region still lags behind in regulatory reform to open services to competition. MENA country commitments for market access for broad groups of service sectors (median of five sectors) are in the middle range among other country groups (figure 5.2). Countries in Eastern Europe, also geographically close to the EU, have been more eager to commit to service liberalization, with little variability among countries, almost on par with high-income OECD countries.

MENA countries have granted more commitments for tourism and financial services (table 5.1). This will help further realize the substantial tourism potential of the region and improve the efficiency of financial transactions, laying the groundwork for the development of domestic financial markets. But the lukewarm commitments in the transport and distribution sectors do not bode well for expanding trade in the region. Moreover, in view of the education and knowledge gaps singled out by the United Nations Development Programme (2002), the absence of commitments in education is not encouraging.

Without further in-depth analysis of the commitments by country (limits, most favored nation exclusions, and other), it is hard to evaluate the likely impact of current policies on MENA trade performance. But even this crude measure of counting open sectors reveals that only four GCC countries—excluding Bahrain, with an opening only in the financial sector, and Saudi Arabia, which is not yet a member of the WTO—are in the forefront of service liberalization. In the rest of the region, the

FIGURE 5.2

Market Access Commitments under GATS

Number of commitments

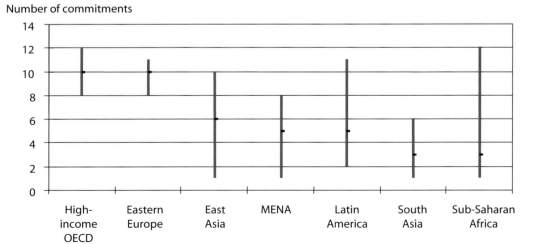

Note: The chart displays minimum, maximum, and median number of sectors for which countries have granted market access commitments under the GATS. Important omissions because of the cutoff date (January 2000) are Jordan and China. The high-income OECD country average excludes the EU.
Source: WTO 2000.

TABLE 5.1

GATS Market Access Commitments by MENA Countries

Commitment	Kuwait	Morocco	Qatar	United Arab Emirates	Djibouti	Egypt, Arab Rep. of	Tunisia	Bahrain	Total
Financial services	X	X	X	X		X	X	X	7
Tourism and travel-related services	X	X	X	X	X	X	X		7
Business services	X	X	X	X	X				5
Communication services		X	X	X	X		X		5
Construction and related engineering services	X	X	X	X		X			5
Environmental services	X	X	X	X					4
Recreational, cultural, and sporting services	X				X				2
Transport services		X				X			2
Distribution services	X								1
Health-related and social services	X								1
Educational services									0
Other services not included elsewhere									0
Total	8	7	6	6	4	4	3	1	

Source: WTO 2000.

agenda is pretty much open, and more ambitious moves could elicit significant rewards.

Transport Services

In the MENA region—and particularly in North Africa—most trade outside the region is by sea or air. Transport by road and rail is used primarily for domestic and regional trade. But because it is needed for door-to-door delivery, the efficiency of the land leg determines the overall efficiency of multimodal transport logistics.

Sea transport is most important, accounting for 83 percent of southern Mediterranean country trade by weight in 1997 (Muller-Jentsch 2002), but only for 53 percent by value, with products having a higher value-to-weight ratio tending to go by air. Transport by air is also important for MENA tourism. In Egypt the share of air transport in foreign arrivals is about 74 percent, and in Morocco, 66 percent. Intensive in labor, tourism generates jobs. Tourism receipts amounted to US$10.5 billion for the region in 1999–2000—about 29 percent of total export earnings in Egypt, 23 percent in Jordan, and 18 percent in Morocco and Tunisia.

Calculating transport-related costs for an economy is not straightforward, but proximate indicators can be constructed by comparing CIF and free on board (FOB) values of trade flows. The difference between the CIF and FOB values of imports, as a share of the FOB value of imports, indicates the ad valorem freight and insurance costs. For seven MENA countries freight costs amounted on average to an estimated 11.8 percent of imports in 2000. Transport costs are particularly high in Jordan, Morocco, and Syria, and are much lower in Tunisia (figure 5.3). Transport costs in the MENA region are higher than in other regions. They also surpass costs in geographically more isolated developing countries, such as Chile. The efficiency of transport would benefit from regulatory reform in the sector as outlined below, but also from improvements in other network industries—especially in ICT (box 5.2).

Air Transport

Despite some progress, the regulatory reform of air transport is still at an early stage. Services remain largely provided by state-owned airlines and airports, with competition restrained by restrictive licensing regimes for domestic flights and international air service agreements. Public ownership, combined with restricted competition, mean poor management and low efficiency for most MENA carriers (Muller-Jentsch 2002). Efficiency indicators, such as freight and passenger capacity use while planes are airborne, suggest that MENA carriers fall short of interna-

FIGURE 5.3

MENA Trade Is Burdened by High Transport Costs

Freight costs in percentage of the value of imports, 2000

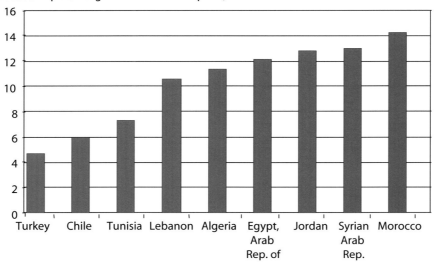

Source: UNCTAD, adapted from Muller-Jentsch 2002.

BOX. 5.2

Transport's Symbiosis with Information and Communications Technologies

Transport logistics are intensive in information. Fast and reliable information processing is a prerequisite for the efficient flow of goods, since transport is "perishable"—the spare capacity of a plane or ship cannot be sold once the trip has been made. Information flows in transportation are facilitated by a variety of ICT applications, such as inventory and warehouse management systems, route optimization, tracing and tracking software, and satellite-based fleet management systems.

So far, MENA countries have largely missed out on these developments. Throughout the region, state-owned airlines, airports, ports, and railways have failed to introduce state-of-the-art ICT applications, reducing their own efficiency, but also disrupting the systemwide flow of information and increasing frictions in trade. On the demand side, widespread use of ICT applications in transport logistics has been hampered by weak incentives to improve efficiency, because of the lack of competition in transport markets. Lack of commercial management in state-owned transport companies has also been a factor, as outdated company structures and cumbersome working procedures have been unfriendly to modern ICT. On the supply side, the high cost and limited availability of ICT services—such as leased lines, networking services, and the Internet—have also been factors, partly reflecting limited competition in telecommunications markets and data transmission in most MENA countries.

---

tional standards by an estimated 15 to 20 percent (figure 5.4). And since the marginal cost for additional passengers and cargo is low, the low capacity use rates suggest that there is much room for improvement in those carriers' poor financial health. Regulatory reform should aim at strengthening competition and the transparency of the regulatory regime (box 5.3).

Air cargo would merit even greater attention in regulatory reform, as it is one of the fastest growing segments of the air transport market—with an estimated 40 percent of global manufactured exports by value now being carried by air. Goods with a high value-to-weight ratio, as well as perishable products, find their way to the markets by air. The expansion of global production-sharing networks—and the widespread use of just-in-time production methods and supply-chain management—have increased the importance of reliable and low-cost air cargo services.

In the MENA region the growth of air cargo has been below the global average—partly because MENA countries find it difficult to diversify their exports into high-value-added products, and partly because of regulatory barriers (Muller-Jentsch 2002). In many MENA countries

FIGURE 5.4

MENA Carriers Underperform by International Efficiency Standards

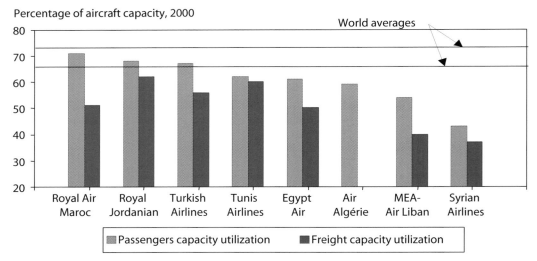

Percentage of aircraft capacity, 2000

Source: Adapted from Muller-Jentsch 2002.

restrictive air-service agreements prevent free route development and network optimization. Leasing constraints, customs delays, and inefficient ground handling add to the barriers. Reforms that encourage more competition and improve performance in air cargo would strengthen the region's links to global markets, attract more FDI, and diversify MENA exports toward higher-value-added products.

Regulatory reform in air transport also needs to encompass airports—particularly ground handling, which is inefficient and costly and frequently identified as a key bottleneck (box 5.3). Several MENA countries are encouraging private participation in the operation of airports—which, coupled with procompetitive regulation, should increase the efficiency of airport service provision. Egypt has awarded build-operate-transfer concessions for three new airports. Algeria is considering similar steps.

Maritime Transport

The speed, cost-effectiveness, and reliability of maritime transport are critical for the promotion of exports and the integration of MENA into global production networks. This is especially true for the shipment of containers, the fastest growing segment in maritime transport, both around the globe and within the region. A high rate of containerization is critical to improving not only the efficiency of maritime transport, but

BOX 5.3

Priorities for Regulatory Reform in MENA's Air Transport

International experience suggests that to foster competition—especially in domestic air transport—routes, capacity, and flight frequency should be determined by market conditions, not rigid licensing regimes, and national ownership and control rules should be kept to a minimum. In most MENA countries, the licensing regimes protect flag carriers. And despite the entry of private airlines, few can compete with the incumbents because they are often confined to niche markets. Cross-border air transport regulation in MENA is still dominated by traditional bilateral air-service agreements that regulate traffic rights, capacity, and routes.

Because the domestic air transport markets in MENA are small—limiting potential efficiency gains—reform should focus on international air transport. Liberalization toward the EU should be a priority, given its importance as a market for MENA countries. The most comprehensive strategy for cross-border liberalization would be the gradual creation of a common Euro-Mediterranean air transport space, eventually to match the free trade area aimed for in the association agreements with the EU. This could involve the gradual accession of MENA countries to the European Civil Aviation Area (ECAA) agreed on in 2001—which will extend to the Central and Eastern European countries the single market for air transport in the EU (Muller-Jentsch 2002).

Extending the ECAA to the southern Mediterranean would greatly facilitate tourism, trade, and business travel within the region. Removing existing barriers to competition would also encourage foreign investment and create opportunities for domestic operators to participate in cross-border alliances. Greater competition would also improve carriers' efficiency and help in passing on cost reductions to users. The benefits could be substantial. A study in the United States found that fares on routes with three competing carriers were on average 8 percent lower than those on routes with two competitors, which in turn were 8 percent lower than those on routes with only one airline.

Procompetitive regulation in airports affects the cost structure of carriers and competition in the market. To achieve more competitive outcomes, ground handling would need to be unbundled from airport and airline operations, with third-party handling licensing liberalized. Airport charges and airport slots would need to be carefully regulated in a procompetitive way—especially the slots, a key determinant of market access and competition.

Source: Muller-Jentsch 2002.

also that of the multimodal transport system, as containerization lowers the cost of cargo modal transfers. Despite recent progress, the efficiency of maritime transport in the MENA region remains low by international standards. Ports—the entry points for the region's trade—remain a weak link in the intermodal transport chain.

MENA countries still lag behind in the rate of containerization in general cargo traffic. At the end of the 1990s, the containerization of Egypt's general cargo was 27 percent for imports and 36 percent for exports. Algeria's average containerization for trade was estimated at 16 percent, and Tunisia's at 37 percent. International averages range from 50 to 60 percent, with much higher rates for most high-income countries (Muller-Jentsch 2002).

Competition in port services remains limited throughout the MENA region, and the absence of private participation in port operations reduces the incentives to improve efficiency. This situation lowers the quality and increases the cost of cargo handling, warehousing, and bunkering, lowering the containerization of cargo traffic. Performance indicators of MENA ports—such as cargo-handling costs and customs clearance times—are elusive, but case studies and anecdotal evidence point to substantial scope for efficiency improvements. A study found that container freight rates to Alexandria in 1998 were generally 15 to 20 percent higher than to other Mediterranean destinations (World Bank 1998). In Casablanca, Morocco's main port, ship handling times could be reduced by about 75 percent if productivity were to match international standards.

Most ports in the region are run by public authorities, on the model of the "service port," in which the authority regulates the port and provides all commercial port services. Government budget constraints, combined with obstacles to private participation, prevent the modernization and adequate maintenance of port facilities. Red tape adds to the bottlenecks, causing delays and disrupting the maritime transport chain. Elsewhere in the world the "landlord port" is becoming the standard operating model, unbundling the regulatory functions (linked to natural monopoly elements, such as provision of basic infrastructure) from the potentially competitive commercial services. More competition in commercial port services, coupled with appropriate regulation, would increase the efficiency of MENA ports in cargo handling, reducing the cost of cargo movements and increasing the containerization of trade.[4]

Land-Based Transport Services

Because of the closure of several borders, land-based transport plays only a minor role in cross-border merchandise transport in MENA, with road transport dominating rail by far. Restrictive regulations in the trucking industry increase transport cost and reduce efficiency in many MENA countries. Red tape at border crossings also hampers efficiency. Moreover, fuel prices, taxes, and user fees do not reflect the negative externalities generated by trucking—such as congestion, environmental costs, and damage to infrastructure. But there have been some attempts to re-form trucking. Tunisia removed legal barriers to market entry, deregu-lated rates, and sold government-owned trucking companies.

Railways, particularly well-suited to provide efficient hinterland con-nections for ports, especially for containerized cargo, have a potential cost advantage over trucking for long-distance transport. And the 1990s saw the reemergence of private rail operations in developing countries, after more than half a century of nationalization and public sector man-agement. By the end of the decade, the governments of 14 developing countries had taken steps of varying magnitudes to spin off rail opera-tions from government to private control. In the MENA region, as a re-sult of decades of state ownership, railways suffer from underinvestment, overstaffing, and lower competitiveness than trucking. In most countries, performance indicators compare unfavorably with EU averages (figure 5.5) (Kessides 2002). But there are exceptions, as in Egypt and Jordan where productivity indicators are satisfactory—probably reflecting the peculiarities of their rail networks.[5]

Outsourcing noncore railway activities, streamlining organizational structures, and introducing concessions to operate infrastructure and provide rail services would improve efficiency and reduce costs. Morocco has taken the lead in railway restructuring. In 1995 it launched an ambi-tious reform program, which turned around the inefficient and loss-making Office National des Chemins de Fer into a profitable company by rationalizing operations, reducing surplus staff, and introducing com-mercial management. Jordan too has taken steps to improve efficiency, privatizing its railway freight operations.

FIGURE 5.5

Considerable Scope for Improving Railway Efficiency in MENA Countries

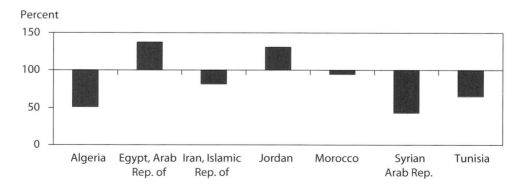

Note: Thousands of traffic units (TUs) per employee: percentage deviations from EU average (1990–99, EU average = 100%).
Source: World Bank staff.

Telecommunications

Telecommunications provide backbone services that affect efficiency and growth of a wide range of user industries. The quality and price of such key services shape overall economic performance, affecting the capacity of businesses to compete in foreign and domestic markets and the scope for integration in global production-sharing networks. Reflecting the rapid pace of innovation in ICTs, competitive market forces are becoming more important in the provision of telecommunications and networking services, moving the sector away from the old "natural monopoly" market model.

Many developing countries have fast-tracked their opening of telecommunications to competition, with Latin America in the lead, closely followed by South Asia and East Asia and the Pacific (Cowhey and Klimenko 2000). But regulatory reform in telecommunications has been slow in the MENA region, where markets remain on average less competitive than in other developing countries. This gap can be measured by an indicator that takes into account the competition in networks and service provision in different segments of the telecommunications markets, the openness to FDI, and the existence of procompetitive regulation and an independent regulatory body (Varoudakis and Rosotto 2001) (figure 5.6). The pace of regulatory reform has recently increased in MENA countries—especially in Algeria, Jordan, and Morocco, which has taken the region's lead in market openness. But there still is considerable scope for freeing up telecommunications markets (box 5.4).

BOX 5.4

Opening Telecommunications Markets to Competition in MENA: Some Progress—with Hesitant Steps

MENA countries have recently stepped up the pace of telecommunications reform. But progress has been uneven, with only five countries having moderate market openness. Morocco, Jordan, and Tunisia illustrate the differences in the pace of reform.

Morocco's liberalization is most advanced. The test bed for effective competition in Morocco was the award of the second global system for mobile communication (GSM) license. After a highly competitive bidding process, the license was awarded to the Telefonica-led consortium, which paid more than US$1 billion, a record for the region. The threat of competition stimulated the incumbent operator, IAM, to lower tariffs four times in one year. This produced unprecedented growth in the mobile market, from 150,000 customers at the beginning of 1999 to 4,000,000 at the end of 2000. Morocco capitalized on the success achieved in the mobile market to move forward on the privatization front. The incumbent operator has been corporatized, and after a long tender process, a 35 percent stake

BOX 5.4 (continued)

was sold in December 2000 to France's Vivendi Universal—for US$2.2 billion. Morocco started to award fixed-line licenses in 2002, but no bidder presented final offers, partly reflecting the adverse international financial situation for telecommunications and partly the license's restrictive obligations in view of the market's saturation by GSM services.

In Jordan the 1995 Telecommunications Law introduced the main regulatory principles of independent regulation, competition, and sector reform. The privatization of Jordan Telecom was completed in 1999, with the acquisition of a 40 percent share in the company by

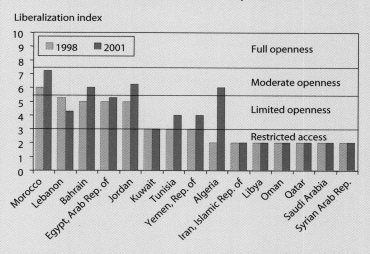

Liberalization index

France Telecom. In parallel, the government has made good progress in liberalizing mobile communications. In 1995 a private provider, Fastlink, owned by Egypt's Orascom Telecom, was licensed to provide GSM services. A second license went to Mobilcom, owned by Jordan Telecom. The competition between Fastlink and Mobilcom led to several reductions in the price of mobile telecommunications and to an expansion of services, reaching 9 percent penetration at the end of 2000. Further competition in the mobile market, with the award of a third license, is being considered for 2003.

Tunisia has a higher GDP per capita than Morocco and Jordan but is less advanced in market liberalization, even with recent efforts. The Tunisian telecommunications market was long characterized by the monopoly of Tunisie Telecom and the extensive role of the state as policymaker, regulator, and operator. Although Tunisia has relatively high fixed-line penetration, a well-balanced network between major cities and rest of the country, and good quality in the basic network, it is clearly below its full potential in some areas, such as wireless communications and Internet penetration. The government enacted a new Communications Code in February 2001, which abolishes the monopoly of the state in the sector, states basic regulatory principles, and creates regulatory agencies. A second GSM license was awarded to Orascom Telecom Tunisia in March 2002 for US$454 million. In early 2003 the incumbent operator, Tunisie Telecom, lowered its prepaid activation fees in response to the lower activation fees of the new entrant. Reflecting considerable pent-up demand for mobile phone lines and fast-rising per capita income, the mobile network in Tunisia could expand almost ninefold by 2006, reaching a penetration rate of 43 percent.

Source: World Bank staff.

International evidence suggests that greater market openness in telecommunications, coupled with a high-quality regulatory regime, drives ICT development. Greater market openness props up expenditure in telecommunications—by encouraging expansion of the network at lower cost, while improving the efficiency of incumbent operators, thus expanding the array of services offered to users and lowering the costs of services to ICT-using sectors (Boylaud and Nicoletti 2000; OECD 2000; Mattoo, Rathindran, and Subramanian 2001; Varoudakis and Rosotto 2001). Because MENA telecommunications markets are less competitive, the overall quality of services is also below the average in other developing countries, despite the potential in the region's high per capita income. Quality is measured by a composite indicator encompassing the density of fixed and mobile telephone networks, the cost of local communications, and the average waiting time for a fixed line (figure 5.6).

More efficient and lower-cost telecommunications could help improve the weak position of MENA countries in global production networks, boosting the region's participation in global trade. Evidence from developing countries over the 1990s suggests that the share of manufactured exports in GDP increases with improvements in the overall quality of telecommunications (figure 5.6). The impact of telecommunications is significant after accounting for other structural determinants of manufactured exports, such as real effective exchange rate competitiveness and GDP growth of the main trade partners (Rosotto, Sekkat, and Varoudakis 2003). On the basis of these estimates, forgone export earnings for MENA—resulting from the gap in the quality of telecommunications with, say, Central and Eastern European countries—are estimated at about 40 percent of total manufactured exports, or 3 percent of GDP. The impact could be even greater, with greater know-how and productivity of exporting firms and the high leverage of telecommunications liberalization in strengthening the investment climate and fostering FDI in other economic sectors.

More competition in leased lines and backbone networks, along with appropriate pricing policies to stimulate demand, would facilitate Internet penetration and ICT sector development. The spread of the Internet—after accounting for other structural determinants—turns out to be greater in countries with more open telecommunications markets, with MENA again lagging behind (figure 5.6).

ICT development, spurred by low-cost and high-quality telecommunications, can also bridge part of the "quality gap" in MENA trade. International evidence suggests that a good level of Internet connectivity (measured by Internet host penetration) is associated with larger high-tech shares in total manufactured exports (figure 5.6). Better Internet connectivity, by facilitating assimilation of existing technologies, enables

FIGURE 5.6

Telecommunications Liberalization in MENA: What's at Stake?

Telecommunications markets remain less competitive,

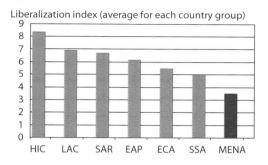

Liberalization index (average for each country group)

partly accounting for the unrealized potential,

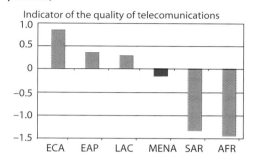

Indicator of the quality of telecommunications

which is at the origin of forgone manufactured export earnings.

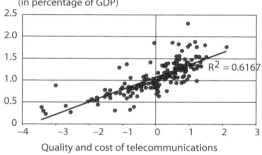

Manufactured exports unexplained by structural factors other than the quality and cost of telecommunications (in percentage of GDP)

$R^2 = 0.6167$

Quality and cost of telecommunications

Internet penetration improves with market openness in telecommunications,

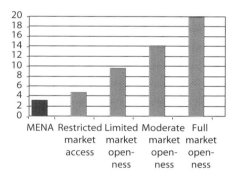

Predicted internet hosts per 10,000 people (average for each country group)

and high-tech exports increase with Internet connectivity,

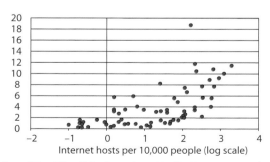

Internet hosts per 10,000 people (log scale)

but manufactured exports in MENA still have light technology content.

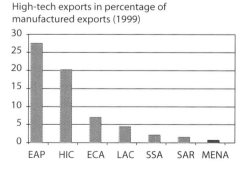

High-tech exports in percentage of manufactured exports (1999)

Note: AFR = Africa, EAP = East Asia and Pacific, ECA = Europe and Central Asia, HIC = high-income countries, LAC = Latin America and the Caribbean, MENA = Middle East and North Africa, SAR = South Asia, and SSA = Sub-Saharan Africa. Predicted rates of Internet penetration are calculated after controlling for differences other than telecommunications market openness in structural determinants across countries . High-tech shares are calculated after controlling for structural determinants other than Internet hosts.
Source: World Bank staff.

exporters in developing countries to move up the scale of technological specialization and position themselves in global high-tech markets. It also facilitates business-to-business e-commerce, improving the links of domestic producers to the cross-border chains of transnational corporations (World Bank 2001b).

Many developing countries have taken advantage of the specialization opportunities in high-tech exports created by global production links. In the late 1990s manufactured exports from countries in East Asia and the Pacific were more tech heavy than high-income countries' exports (figure 5.6). But the high-tech content of MENA countries' manufactured exports remains low—the lowest, on average, among developing regions. One major obstacle to greater use of ICT in MENA—especially the Internet—is the high cost of telecommunications, Internet services, and networking infrastructure. Content controls also impede the spread of the Internet. Lower costs would spur traffic and demand for infrastructure—which, thanks to economies of scale, would further lower the cost of delivering the service. And higher demand would attract new investments in infrastructure, further improving connectivity.

Power

Ensuring reliable provision of electricity at low cost improves the competitiveness of industry in both domestic and foreign markets. Indeed, electricity costs make up a significant share of costs in many manufacturing industries. In addition, access to reliable electricity supply in rural areas is a major development challenge, as just over one-third of the rural population in developing countries have access to electricity—a figure that has not changed significantly over the past 20 years. Most MENA countries have achieved high levels of electrification—90 percent on average for the whole region in 2000. In Egypt the favorable geographic distribution of the rural population—along the Nile—has permitted cost-effective supply of hydro power. But an estimated 25 million people elsewhere remain without access to power, with electrification rates as low as 42 percent in the Republic of Yemen and 55 percent in Morocco.

Until recently the electricity supply industry typically was vertically integrated, with a franchise monopoly as the sole supplier of electricity, under public ownership, either by the state or municipal governments. The past decade has seen a dramatic change in views about how the industry should be structured and regulated (Newbery 1999). The challenge now is to meet fast-growing demand through greater private participation in the sector—and to introduce competition to improve efficiency. This requires restructuring the industry according to local conditions (in some cases unbundling services) and taking steps to improve the creditworthiness of operators—through better cost recovery, price structures, and fee collection. But experience suggests that choosing the right reform strategy is more challenging than early optimists claimed. Countries that have not restructured their electricity systems can now reflect on the lessons and consider the options (box 5.5).

BOX 5.5

Restructuring the Electricity Supply Industry without the Lights Going Off: Lessons from Two Decades of Reform

Since 1980, when Chile commenced a radical program of restructuring and privatization, more than 60 countries have introduced reforms in the electricity sector. Today, what may be termed the standard reform model separates the potentially competitive parts from the core natural monopoly for transmission and distribution, with a regulatory agency setting the transmission and distribution tariffs. Competing generators offer electricity to the wholesale market. Eligible customers are free to choose their supplier. And new entrants are free to build new capacity with nondiscriminatory access to the grid and final customers.

In most countries, regulatory reforms in the electricity sectors have brought about several of the expected benefits—enhanced productivity and cost-effectiveness, improved output quality, greater responsiveness to consumer needs, and increased investment driven by market incentives rather than bureaucratic preference. Still, the postreform experience reveals substantial cross-country differences in market behavior and performance in restructured electricity markets. For example, new entry, private sector investment, price changes, and price volatility have all been mixed. And in some countries the unintended consequences of reforms seem to have caused significant problems.

Perhaps the single most important lesson is that models that appear to work well in some circumstances and places may not be easily transferable to countries in different circumstances. Various empirical assessments suggest that several factors may be responsible for the observed variance in performance: the structural option adopted, the extent of market liberalization, the speed and sequencing of reforms, the quality of regulatory governance, and the interaction between market rules and market structure. But it is widely claimed that the sector's "regulatory governance" regime is more important for attracting long-term private investment than the specific choice of industrial structure.

Several basic questions and contentious issues remain:

• How to improve incentives for efficiency in availability and operation while maintaining incentives for and ability to finance efficient expansion.

(Box continues on the following page.)

BOX 5.5 (continued)

- Whether the presence of coordination economies implies that vertical separation of transmission from generation will undermine the ability to undertake investment based on long-term systemwide planning.

- Whether there are significant gains from restructuring systems that are moderately well run in terms of availability, dispatch, and grid adequacy.

- Whether all asset types should be privatized or private ownership should be limited to the structurally competitive segments of the industry.

- Whether economies of scale in generation limit the potential for introducing competition in relatively small markets.

- Whether large economies of scale in distribution imply that that too much fragmentation of distribution facilities will increase distribution costs, whether the supply function (or retailing) should be separated from distribution, and the extent to which the supply function should be liberalized.

- What minimal set of regulations is needed under ideal circumstances, and how this set should be expanded in response to equity concerns, consumer protection, and other social goals.

Source: World Bank staff.

In MENA countries the industry still comprises mostly vertically integrated state-owned monopolies with weak financial health, low operating efficiency, and extensive government interference in their operations. Regulatory frameworks are not characterized by independence, transparency, and accountability. Regulatory and operational functions are not sufficiently separated to assure potential private investors and new entrants that the future policy developments in the sector will be fair and competitively neutral. Until the end of the 1990s MENA's reform scorecard in the industry was thus very low, ahead only of Africa (figure 5.7).[6]

The lack of comprehensive regulatory reform is reflected in poor operational efficiency throughout the region, resulting in high electricity costs or in sizable operational losses when electricity prices are controlled. Indeed, several of the region's electricity systems are plagued by high transmission and distribution losses, which in 1990–98 exceeded the world average in most countries (figure 5.7). Notable exceptions are Morocco and Jordan, which are ahead of the others in regulatory reform.

Some countries are taking promising steps. Algeria, Jordan, and Lebanon have new electricity laws, which include corporatizing the in-

FIGURE 5.7

Electricity Supply Industry Reform and Performance

The electricity supply industry remains less
competitive in MENA,   leading to low network efficiency.

Regulatory reform indicator as of 1998 (maximum 6)

Electricity transmission losses in percentage of domestic supply (2000)

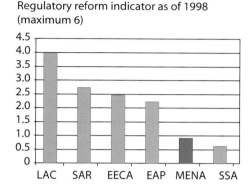

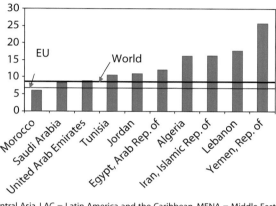

Note: EAP = East Asia and Pacific, EECA = Eastern Europe and Central Asia, LAC = Latin America and the Caribbean, MENA = Middle East and North Africa, SAR = South Asia, and SSA = Sub-Saharan Africa.
Source: World Bank staff.

cumbent and setting up a regulatory body. Egypt has created a holding company with corporate subsidiaries and established a regulatory agency. Egypt, Morocco, Tunisia, and West Bank and Gaza have independent power producers. Jordan, which has had a locally privately owned distribution company for many years, has fully unbundled and is preparing to privatize the other entities as well. In Morocco, about 50 percent of distribution is operated through private concessions, with steps taken to rationalize energy consumption through appropriate tariff reform.

Financial Services

Access to finance at competitive costs enables new firms to expand capacity and take advantage of export opportunities—or compete more successfully in less protected domestic markets. Better access to finance also helps businesses head off the shocks associated with participation in more open global markets. Many developing countries have implemented important financial sector reforms, with the aim of mobilizing savings, facilitating access to finance, and improving the allocation of financial resources.

Most MENA countries embarked on financial sector reform only in the 1990s, almost two decades after East Asia and Latin America. Banking systems were state dominated and excessively regulated—and they remain so in Algeria, the Islamic Republic of Iran, and Syria, where state-owned banks still account for more than 95 percent of domestic bank assets (Lee 2002; Nashashibi, Elhage, and Fedelino 2001). In some cases state-owned banks have extended soft loans to loss-making public enterprises, creating contingent liabilities for the public sector and credit bottlenecks to private sector investment.

In Algeria the successive buybacks by the government of bad bank loans to state enterprises over 1993–97 represented more than 50 percent of the average outstanding loans to the economy, and close to 30 percent of average GDP. A fresh cleanup in 2001 cost an additional 15 percent of GDP. But in the region as a whole, the share of bank lending to the public sector has come down from nearly 40 percent in 1990–95 to about 25 percent in 1996–2000, allowing more room for private sector financing.

Foreign bank entry in developing countries, through establishing branches and subsidiaries in the context of the GATS framework, can enhance internal financial liberalization as it injects more competition into domestic banking systems. Spurred by growth in trade and the liberalization of financial services around the globe, international banks have been lured to economies in transition and countries in Latin America (Mathieson and Roldòs 2001).[7]

The foreign bank presence remains low in MENA (figure 5.8). But foreign bank entry is on an upward trend, at about 9 percent of total bank assets in 2000, up from 4 percent in 1995.

In Gulf countries the foreign bank presence is higher, at an estimated 14 percent, but was constant throughout the 1990s. Lebanon, Morocco, and Tunisia are ahead of other countries in the region in foreign bank participation.

Because local banks in protected banking markets charge high prices for their services and lack incentives to improve efficiency, the entry of foreign competitors can improve the quality of financial services in a number of ways (World Bank 2001a): (1) by limiting excess pricing by incumbent banks; (2) by enhancing the efficiency of domestic banks, because foreign bank presence may enable domestic banks to cut costs by assimilating superior banking techniques and rationalizing their networks; and (3) through spillovers, by training staff in modern banking techniques.

Despite these potential benefits, concerns are often voiced that access to credit may be impaired for some sectors of the economy—particularly small and medium-size enterprises—because foreign banks tend to serve large customers. But evidence from a survey of more than 4,000 enterprises in 38 developing and transition economies suggests that, although large enterprises seem to take better advantage of foreign bank presence, benefits also appear to accrue to small and medium-size enterprises (Barth, Caprio, and Levine 2001; Clarke, Cull, and Martinez Peria 2001).

FIGURE 5.8

Financial Reform and Foreign Bank Presence in MENA

Foreign bank presence remains limited in MENA.

Participation of foreign banks from non-MENA, high-income countries is weak.

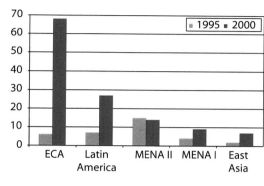

Foreign bank assets in percentage of total bank assets

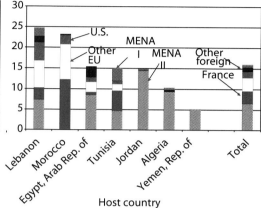

Foreign participation in the equity capital of domestic banks (in percent by home country, 2000)

Notes: ECA = Europe and Central Asia; MENA I = Algeria, Egypt, the Islamic Republic of Iran, Jordan, Lebanon, Morocco, the Republic of Yemen, Syria, and Tunisia; MENA II = Bahrain, Kuwait, Libya, Oman, Qatar, Saudi Arabia, and the United Arab Emirates.
Source: World Bank staff estimates; Bureau van Dijk, various years.

First, the lower interest margins spurred by foreign bank entry may help expand the amount of lending to small and medium-size enterprises, even if the share of lending to them declines. Second, foreign bank competition for large customers may displace some domestic banks, forcing them to seek new market niches, improving the access for small borrowers.

In MENA such benefits may be rather limited at present—because of the low overall presence of foreign banks and the relatively limited participation of banks from high-income countries outside the region (figure 5.8). Stepping up domestic bank restructuring, privatization, and modernization would increase the presence of foreign banks and be necessary to safeguard the soundness of domestic banks in the face of stronger competition. Foreign banks could also contribute to the restructuring and modernization of the domestic banking system as strategic partners, facilitating the privatization of state banks.

Services Reform and Private Investment: Opportunities and Pitfalls

Because services often cannot be traded, increasing access to service markets generally requires the entry of foreign competitors through FDI.

This will lead to the introduction of new technologies that improve efficiency and competitiveness, but that also increase the hiring of domestic labor. Investment in services now accounts for about half the inward FDI stock in the world (UNCTAD 2001).

Traditionally, developing countries used to be recipients of FDI in manufacturing and the primary sector. This changed drastically over the 1990s. The shift to the private provision of infrastructure services in the 1990s was much more rapid and widespread than originally anticipated. By 2001 developing countries had seen more than US$755 billion of investment flows to nearly 2,500 infrastructure projects (Harris 2003) (figure 5.9). Investment was concentrated in Latin America, where investments were largely associated with the sale or concessioning of existing assets, and East Asia, which saw a far higher proportion of greenfield projects. The bulk of this was in power and telecommunications, but other sectors also saw substantial private participation—especially water and transport (figure 5.9).

MENA countries find it difficult to benefit from these global trends because they have approached service reform in a piecemeal fashion—with privatization slower than in other parts of the world and barriers to entry often remaining forbidding, for both domestic and foreign investors. That is why cumulative FDI in infrastructure in the MENA region constituted only 3 percent of the world total in 2001, a meager US$23 billion (figure 5.9).

MENA countries attracted only about US$6 billion of private investment in the electricity supply industry in the 1990s. Compare that with US$64 billion in Latin America and US$56 billion in East Asia. The region's poor record in attracting private investment is especially problematic because of the continuing growth in electricity demand, expected to average 6 percent per year up to 2010. To meet this demand, the region's electricity systems will require new investment in excess of US$30 billion (Kessides 2002). In view of the severe fiscal constraints facing many of the region's countries, any attempts to meet these investment requirements with public funds will divert scarce resources from health, education, and other pressing social needs, increasing the opportunity costs of state ownership in the electricity sector.

With hindsight of more than a decade, it is now becoming clear that private sector participation in infrastructure is no panacea. First, investment flows in infrastructure are unstable. They began to decline after 1997, in the wake of the East Asian financial crisis, and by 2001 were only 44 percent of their peak—although still much higher than in the early 1990s (figure 5.9). Power has seen the largest decline from its peaks, followed by telecommunications. The declines have been accompanied by the cancellation or renegotiation of some projects, and, in some parts of the world, by a shift in public opinion against the private provision of infrastructure services (Harris 2003).

FIGURE 5.9

Private Participation in Investment in Network Industries
(in 2001 US$)

Private investment in infrastructure remains low in MENA.

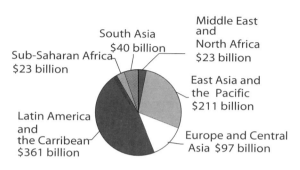

Total private investment = US$754 billion

Private sector participation is larger in power and telecommunications.

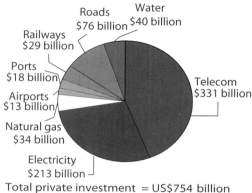

Total private investment = US$754 billion

Private sector investment in infrastructure in developing countries lost steam in the late 1990s.

Investment (2001 US$ billion)

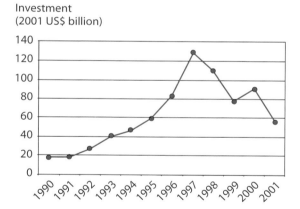

Low-cost recovery by incumbent public utilities sometimes compromised the viability of private infrastructure ventures.

Ratio of revenue to costs

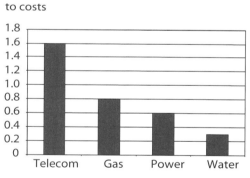

Source: World Bank staff, based on Harris 2003.

Several factors explain the subdued interest. Pessimism about emerging markets is on the rise, following the East Asian, Russian, and Argentine crises. Owing to declines in high-income country stock markets, some of the leading investors in infrastructure have become bankrupt or remain saddled with debt, mainly as a result of their earlier aggressive strategies. In some middle-income developing countries demand for infrastructure services fell as real incomes contracted, following large exchange rate devaluations. Some investors overestimated the ability of governments to manage the reform and honor their tariff and other build-transfer-operate commitments. Pricing policies implied by pass-through clauses and indexation, introduced to handle the risks of devaluation, were not politically sustainable. In addition to inciting renegotiations in many projects, the shocks led investors to reevaluate the risks of emerging markets.

Implementing and sustaining reform has tended to be more difficult in some sectors than others. In telecommunications, where prices before liberalization were often high—and in ports, airports, and rail freight, which are frequently export oriented and do not serve the general public—there has been less boom and bust. Electricity and water, which on average had to make the largest adjustments because of low cost recovery (figure 5.9), have often seen severe malaise. In many cases, reductions in cost brought about by private participation through improved efficiency led to lower user costs and expanded service provision. But where prices were way below costs, efficiency improvements could not offset the need for price increases, at least without continuing subsidies by taxpayers. Indeed, regardless of who owns the assets, infrastructure services must in the end be paid for either by users or taxpayers. Private participation does not alter this equation.

Overall, developing countries could be better served with a sound design of private participation schemes that develop procompetitive regulatory regimes and strengthening regulatory capacity, improve the targeting of subsidies to reach the poor, and ensure the transparency of privatization and award processes in concession-type contracts (Klein 2003).

Notes

1. Based on WTO (2002).

2. This impact accounts only for growth effects driven by stronger domestic and foreign demand. The total impact could be greater when accounting for cost reductions in ICT-using sectors, as well as efficiency and productivity improvements forthcoming in the long run.

3. According to the Business Software Alliance, the average software piracy rate in the Middle East in 2000 was 57 percent of total packaged software sales, far higher than the 37 percent worldwide average. Also see University of Napoli Federico II (2001).

4. The regulatory approach has to be differentiated, depending on the type of cargo. Container handling usually requires specialized heavy equipment. It thus involves sizable fixed costs and vertical integration of infrastructure investments and service provision that limit the degree of

competition. Appropriate regulation in such concessions should be designed with the aim of preventing the abuse of monopoly power. General cargo handling involves fewer economies of scale, so that infrastructure investment and service provision could be unbundled—with the service open to competitive provision. A detailed analysis is provided in Muller-Jentsch (2002).

5.   Egypt has the largest rail network in the MENA region, but operations are facilitated because there is one primary line that spans the length of the Nile. Jordan's 620 kilometers of track are mainly used to transport mined phosphate to the port of Aqaba. Despite the apparently good productivity indicators, the Egyptian National Railways is not profitable, with income covering only about 60 percent of operating costs.

6.   The ranking is based on the following six criteria: Has the electric utility been commercialized and corporatized? Has an energy law, which would permit unbundling and/or privatization in part or in whole of the industry, been passed by parliament? Has a regulatory body that is separate from the utility and from the ministry started work? Is there any private sector investment on greenfield sites in operation or under construction? Has the core state-owned utility been restructured or separated? Has any of the existing state-owned enterprise been privatized? See Kessides (2002).

7.   The share of bank assets controlled by foreign banks in Central Europe (the Czech Republic, Poland, Hungary) rose from 12 percent in 1994 to 57 percent in 1999. Similarly, in Latin America, by the end of the decade, foreign banks accounted for nearly half or more of the banking systems of several countries (Argentina, Chile, Mexico, and República Bolivariana de Venezuela), up from between 10 and 20 percent in 1994. However, in low-income countries too, foreign banks participate increasingly in domestic banking systems (World Bank 2002b).

CHAPTER 6

From Adversity to Opportunity: Agriculture, Trade, and Water

The reform of agricultural trade presents governments around the world with difficult choices and great opportunities. The benefits can be large—increasing efficiency in agriculture, improving living standards, and ensuring more sustainable development. But the transition costs can also be large.

Many of the MENA region's people, 40 percent in 2000, live in rural areas, the majority of them poor. Water is scarce, and today's patterns of agricultural water use and cropping are unsustainable. Consider the exponents. Drinking water uses only 1 cubic meter (m^3) of water per person a year. Municipal and industrial uses consume 100 m^3 of water per person a year. But food production uses upward of 1,000 m^3 of water per person a year—more than 80 percent of the region's water use. Yet the region's food production is in deficit, and trade is essential to ensure the region's food needs.

The challenge is to turn these adverse conditions into opportunities—through trade. This chapter looks at some of the potential for improving agricultural trade in MENA—in the ongoing WTO negotiations for global agricultural reforms—and trade arrangements with Europe. The main messages are as follows:

- It is in the MENA region's interests to subscribe to an equitable, liberal, and open rules-based multilateral trading system within the WTO framework. But sustainable development in agriculture requires gradual reforms in agriculture and in rural areas. It also requires much faster opening of market access in richer countries and a commitment from MENA's trading partners to mitigate the substantial welfare losses from freer global trade. Closer to home and within the context of trade relations with the EU, revitalized regional trade agreements can begin to address market access and trade reforms.

- With substantially better access for its exports, and with substantial trade and domestic price reforms, MENA could have large welfare and efficiency gains of US$2 billion a year. It could also have very large savings in water use, with food security achieved through trade rather than protection. Improvements in agricultural trade should lead to faster and more sustainable growth, reducing poverty along the way.

- The consequences of trade-related job losses are a serious issue. The benefits of freer trade will go mainly to better-off farmers in irrigated areas and urban consumers. But large losses will be borne by the more vulnerable segments of the rural population—small field crop producers, subsistence farmers in rainfed areas, and poor livestock herders. Their earnings losses will have to be dealt with in ways different from those envisaged for the "average" displaced manufacturing worker. The displacement process should avoid putting the burden disproportionately on women. Packaging the transition process to accommodate those constraints and designing adequate safety nets could ensure that trade reform in agriculture is politically viable.

Agriculture's contribution to GDP ranges from a high of more than 20 percent for Syria and Morocco to a low of less than 5 percent for Jordan (table 6.1). Contrast that with a rural population of 30 to 60 percent (with such exceptions as 10 percent in Lebanon) and agriculture's share of around 28 percent of the labor force. Increasing agricultural production, greater volatility, and stagnating per capita food production attest to the sector's inability to contribute to a more sustainable growth path under current circumstances.

Water and Land Are Scarce throughout the Region

MENA countries face serious environmental and natural resource problems. Rapid population growth (more than 2.5 percent a year in the past decade) and economic development have increased the pressure on the region's natural resource base. Rising demand for food and feeds has increased land and water degradation. Future economic and population growth will put further pressures on MENA agriculture and the environment unless distorted pricing measures and water and fuel subsidization schemes are phased out and resource losses are addressed more aggressively. Typical agricultural water tariffs in the region are less than 5 cents per m^3, a fraction of the cost for production and distribution (much less the depletion costs).

A large net food importer, the region relies on the rest of the world for about 20 percent of its food needs. Agricultural exports (mainly fruits, vegetables, cotton), valued at about US$6 billion in 2000, represent

TABLE 6.1

Selected Agricultural, Water, and Social Indicators in MENA

Region/country	Rural population (percent of total)	Rural poverty (percent of total poor)	Agricultural labor force (percent of total labor force)	Contribution to GDP by agriculture (percent)	Total renewable water resources (m³/capita/yr)	Agricultural water productivity— agricultural GDP/water use (US$/m³/year)
MENA countries						
Labor abundant, resource poor						
Egypt, Arab Rep.	55	61	33	17	859	0.28
Jordan	26	29	11	2	179	0.27
Lebanon	10	17	4	12	1,261	2.11
Morocco	44	65	36	16	971	0.37
Tunisia	34	36	25	12	482	1.04
Labor abundant, resource rich						
Algeria	40	53	24	12	473	1.26
Iran, Islamic Rep. of	38	48	26	19	1,955	0.29
Syrian Arab Rep.	46	68	28	24	1,622	0.24
Yemen, Rep. of	75	72	51	15	223	0.21
GCC						
Bahrain	8	0	1	1	181	0.37
Kuwait	2	6	1	1	10	1.40
Qatar	7	28	1	1	94	0.67
Saudi Arabia	14	34	10	7	118	0.78
Eastern European countries						
Poland	34		22	3	1,596	4.65
Turkey	25		46	15	3,439	1.10
Latin American countries						
Brazil	19	44	17	8	48,314	2.01
Chile	14	18	16	11	60,614	0.93
Costa Rica	52	60	20	9	27,932	1.07
Mexico	26		21	4	4,624	0.39

Note: GDP is in US$2,000.
Sources: FAO 2002a, 2002b.

about one-fourth of agricultural imports of approximately US$24 billion (dominated by cereals, meat, sugar, oils, and fats). Per capita, the region is the world's largest grain importer, with Algeria, Egypt, the Islamic Republic of Iran, Morocco, and Tunisia alone taking one-quarter of world wheat imports. Agricultural imports declined from 20 percent of total imports in 1987 to 13 percent in 2000 because of falling global cereal prices and rising domestic food production. Cereal imports actually exceeded domestic production in some years (figure 6.1).

Concerns about food security explain the significant support for input and output prices. MENA countries use various combinations of production, consumption, and tariff measures to support agricultural production. Tariffs in the region tend to be higher than in other developing

FIGURE 6.1

MENA: Production, Net Imports, and Consumption of Cereals, 1975–2001

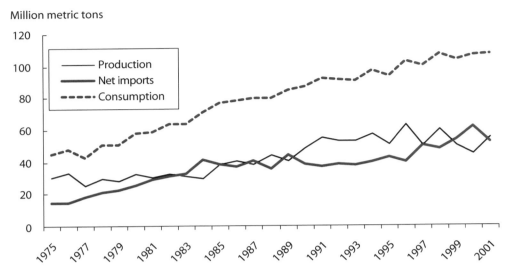

Source: FAO 2002b.

regions (figure 6.2), although border protection is greater for meat, vegetable oils, and processed foods than for sugar or cereals, the products with the lowest custom duties. Tariff protection is compounded by nontariff barriers in various forms. Support measures on the production side include high producer prices, production input subsidies, and water subsidies. The need to provide cheap food to consumers and weak market access for noncereal exports also make it difficult to allocate resources efficiently, equitably, and sustainably. This is not exceptional in the MENA region. Many countries, especially the industrial ones, have similar (or higher) levels of protection for import-substitution agriculture. But the urgency for reform is much more acute in the MENA region, given its limited water resources and large rural populations.

The region's main trading partner is the EU, which is the main market outlet for its agricultural exports and the origin for a large part of its agricultural imports. Algeria, Egypt, Jordan, Lebanon, Morocco, and Tunisia have the highest shares of trade with the EU, reflecting the proximity and the closeness of their economic ties.

WTO Negotiations Promise Large Global Welfare Gains

The November 2001 declaration of the Fourth Ministerial Conference of the WTO in Doha provided the mandate for a new round of multi-

FIGURE 6.2

Average Applied Tariffs for Agricultural Products

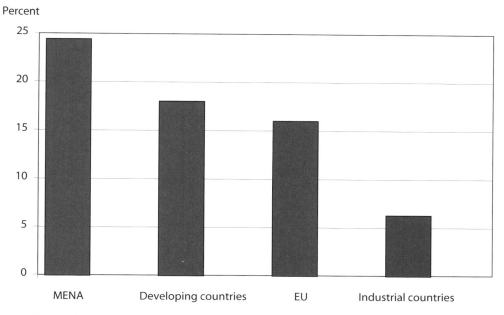

Sources: MENA (includes only Egypt, Jordan, Morocco, and Tunisia): Agricultural Market Access Database 2001 and Jordan Ministry of Industry and Trade; EU: WTO 2002; developing countries: Wilson 2002; and industrial countries: Wilson 2002.

lateral trade negotiations in agriculture—to be concluded by 2005. Countries are being asked to reduce their trade restrictions in exchange for better market access in other markets. The declaration also provides for special and differential treatment for developing countries to meet their needs in food security and rural development. The benefits are expected to be substantial for all, but there will also be significant adjustment and transition costs for individual countries and regions.

The next WTO ministerial meeting is slated for September 2003 in Cancun, with global trade reforms in agriculture to take center stage. Major agricultural exporters in industrial and developing countries (the so-called Cairns group, the United States, and others) are pushing for sharp reductions in global agricultural protection and better market access. Other industrial countries (Japan and those in Europe) want to maintain high domestic protection. And large net food importers in developing countries are pressing for their special needs. The implications are significant for the MENA region because it is a large net food importer, because it heavily protects its agricultural sector, and because it needs better market access in key export markets, especially in Europe. The new round will directly affect only WTO members in the region, but indirectly it will affect all other MENA countries.

On a parallel track, and closer to home, the Euro-Med association agreements essentially exempt agriculture by granting special status to agricultural trade. Export market access rules are governed by preferential access clauses, mostly under quotas, and generally reflect continuing large restrictions on MENA's access to European markets. But they do contain specific provisions to implement progressively greater liberalization of agricultural trade over time. The WTO negotiations are also likely to affect the EU's choices in its regional trade arrangements.

Historically, global trade in agricultural products has attracted higher tariffs than all other products; it is restrained by numerous and complex nontrade barriers and is affected by domestic support policies. Partly as a result, the share of agriculture in world merchandise trade has been on a declining trend, falling to 9 percent in 2000 from 15 percent in the early 1980s. During 1990–2000, world agricultural exports grew in current dollar terms at about a 3 percent annual rate, half as fast as overall merchandise trade. After the conclusion of the previous Uruguay Round negotiations in 1994, world agricultural export growth picked up, only to falter after the onset of the Asian crisis in 1997. Against this backdrop, world agricultural export market shares of MENA countries remained under 1 percent throughout 1974–2000.

The Uruguay Round Agricultural Agreement concluded in 1994 initiated the first steps toward liberalization of global trade in agriculture by negotiating improvements in market access through tariff reductions, cuts in national support for production and exports, and setting bounds for protection. The progress on new agricultural negotiations is turning out to be slow and contentious. The full round of negotiations, although planned to start in 1999, a year ahead of full implementation for industrial countries, could begin only in March 2000. The implementation has not been encouraging. The agricultural reforms are proving fragile, with bound tariff rates remaining high and domestic support levels increasing because of the declines in market prices. By 1998 agricultural support in OECD countries exceeded by US$36 billion the level in 1994 (Anderson and Morris 2000). Although the share of agriculture in industrial economies is about half that of 20 years ago, and in most countries represents less than 3 percent of GDP, the political power of agricultural lobbies remains strong.

At Doha, agriculture remained the single most divisive issue facing negotiators. And it remains the single most significant agenda item in post-Doha world trade negotiations. The potential benefits of a full liberalization of agriculture and food for both developing and industrial countries are estimated at US$250 billion, six times those of abolishing the MFA (figure 6.3).

The high stakes for developing countries are obvious in the annual subsidies to production and exports in OECD countries: US$362 billion,

FIGURE 6.3

Static Welfare Gains from Agricultural Liberalization Exceed Those from Merchandise Trade
(incremental income in 2015, compared with 1997)

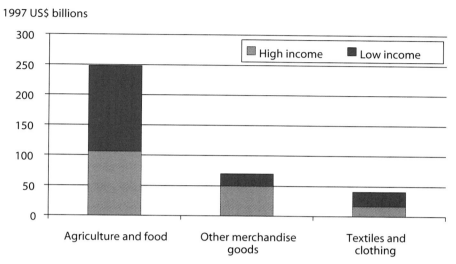

Source: World Bank 2002.

far exceeding official aid flows of US$53 billion.[1] Dynamic welfare gains, after allowing for investment growth and productivity gains, are valued at US$46 billion a year, with 65 percent to developing countries and 35 percent to industrial countries.[2]

MENA, a Large Net Food Importer, Could Be Hurt

As a large net importer of agricultural products, MENA depends on imports for cereals, sugar, cooking oil, and other foods (figure 6.4). Over the past two decades, MENA net annual agricultural imports have ranged between US$16 billion and US$20 billion.

By most counts, eliminating international trade barriers and national subsidies for production and exports causes the long-run real food prices to rise by as much as 12 percent. In three products critical for MENA countries, expected price increases are 16.4 percent for sugar, 11.2 percent for vegetable oils, and 16.3 percent for cereals. But for vegetables and fruits, a product group important to MENA exports, prices are expected to rise by only 8.3 percent. So in net terms, MENA's terms of trade would worsen, with higher import prices relative to export prices making consumers worse off because they have to pay more for their purchases of food. And given the large distortions in MENA's agricultural sector, there

FIGURE 6.4

MENA Net Agricultural Exports, Average 1998–2000

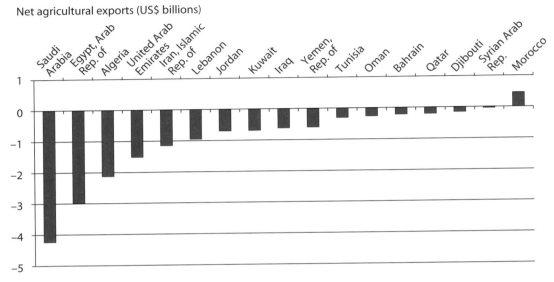

Source: UN 2001.

will also be the effects of attracting more resources into already inefficient domestic production. The combined effects of these two factors are estimated to account for a static welfare loss of about US$3 billion in 1995 prices by 2005 (Anderson, Hoekman, and Strutt 2001) (figure 6.5). China is the only other country that loses as a food importer. Much of the loss in the MENA region originates in inefficiencies that could be corrected by removing distortions in domestic agriculture (figure 6.6).

The analyses cited rely on the Global Trade Analysis Project (GTAP) database version 5, which does not adequately capture domestic distortion in MENA.[3] With better estimates of the distortions in the MENA region, the welfare gains from removing domestic distortions are likely to be even larger, but because of high protection enjoyed by field crops and livestock, eliminating or significantly reducing tariffs in these sectors will pose serious challenges (see the discussion below on managing the transition).

The greatest benefits for the MENA region will come from comprehensive domestic reforms—in tandem with greater market access in European and world markets. MENA governments face issues of timing and sequencing of reforms. The heaviest domestic and border distortions are in the livestock, dairy, oilseeds, and cereal markets. Programs have to be put in place for these markets in a gradual way and according to some preannounced plans. Estimates of various sequencing strategies show that the biggest welfare gains (up to 4 percent of GDP) are obtained when agricultural trade is liberalized gradually as opposed to a

FIGURE 6.5

MENA Loses under Global Agricultural Trade Liberalization if It Does Not Change Domestic Subsidies and Distortions

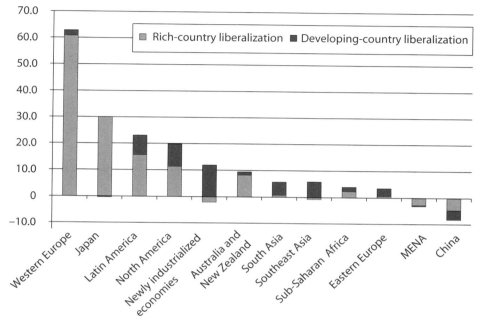

Welfare gain in 1995 US$ billions

Legend: ▨ Rich-country liberalization ■ Developing-country liberalization

Categories (left to right): Western Europe, Japan, Latin America, North America, Newly industrialized economies, Australia and New Zealand, South Asia, Southeast Asia, Sub-Saharan Africa, Eastern Europe, MENA, China

Source: Anderson, Hoekman, and Strutt 2001.

one-shot unilateral implementation at the beginning of the reform program (Elshennawy 2001). But countries have to pay particular attention to the implications of this gradual approach for government revenues, adjustment costs, and the credibility of reform.

Domestic Reforms, and Greater Access to European Export Markets, Would More than Offset the Losses

The process will involve substantial losses. Agricultural trade liberalization will mean painful changes in the rural world. Although the benefits are widespread, the costs will be concentrated on the most vulnerable and least competitive. Production in sugar, livestock, dairy, and cereals is expected to drop by an average of 10 to 65 percent in Morocco (Rutherford, Rutstrom, and Tarr 1997). The agricultural sector in Tunisia could lose annually around 3 percent of its value added (Cockburn, Decaluwe, and Dostie 1998). These large losses are set against positive national welfare improvements that could reach up to 1.5 percent of GDP.

FIGURE 6.6

Gains in MENA from Removing Agricultural Trade Distortions in Addition to Export Subsidies

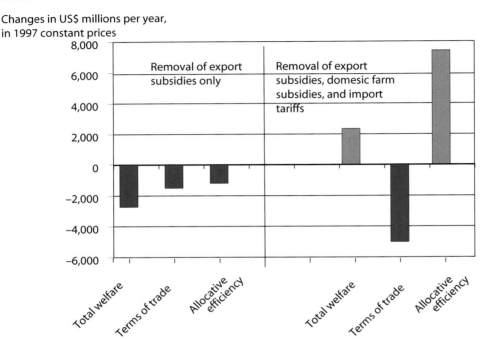

Changes in US$ millions per year, in 1997 constant prices

Source: Elbehri and Leetmaa 2002.

Improved EU market access will be critical. Greater market access is crucial for products in which MENA countries have comparative advantage. It must go beyond the current reference-based seasonal tariff quotas and reference quantity system. The EU simple average tariff on agricultural products, now 16.1 percent, remains higher than that for nonagricultural products. It also hides evidence of tariff escalation, particularly for processed food and agricultural products (WTO 2002). This has implications for MENA's trade with the EU. When liberalization explicitly takes into consideration the higher tariffs on processed food than on raw commodities, MENA is the region with the highest incremental welfare gains,[4] with an additional 10 percent (Gehlhar and Wainio 2002). Given the fast-growing world market, processed food trade could provide the region with an opportunity to invest more in the sector if concrete steps are taken by its major trading partners, particularly the EU, to reduce their border protection against MENA's exports.[5]

Agriculture Trade and Its Implications for Water

Greater efficiency in domestic agriculture, combined with agricultural trade liberalization, might also allow MENA countries to begin to address acute water scarcity and the reallocation of water uses. The region tends on average to have lower agricultural output per unit of water consumed in the sector than countries in the same income group (figure 6.7). So water scarcity in the region is greatly influenced by the inefficiency of water consumption in the agricultural sector.

Trade in agriculture already provides large gains in water use in the MENA region. Allan (1997, 2001a, 2001b) proposes a "virtual water hypothesis," which asserts that the presence of water embedded in agricultural crops or "virtual water" is the prime reason why water-scarce regions such as MENA have been able to avoid severe water shortages. In essence, countries that are scarce in water choose to import agricultural crops in order to save on water required for production. The hypothesis makes the case for a strong link between water-scarce regions and import of water-intensive crops such as wheat. Hakimian (2003) tests Allan's hypothesis by a regression analysis on a cross-country dataset of 100 countries, including 14 MENA countries.

FIGURE 6.7

Agricultural Water Productivity by Country

(nominal US$ per m³/year of water)

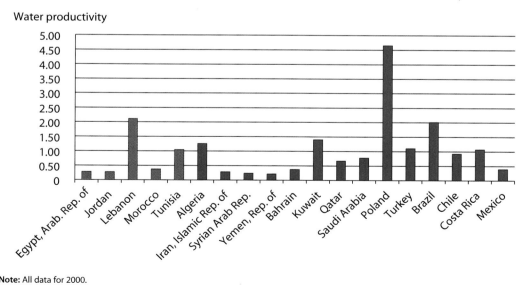

Note: All data for 2000.
Sources: FAO 2002a; World Bank 2003.

Although it may seem that crops with high water content, such as tomatoes, require more water to produce than "dry" crops such as wheat, by considering the longer cultivation season for cereals compared with vegetables, water requirements per unit weight of production are actually higher for cereals than for vegetables (table 6.2). Since water requirements vary greatly depending on various conditions, such as climate, soil conditions, and the specific varieties of crops, these figures should be viewed with caution. For water-intensive agricultural crops, such as meat (beef), vegetable oil, and milk, a range (low, average, high) was specified because of the variability and uncertainty in the water requirement estimates. The data show that meat, vegetable oils, and milk are far more water intensive to produce than vegetables, fruits, or cereals. For example, producing 1 kilogram of meat requires approximately 30 times more water than producing the same unit of cereals.

Figure 6.8 presents the aggregate water required to produce the trade volume for seven MENA countries, using trade data for representative food crops for the MENA region and their average water requirement data (table 6.2).[6] The water content in agricultural trade or the "virtual water hypothesis" is assessed. Given the sheer size of imports, all MENA countries are large net importers of water through agricultural trade. Algeria, Egypt, and the Islamic Republic of Iran import particularly large volumes of water through food. The total import of water ranges from approximately 5,000 million m^3 of water per year in Lebanon to 55,000

TABLE 6.2

Water Requirements of Agricultural Products

(m^3 of water/metric ton of food)

Product	Water
Tomatoes[a]	450
Olives[a]	500
Vegetables[a]	1,000
Maize	1,400
Wheat	1,450
Barley[a]	1,450
Fruits[a]	1,500
Bananas[a]	1,750
Rice	3,450
Sugar[a]	5,000
Milk[b]	6,000
Cotton[a]	7,000
Vegetable oil[c]	22,000
Beef	42,500

Sources: a. Staff estimates; b. water requirements for milk cows from Department for Environment, Food and Rural Affairs (DEFRA) 2002 and Government of Ontario, Canada 1992 and c. FAO 1996. All other crop water requirement data are from Gleick 2000 and Barthelemy 1993.

FIGURE 6.8

Water Content of Trade, Selected MENA Countries

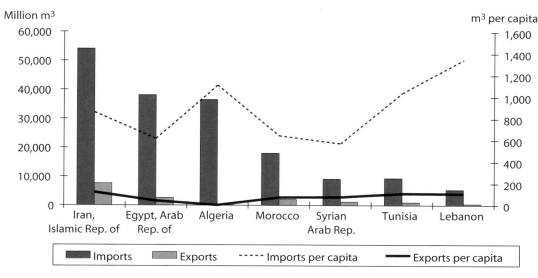

Sources: FAO 2002b for trade data; table 6.2 for water requirement data.

million m³ of water per year in the Islamic Republic of Iran. For exports, the water content ranges from 500 million m³ in Lebanon to 7,500 million m³ in the Islamic Republic of Iran.

But the water requirements in table 6.2 provide only a physical input-output transformation to show the relative intensity of water use by different agricultural products. To illustrate the differences in the economics of water use requires factoring in differences in output prices or the value of the physical transformation. One easy and simple way to do this is to adjust the water use by relative final product prices. For example, wheat prices in world markets are about US$120 per metric ton, while the price of vegetables is about 5 times larger (US$500 per metric ton) and that of beef 10 times higher (US$2,150 per metric ton). So the cost of water transformed into beef becomes much less when adjusted for the higher prices, and the cost of the water transformed into vegetables becomes even lower (figure 6.9).

The relative inefficiencies in water use for different agricultural products are evident when differences in physical use of water per ton of production and the relative final product prices are taken into account (figure 6.9). First, irrigated crop production of rice and sugar is inefficient, using twice the water of producing wheat at world prices. There is little justification for producing these crops in the water-scarce MENA region. Second, livestock and dairy production is also hugely inefficient in water-scarce environments. Third, irrigated wheat and other cereals do

FIGURE 6.9

Relative Costs of Water Use for Different Agricultural Products, MENA Region, 2003

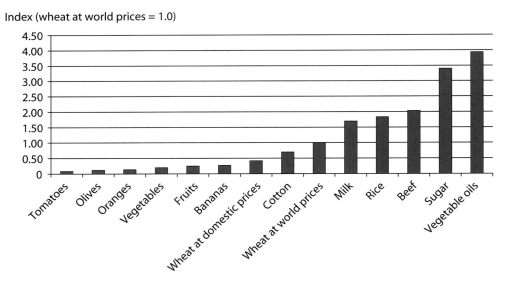

Index (wheat at world prices = 1.0)

Sources: Staff estimates and table 6.2; USDA and World Bank commodity price data.

better, in the middle of the picture. But they still do considerably worse—five times or more inefficient—than producing export crops, such as cotton, fruits and vegetables, and arid-area crops, such as olives. Cotton is much more efficient than wheat production at world prices, even though it uses much more water than wheat per metric ton of production. Indeed, estimates suggest that the elimination of protection in Egypt would dramatically improve the relative returns to cotton cultivation relative to those of wheat and rice.

None of these calculations price water or the other input subsidies and farming price support mechanisms. Once these are factored in, it is no surprise that farmers in the region grow water-intensive inefficient crops.

Although MENA countries do not export cereals, they produce cereals domestically on both rainfed and irrigated lands, with high producer support from the government provided for food security purposes. On average, about 41 percent of wheat and 34 percent of barley are produced on irrigated land. Saudi Arabia and Egypt produce all their cereals on irrigated land (table 6.3).

A large proportion of domestic cereal production that takes place is in mixed rainfed conditions, using ground moisture and some irrigation water use, during the wet winter season. These are less water-intensive methods and are probably relatively efficient. So moving to world prices

TABLE 6.3

Cereal Area under Irrigation, 1995

Country	Share of irrigation in total cereal area (percent)
Labor abundant, resource poor	
Egypt, Arab Rep.	100
Jordan	30
Lebanon	39
Morocco	15
Tunisia	3.5
Labor abundant, resource rich	
Iran, Islamic Rep. of	61
Syrian Arab Rep.	45
Yemen, Rep. of	19

Source: Staff estimates.

progressively over time and pricing water better will induce a relative shift out of import-substituting cereals and into more efficient, exportable crops. But it will not necessarily induce a drastic shift out of domestic cereal production. Cereal production on fully irrigated lands may be under greater pressure, considering the region's water scarcity and the move to adopt lower protection. That lowering of protection can be calibrated to permit efficient shifts in cropping patterns.

Market Access, Employment Impacts, and Managing the Transition

The benefits of agricultural trade liberalization in the MENA region will depend greatly on improved market access, especially in the EU. The impacts of reform will be large, and the transition costs significant. Labor and employment impacts will be more adverse in rainfed areas. Transition costs will need to be managed through a number of different instruments.

Regulations on market access in industrial countries (the EU, United States, and others) are particularly important for MENA. There are important patterns of protection in favor of agricultural products in industrial countries that are stronger for processed goods with higher-value-added content. For current WTO members, further trade liberalization will have to pass through further cuts in bound and applied tariffs. For those negotiating entry in the WTO or unilaterally modifying trade policy, the conversion of nontariff measures affecting agricultural imports into ad valorem or specific tariffs will rank high on the agenda. With the current patterns of protection and the differences existing between MENA countries, it will be difficult to predict the effects of further trade liberalization unless how, what, and when market access regulations are to be implemented are examined, taking into account the expected behavioral responses from producers and consumers. The net effect on the agriculture sector will depend on both what is offered by and to trading partners.

Reduced distortions in the EU market are in the common interest of most of the developing countries, including those in the MENA region (Diao, Roe, and Somwaru 2002). Export markets for MENA are concentrated in the EU because of geographic proximity, historic linkages, and preferential trade arrangements. There is a widespread belief within MENA countries with important trade flows with the EU that agricultural trade liberalization has not yielded symmetrical benefits, because key potential EU agricultural and food markets for southern Mediterranean countries remain heavily protected. Policymakers in the region should note that this is in sharp contrast to the large benefits reaped by commercial farmers on the northern shore as a result of the generous EU subsidies and the opening of markets on the southern shore. Further liberalization of agricultural markets could be threatened if this imbalance is not rectified.[7]

Finally, protection measures are complicated by the constraints posed by large actors in the market. These are private operators, namely supermarket chains and food processors that impose their own standards and criteria on product quality, time of delivery, stability of supply flows, and so on. These criteria are binding and can be more restrictive than government or trade bloc restrictions. Under market conditions, it is difficult to develop regulations to force these private agents to change their purchasing practices, assuming that there are no discriminatory processes involved, and the onus of adaptation is on the suppliers, and in the case of MENA, the exporters to these markets.

Yet, trade liberalization can provide opportunities for agricultural and food product exports from MENA countries (box 6.1). However, internal marketing processes and structures in MENA face serious structural and policy constraints in the context of standards, price formation, information, storage, and transport, all of which are invariably hindered by bureaucratic interventions and inefficient public enterprises (box 6.2). These constraints prevent a flexible response to agricultural trade liberalization and thus reduce the potential benefits expected. Exporters invariably depend on vertical integration from production to shipping in order to ensure products of adequate quality and quantity. This increases risks as specialization in the different stages of transport, storage, conditioning, and packaging is not feasible under all circumstances. Thus, internal reforms in market organization and marketing are critical to enhancing the possibility of opportunities of market access.

BOX 6.1

Horticultural Export Promotion in Jordan

Jordan's agricultural exports to non-Arab countries are small, amounting to only 4 percent of the total exported in 2000. In 1998, Jordan's exports to Europe amounted to about 4,249 tons (mainly cucumbers, green beans, peppers, and grapes) valued at US$5 million. These amounts are less than 0.5 percent of Israel's agricultural exports to these countries. There is considerable scope to increase Jordan's exports to Europe and also to other Gulf countries by expanding the access of small-scale and medium-scale producers to these markets. This would require not only linkages through contract farming with large-scale farmers but also the adoption of more efficient production practices. For example, the use of drip irrigation, plastic greenhousing, efficient application of fertilizers and pesticides, and high yielding varieties of green beans, sweet peppers, strawberries, and seedless grapes could provide between US$8,500 and US$30,000/hectare without requiring high levels of water usage if saving techniques are put in place (World Bank 2002). Labor requirements for these crops in terms of land preparation, sowing, planting, husbandry, pruning, and harvesting indicate that these activities are labor intensive and could have important implications in terms of labor generation (between 1,000 and 7,000 person-hours per hectare is needed for the farming conditions in the Jordan Rift Valley).

BOX 6.2

Nontraditional Export Crops in Egypt

Promotion of fresh, nontraditional export horticulture crops is considered an important intervention area for agricultural production development in Egypt. Crops selected as having a potential for further production and export include table grapes, strawberries, fine green beans, green onions, galia melons, and cut flowers. Development of these nontraditional crops would require further efforts in terms of technical, transportation, and marketing assistance. Analysis conducted in the Agricultural Technology Utilization and Transfer (ATUT) Project indicate that Egypt has a strong comparative advantage in these products but faces significant competition from countries such as Kenya, Zimbabwe, Ecuador, and Chile (Development Alternatives, Inc. [DAI] 2002). Specific constraints to further development in the sector include high transportation costs as well as quality considerations. Egyptian exporters will have to add value to their products to be able to grab higher market shares. This could be done by aggressively moving into niche markets, such as organic produce and shipping products in packages that can be put directly on supermarket shelves.

Labor and Employment Impacts of Agricultural Liberalization

Agriculture in the MENA region is characterized by high dependence on rainfed production systems, usually for cereals (wheat and barley, the latter mainly as feed) and livestock. Another feature is the high share of labor employed in agriculture. A paradox exists: for social and economic reasons, both MENA governments and the EU prefer that agriculture absorb labor. Yet, agricultural policies also encourage capital-intensive development through investment and interest rate subsidies, with the assumption that mechanized agriculture is efficient.[8] Thus, there are significant complementarities between the current policy emphasis on food security—self-sufficiency focusing on cereal production with the concomitant producer price supports—and the long-term trends of subsidized mechanization.

Part of the drop in internal prices from trade reform will be offset by the increase in international prices for the same commodities, as subsidized exports from developed countries decline with the liberalization of agricultural trade. But this effect will be limited by the high price supports provided in MENA countries, particularly to cereal producers. Results show that, in general, as a consequence of agricultural trade liberalization:

- The economy as a whole will gain as investments and labor are diverted to activities more productive and efficient in their use, increasing overall GDP growth rates.

- Labor and capital would be transferred out of the agricultural sector.

- Overall, the agricultural sector will thus be affected adversely as agricultural and agro-industrial production declines, but also positively as production becomes more competitive.

- The cereals sector, now strongly protected through producer subsidies, would be hurt disproportionately. Competitive cereal production, mostly on medium-size and large farms, is concentrated in the high-potential humid and subhumid zones.

- Fruit and vegetable production under irrigated conditions remains flexible and competitive, and tree crops appear to be the solution for the arid and semiarid zones, where they remain competitive, a viable substitute for cereal production.[9]

Among the diverse effects of agricultural liberalization, the impact of greatest concern to policymakers is that on rural labor and employment. Trade liberalization will displace labor out of agriculture, but the adaptive process is complex. There will not be automatic and massive out-migration to cities. The adjustment of the different farm households will depend on the opportunities, the constraints, and the costs of migration.

- Part of the farm labor force will adapt within the agricultural sector, mainly by shifting from the production of subsistence crops to the production of higher-value cash crops.

- Part will shift into the nonagricultural sectors (manufacturing, services, construction). Pressure on wages could cause economic and social problems. Some of the established and unskilled or semiskilled nonagricultural labor will be pushed out by the incoming displaced agricultural labor and migrate or join the pool of unemployed.[10]

- Part will not be able to adapt, mainly the older members of the labor force.

The expected decline of agricultural prices (relative to nonagricultural prices) associated with trade liberalization will thus be felt differently across rural household types. The resulting adaptive process can be assessed in five dimensions: the farm; the proximate geographic region; the agroclimatic region; the farming system, particularly irrigated and rainfed agriculture; and the agricultural and nonagricultural sectors, the latter rural or nonrural. The adaptive process will diffuse the impact of liberalization on labor displacement through these five dimensions.[11]

Farmers, or farm families, can be described as risk-averse economic agents managing a portfolio of resources. This portfolio comprises land for crop production and livestock production and labor for on-farm and off-farm employment, the latter in a temporary, seasonal, or permanent manner, in the rural or nonrural sectors, in the country or abroad. The objective is to manage this portfolio in such a manner as to stabilize income and consumption flows.

The reallocation of labor within a farm in response to liberalization will be through adjustments in the product mix, within the perspective of the portfolio optimization process discussed above. The reallocation of labor in the farm family in response to agricultural price liberalization is a function of the efficient use of the portfolio of farm resources and the stability of income and consumption flows. While resources would be expected to move away from the protected cereal crops, consumption needs would buffer the magnitude of such an impact. Furthermore, there would be limits to the expansion of cash crops given marketing, storage, and perishability constraints and market risks. Labor would be reallocated among farm products and off-farm employment.

For one group, adjustments take place only in the patterns for reallocating family labor. This is the case of landless farmers, defined as laborers in the strict sense, used in agriculture as hired labor. This labor force can be skilled in specific agricultural activities (grafting, cotton picking) or unskilled, and can also work in the nonfarm and nonagricultural sectors.[12]

In the labor reallocation process one critical question is whether there would be any systematic relationship between farm size and labor displacement. This will depend on the change in the crop mix and the technology of production. Smaller farms, using large amounts of labor in labor-intensive technologies, would face redundant labor on the farm. Larger farms using capital-intensive technologies would reallocate resources toward abundant and cheaper labor, but would not be able to absorb all the displaced labor.

Part of the labor reallocation process would be limited to movements within proximate areas, because of the familiarity of workers with regional production patterns, lower transfer costs from shorter movements, and so on. The employment impact on different farm sizes can be assessed within a level of aggregation, such as an administrative unit, groups of provinces, and river basins. This should not be done mechanically because skill requirements are a critical factor in labor mobility. For example, an area with predominantly irrigated agriculture can reabsorb displaced labor within its borders, but labor transfers between rainfed and irrigated areas may not be that easy.

Agroclimatic classification is important for agriculture as the determining factor in cropping patterns. Most likely, farmers in low-rainfall areas will be hurt more by agricultural trade liberalization because they can grow fewer alternative crops. To the extent that an agroclimatic region is characterized by similarities in farming systems, labor displacement and absorption would follow similar patterns.

As the protection of rainfed cereal crops decreases, labor would move out of cereals and into more labor-intensive cash crops, which dominate the irrigated sector. The rainfed sector would face higher numbers of displaced workers. But these workers can be absorbed into the irrigated sector to only a limited extent. The irrigated sector would also shed labor, because it uses labor-intensive methods to begin with. As capital also leaves agriculture, particularly irrigated agriculture, some labor associated with capital in fixed proportions will also be displaced.

Labor displacement is best interpreted through the direction of changes. Some of the displaced workers can be reabsorbed in the agricultural sector. So the net labor displacement in agriculture could be relatively low, but it is inevitable. The relative share of agriculture in the total labor force has been declining, and the labor and employment impact of agricultural liberalization has to be put in the context of this long-term trend. What is more important is that the process will entail significant costs both for reabsorbing labor within agriculture and for transforming labor to other sectors.

If the objective is to achieve efficiency in agriculture (as well as the economy), the agricultural sector and rural areas cannot maintain their traditional role as a buffer for labor and unemployment more than other sectors. So labor transfers from agriculture should be accepted so that adequate measures are taken to manage the transitional issues.

Small rainfed farms, a large group covering limited area, deserve in-depth analysis through new studies. Particularly in the lower-rainfall regions, they are at the margin of production, producing mostly for subsistence, tangential to market forces. They absorb a significant amount of labor, so the way liberalization affects them needs to be assessed carefully.

Land and capital would also be expected to move from agriculture to other sectors—and within agriculture from the protected subsectors to others. Agroclimatic conditions constrain the mobility of land among different products, with water a limiting factor. Land close to urban and semiurban centers would be transferred to nonagricultural uses.

Implications for Women

Women are heavily involved in agriculture in most MENA countries (figure 6.10). That makes it crucial to understand the gender effects of agricultural trade liberalization in the region. Reviews of farming practices by gender in MENA (such as by Kasnakoglu [1999]) reveal that the female labor force in agriculture has greater involvement:

- In livestock than in crop production.

- In middle phases of crop production than in land preparation and seeding or marketing.

- In horticulture than in cereal production.

- In small farms and holdings on marginal lands.

- In areas with large male migration to urban areas.

- In middle-aged and older workers.

- In summer months and harvesting periods.

- In labor-intensive activities, which tend to be disadvantaged when mechanization is introduced.

Trade liberalization will affect the field crops, livestock, and horticulture subsectors differently, hitting the cereal and livestock markets hardest, and giving horticulture and agrofood industries better market prospects. This is an underresearched area that requires supplemental

FIGURE 6.10

Gender Composition of the Labor Force in Selected MENA Countries

Share in agricultural labor force (percent)

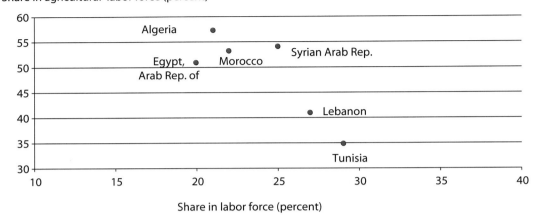

Share in labor force (percent)

Source: Kasnakoglu 1999; World Bank 2003.

analysis. Better micro- and macrolevel information and the availability of new gender-"adjusted" analytical tools for analyzing the relationship between trade liberalization and gender, including the use of computable general equilibrium models (such as in Fontana 2003), can produce new insights on liberalization outcomes.

Implications for Safety Nets and Transition Strategies for the Rural Poor

Trade liberalization implies changes in relative prices and reallocations of resources, but it is more than purely economic. The transfer of resources and factors of production from one sector—or one product to another—has social and political impacts that need to be buffered to avoid social upheaval. The costs of adapting to the effects of liberalization (retraining of labor, building economic and social infrastructure for labor that will migrate to more profitable sectors) have to be assessed. And to avoid shock effects, the process has to be planned and phased.

Farm family strategies for coping. In an environment in which climatic factors can impart a high degree of uncertainty and variability to crop production, livestock production and off-farm employment activities play a crucial stabilizing role, ensuring adequate stability to income and consumption flows. In the southern Mediterranean basin, the importance of off-farm income has been demonstrated in many countries. Part of the farm family's labor resources are allocated in diverse ways to off-farm employment, in temporary, seasonal, or permanent jobs, in the agricultural sector, in rural or urban areas, at home or abroad. The most important aspect of such off-farm employment is that income transfers—from those employed off the farm to those on the farm—are an essential part of farm family income. In Tunisia the incidence of off-farm income is inversely related to farm size, and for smaller farms this income is the more important source for farm investments. In Syria, such income made up an average of 35 to 40 percent of farm income.

Government strategies. Government policies should serve three objectives: production incentives, social transfers, and risk management.

Producer-support policies in the MENA region invariably entail price supports for dominant products, mainly cereals, and input price subsidies, with the main pretext being incentives for production and productivity. These interventions can be guaranteed minimum prices, obligatory delivery prices from state monopolies, or floor prices with a premium over reference prices based on production costs or import prices. The input subsidies aim to promote technology embodied in fertilizers, improved seeds, and the like. But they distort markets and result in an overdetermined economic system. Overall, support policies have had limited impact in raising production and productivity, especially in less favorable arid zones with low and variable rainfall.

The producer price supports are also instruments of social policy because social safety nets and other instruments of social protection, designed mainly for industrial and service workers in urban agglomerations, are not available to dispersed rural beneficiaries. Their effects as instruments of social protection are diluted because they are not targeted to the more needy and poorer segments of the rural society. Indeed, larger farms benefit proportionately more. And smaller farms producing cereals for family consumption, or lacking access to markets or state purchases, do not benefit.

Producer price supports also aim to manage the risks of climatic and market variability. This is a self-insurance policy for the governments, viable under today's macroeconomic conditions.

Overall, the interventions to support and stabilize prices can even hurt farm families. If the commodity whose price is being stabilized is negatively correlated with the other elements of the farm family portfolio, that portfolio would be destabilized, and risk-averse farmers wishing to avoid instability in their portfolio would resist it (Newberry and Stiglitz 1981).

Managing the Transition

Managing the transition requires:

- Accompanying measures for the adjustment of displaced labor.

- Providing producers with predictable, rule-based stability in output markets.[13]

- Promoting technological change.

- Investing in additional social and physical infrastructure.

- Establishing public works programs.

- Improving agricultural marketing.

- Reinforcing economywide liberalization.

Accompanying Measures for the Adjustment of Displaced Labor

Different adjustment scenarios need to be considered, targeting specific measures to different categories of labor.

- The segment of the labor market that will adapt within the agricultural sector, mainly from the production of subsistence crops to the production of higher-value cash crops, would need government assistance in bearing the transfer and conversion costs. Some technical support and even financial incentives may be necessary for farms employing displaced labor.

- The segment of the labor force that will shift into the nonagricultural sectors (manufacturing, services, construction) will require significant training expenditures, particularly for semiskilled and skilled jobs.

- For the segment of the farm labor that will not be able to adapt to the impact of liberalization, problems would need to be addressed through a social safety net program entailing direct transfers.

Providing Producers with Predictable, Rule-Based Stability in Output Markets

Liberalization entails welfare gains, but producers of cereal products will be negatively affected. Liberalization will not eliminate the production of key cereal products overnight. And some support for cereal producers, relying more on market forces and less on direct interventions, can be envisaged. A key principle is that these interventions should be rule-based and predictable to allow markets to operate. For example, price bands or compensatory schemes could be considered. And strategic reserves could be increased, but managing the reserves needs to be rule-based as well.

Promoting Technological Change

Far from automatic, technological change requires a concerted effort by public and private agencies in agricultural research and dissemination, both of which are integral for the transition. The costs of public and private research and disseminating technologies to farms are considerable, but the returns are high enough to justify them.

Investing in Additional Social and Physical Infrastructure

Physical infrastructure needs will increase and change as markets demand more efficient services (communication, energy, roads). On the social side, labor transfers will require investments in education, health, and housing as families move from dispersed rural locations to intermediate and higher population centers, or to urban and semiurban agglomerations.

Establishing Public Works Programs and Associated Safety Nets

In the transition, there will have to be strong reliance on public works programs, especially those in infrastructure. Public works and social safety nets can be directed toward the creation of physical and social infrastructure by displaced agricultural workers and their families seeking employment in urban and industrial areas.

Improving Agricultural Marketing

The agricultural marketing system—comprising collection, transportation, conditioning, packaging, transformation, storage, and wholesale and retail market systems—has to transmit information through prices, so that farmers can make investment and production choices based on accurate reflections of market conditions. The system needs to be reinforced by regulatory institutions, such as laws for market conduct and the enforcement of contracts, grades, and standards.

In MENA countries today, markets are not functioning efficiently, particularly in price formation, information creation and transmission, and arbitrage. The main reason is the administrative intervention in wholesale markets to stabilize urban food prices. This intervention needs to be eliminated to permit markets to promote stability through arbitrage and to allow for market segmentation.

Reinforcing Economywide Adjustment and Liberalization

The required adjustments in the nonagricultural sectors will also need to be carefully considered. Public enterprises are subjected to market rules through restructuring and privatization, but the private sector has to adapt and improve its efficiency as well. Equipment and technologies need to be updated. Labor has to be trained and retrained. Marketing efficiency has to improve. And market regulations and standards need to be modernized.

Covering the Costs of Transition

The costs of transition are not small. For example, the long-term cost of total liberalization in Tunisian agriculture was estimated at US$1.25 billion, with a third for transitional costs associated with labor and capital and two-thirds for *mise à niveau*. But the present value of the benefits was estimated at about US$9 billion, using a discount rate of 5 percent. So the benefits of liberalization would be more than adequate to finance the costs of transition, if those benefits can be captured to finance the transition.

Trade liberalization in MENA, including agricultural trade liberalization, should not be viewed in a short-term perspective. It is a longer-term process, requiring adequate consideration of social and political consequences, and careful planning of the sequencing, adaptation, financing, and implementation of actions. That is why MENA countries have to consider the possibly destabilizing social ramifications of agricultural liberalization. Neither MENA countries nor the international community wants social and political destabilization. So mutually acceptable solutions need to be found with appropriate cost sharing.

Notes

1. The estimates for subsidies, for 1997, are expected to have risen. The Official Development Assistance (ODA) estimate is for 2000.

2. Estimates vary from study to study. Anderson, Hoekman, and Strutt (2001) have an estimate of US$56 billion, Anderson and Morris (2000) estimate US$80 billion.

3. Turkey is also included in MENA, unlike in the standard World Bank classifications. Individual country data are only for Morocco and Turkey. The rest of the GTAP MENA region is aggregated into "rest of Middle East" and "rest of North Africa." Data on domestic input subsidies are reported as zero, except for Turkey in MENA.

FIGURE 7.1

Trends in EU Import Market Shares of Accession and Euro-Med Countries

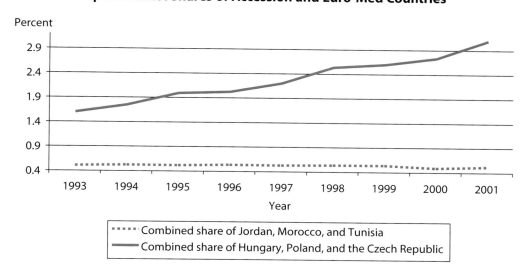

Percent

The trade market shares of another group of countries that signed accession agreements with the EU in the early 1990s have increased sharply—from around 1.5 percent to around 3 percent. The difference is most likely the result of differences in the content of the agreements they entered.

A comparison of the key features of the Euro-Med agreements and the accession agreements (table 7.1) makes it possible to identify four main reasons why the initial economic impact of the former has been modest so far.[2]

TABLE 7.1

Key Features of Euro-Med and EU Accession Agreements

Reforms in the agreements	Euro-Med	EU accession
Free movement		
Industrial goods	Yes	Yes
Agricultural goods	To be negotiated	Yes
Services	To be negotiated	Yes
Capital	No	Yes
Labor	No	Yes, with transition period
Complementary structural reforms		
Competition policy	Included as areas for cooperation and harmonization but with no mechanisms for implementation	Included as preconditions for accession
Privatization		
Company law		
Financial sector reform		
Intellectual property rights		

Source: Adapted from Diwan and others 2003.

- Most MENA countries have not pursued domestic reforms comprehensive enough to realize the benefits of greater market access to European economies.

- The Euro-Med agreements are limited in their coverage of trade in agriculture and services, and they do not cover labor.

- The Euro-Med agreements contain restrictive rules of origin for selected manufactured goods, such as clothing.

- There has been little progress in harmonizing standards across partners.

Limited Domestic Reforms

The first step in expanding trade is liberalizing it in a meaningful way. Various MENA countries have attempted this in fits and starts in the past two decades, but they have not liberalized as much as other regions. Among world regions, MENA has the second-highest average tariff rates and the second-highest incidence of nontariff barriers (see chapter 2). Furthermore, the tariff-reduction schedules in the Euro-Med agreements are backloaded: the larger reductions are to take place in the final years of the agreements. So, very little pressure is placed on the Arab countries to move faster on trade reform.

Structural reforms to improve the investment climate are also critical for trade liberalization. Such reforms typically involve measures to improve factory-to-port transport logistics, customs administration, competition policy (including privatization), company law, intellectual property rights, and financial and insurance services. They can substantially reduce transaction costs, increasing the ability of firms to respond to price signals communicated by trade reforms. MENA countries have made some progress in these areas, but the agenda for reform remains substantial.

Narrow Coverage

Liberalizing services can promote trade, growth, and employment. But the coverage of services is limited in the Euro-Med agreements. Restrictions and special costs continue to apply to cross-border trade in services. For example, several MENA countries apply a national carrier preference in air and sea freight services. Transshipments are often subject to high charges and fees. Similar preferences and charges apply to finance and telecommunications services.

Why the restrictions? MENA countries are reluctant to relinquish government control over banks, insurance companies, transport services, electricity authorities, and telecommunications agencies. They are even more reluctant when the likely sources of private delivery of services would be foreign.

The Euro-Med agreements specify that liberalizing services is to be discussed after a transition period, but no time-bound negotiations have begun.[3] Nor have many MENA countries made unilateral moves to modify foreign investment and domestic regulatory policies in key service sectors. By contrast, several EU accession countries in Central and Eastern Europe have for years been adapting their service regulations to meet EU requirements, and they have been open to foreign investment as well.

Not all of the MENA region's trade problems are self-inflicted. In many cases, its more developed trade partners have taken a deeply protectionist approach to integration agreements—by severely limiting trade in agricultural goods, for example. The lack of EU market access for agricultural goods is quantitatively a significant constraint on export growth for many MENA countries (Chaherli and El-Said 2000). Exports of key unprocessed agricultural products from southern Mediterranean partners are kept out by tariff and nontariff barriers. Tariff escalation in these countries also affects the development of the processed food sector. Sanitary and phytosanitary standard issues, such as pest control and quarantine systems, also affect the exports of agricultural products.

Nor does the coverage of the Euro-Med agreements extend to trade in labor services, a major foreign exchange earner for several MENA countries. Services would become even more important if temporary movements of MENA-origin workers to EU countries were liberalized. That could be of mutual benefit, given the need for additional workers in the EU. In general, however, the agreements limit the coverage of labor services to multilateral obligations offered under the GATS. No special exemptions are offered to MENA countries. By contrast, the accession agreements of the Central and Eastern European countries with the EU have clauses on the movement of workers, with fairly well-defined implementation procedures. The aim, after a transition period, is for free movement of labor within the expanded EU.

Restrictive Rules of Origin

Manufactured goods, which are treated more generously than agriculture and services in the Euro-Med agreements, are allowed in at zero tariffs. But the trade-enhancing effects are limited. First, the nonpreferential tariff rates on many manufactured goods are low to begin with (about 4 percent on average), so the advantage of preferential treatment to MENA countries is small. Second, several potentially important manufactured export items are subject to extremely restrictive rules of origin, again dampening the possibility of expanded trade.

Restrictive rules of origin are particularly important for clothing, textiles, and footwear. They are generally ranked from least to most restrictive as follows: those requiring a change in tariff classification, those stipulating minimum value addition, and those requiring specific production processes. For clothing from MENA countries, the EU applies the most restrictive rule. Thus, for cotton shirt imports, the rules of origin require that two stages of production be undertaken in MENA: the production of fabric from yarn and the stitching of the fabric into a shirt. In addition, the administrative procedures for proving origin are complex and time consuming. Sometimes the costs of proving origin are so high that exporters prefer to pay duties to get their goods in, despite having duty-free access provisions in their country's agreement (Herin 1986). In general, rules of origin have been found to restrict trade by as much as 40 percent (Gasiorek and others 2001).[4]

Lack of Common Standards

Standards for imports are often justified by health and safety concerns, typically for food products and engineering goods. But if standards discriminate against foreign goods—or increase costs unnecessarily—they take on the character of nontariff barriers and reduce integration. The costs of compliance with standards arise largely from the testing procedures. Most MENA countries do not readily accept compliance certificates issued by foreign laboratories. Instead, they require that the relevant testing be done at their national laboratories, which are usually weaker than European testing centers and saddled with cumbersome procedures, pushing up product costs.[5]

When domestic standards and testing procedures differ from those in the EU, MENA exporters are at a disadvantage. This situation also prevents MENA countries from joining global production chains with final outputs destined for EU markets. The incompatibility of standards can be addressed over time by bringing MENA standards and enforcement procedures into conformity with those applied in the EU. This convergence can be facilitated by technical assistance and funding from the EU.

The EU has not pushed hard for the harmonization of standards with MENA countries, unlike the approach with Central and Eastern European countries. The agreements with Central and Eastern European countries cover the need to harmonize standards and provide technical assistance funds to help them achieve this. Central and Eastern European countries are also encouraged to participate in the activities of specialized standards organizations, to make them familiar with EU standards and enforcement mechanisms. The Euro-Med agreements, by contrast, do not specify how standards are to be harmonized (Brenton and Manchin 2003).

Intraregional Integration

There have been numerous attempts to foster intraregional integration among Arab states in recent decades. A major pan-Arab effort was the 1982 Agreement for Facilitation and Promotion of Intra-Arab Trade, superseded in 1997 by the Pan-Arab Free Trade Agreement (PAFTA), which has 21 countries as signatories. Other recent examples of plurilateral agreements include the Arab Maghreb Union (with Algeria, Libya, Mauritania, Morocco, and Tunisia as members) and the Unified Economic Agreement between the Countries of the GCC (UEA-GCC), signed in 2001 by Bahrain, Kuwait, Oman, Qatar, Saudi Arabia, and the UAE (see box 7.2).

BOX 7.2

Subregional Integration through the GCC

The GCC has been relatively successful in implementing integration in the MENA region. It launched the UEA in 1982 to achieve free trade among members and enhance cooperation in factor movements, policy coordination, and services. Free trade was achieved in 1983 for agricultural, livestock, mineral, and industrial products. Since then, efforts have been under way to form a customs union. The first step, in 1988, was to adopt a common band of external tariffs (ranging between 4 and 20 percent). The second major step, in 1999, was to agree that a full customs union would be established by 2005 with a two-tier common external tariff. Further negotiations have proceeded with greater speed and unanimity than expected, and the target date for the customs union was advanced to 2003.

Among intraregional efforts in the MENA region, the UEA-GCC comes closest to a deep integration agreement. It has the widest coverage of goods and services. It has a common external tariff and unified customs processes and regulations. It has achieved substantial harmonization of industrial standards, and allows skilled professionals to register and practice in all member countries. It also aims for WTO consistency in trade policies, and it has begun discussing an association agreement with the EU.

Liberalization within the subregion has been accompanied by structural reform as well, especially in allowing private and foreign investment in several infrastructure sectors (such as power and water), undertaking domestic price reform for electricity and water, and allowing noncitizens to purchase real estate.

The level of trade integration among MENA countries is lower than other intraregional groupings: intraregional exports among Arab countries were just over 8 percent of total exports in 1998, compared with 22 percent for ASEAN (Association of Southeast Asian Nations) and 25 percent for MERCOSUR (Mercado Común del Sur, made up of Argentina, Brazil, and Uruguay) (table 7.2). Apart from an increase in the early 1980s, there has been no upward trend in intraregional trade among MENA countries.

One reason for the low level of intra-MENA trade could be the fact that the region consists of economies with similar production and export structures and thus with low potential for trade. Trade complementarity among countries can be measured quantitatively by indexes that reflect the extent to which goods exported by one country are imported by another. A recent study reports that such complementarity indexes show low values for Arab countries relative to other groupings, such as the European Community and NAFTA (Fawzy 2003).

The small economic size of the MENA region might be another reason for low trade. This is undoubtedly part of the explanation, but quantitative studies suggest that even when size is controlled, the level of intraregional trade is below potential (Al-Atrash and Yousef 2000). This suggests that the various integration efforts in the region have not overcome other barriers to intraregional trade.

Among the economic barriers are high tariff rates, inhospitable investment climates, high transaction costs, and the dominance of the public sector in MENA economies. For example, Arab countries have higher weighted-average tariff rates than other regional groupings such as MERCOSUR, ASEAN, and the EU. Nontariff barriers are also high. As noted earlier, the cost of compliance with non-tariff-related measures in various MENA countries can be as high as 10 percent of the value of the items imported (Zarrouk 2003). Furthermore, the private sector, which often plays a leading role in integration efforts, is likely to be less effective in this function in the MENA region because of the dominance of

TABLE 7.2

Trends in Intraregional Trade, Selected Regions

Regional bloc	Intraregional exports as a share of total exports (%)				
	1980	1985	1990	1995	1998
Arab countries	4.5	7.8	9.4	6.7	8.2
ASEAN	22.4	20.7	20.7	26.4	22.2
MERCOSUR	12	6	9	20	25
EU	60.8	59.2	65.9	62.4	56.8

Source: Adapted from Fawzy 2003.

might find it easier to move faster on liberalizing their finance, telecommunications, electricity, and transport services markets if they were offered enhanced labor access in the bargain.

Relaxing Rules of Origin

One desirable change would be to use the least restrictive rule of origin wherever possible. So rather than use rules requiring specific production processes (as for clothing), the EU should be asked to use either a rule specified in minimum value-added terms or a change in tariff classification. A second desirable change would be to allow diagonal cumulation in determining whether a specific rule of origin has been met. Diagonal cumulation means that intermediate goods produced in any other country that has an association agreement with the EU would qualify as goods produced in the exporting country of immediate concern. At the moment, only bilateral cumulation is allowed, such that only intermediate inputs originating in the EU (including items previously imported into the EU) qualify. But since the EU is often not the least-cost supplier of intermediate inputs for exports of concern to MENA (such as garments), bilateral cumulation is too restrictive.

For diagonal cumulation to be applied, MENA countries must also have free trade agreements and harmonized rules of origin with the supplier countries. This can be a complex and drawn out process, explaining why engaging in multilateral liberalization efforts is often preferred.

Harmonizing Standards

Under the mutual recognition principle, the EU can decide that a trading partner's standards and enforcement mechanisms are equivalent to its own, for a range of products and processes. When such equivalence cannot be assumed, the signatories have to reach agreement on a common set of requirements that may be applied at the product or process level. But agreements of this sort can be complex and time consuming to negotiate. In practice, little progress has been made in harmonizing MENA and EU standards in the past decade or so, a state of affairs no doubt considered satisfactory by import-substitution interests on both sides.

Since it is in the interest of MENA countries to gain more access to EU markets, it would be best for them to take the lead in harmonizing their standards with those of the EU. They could adopt EU standards for all products with significant export potential. Since legislating this might be slowed by vested interests, an initial measure would be to make local or national standards voluntary (rather than obligatory) for a selected range of export products. This would permit eager exporters to immediately adopt

EU standards without running afoul of local and national laws.[7] It would also allow exports to avoid the costs and delay of national certification.

Adopting EU standards would not solve all the technical barriers to trade. To meet these standards, MENA exporters will have to upgrade production facilities in many cases, a matter that can be left to individual or group private sector initiatives. MENA exporters will also have to show, through credible certification mechanisms, that they have met the agreed-on standards. This can be done through private certification companies, but it would be useful to streamline the procedures and upgrade the skills of national certification agencies so that they might perform this role. The EU could help in this process through funding and technical assistance.[8]

Potential Impact of Deeper Integration

The foregoing discussion essentially argues that RIAs aiming at deeper integration are likely to be more effective than the current versions of the Euro-Med and intraregional agreements.

What would deeper integration entail?[9] On the one hand: much greater cooperation to harmonize policies and administrative procedures across a broad range of activities relating to customs operations, health and safety standards, licensing and certification; supervision of financial services; and competition and antimonopoly legislation. On the other hand: much greater openness to trade in services and to the freer flow of labor and capital.

What would deep integration promise? A recent quantitative estimate suggests that the overall gains from liberalizing trade in both services and goods (and removing various regulatory nontariff barriers in the process) are about 6 to 10 percent of baseline GDP in Egypt and Tunisia, respectively (Hoekman and Messerlin 2002).

The dynamic gains from liberalizing trade in goods and services can outstrip the static gains, with productivity improvements as the main driver. Estimating the dynamic benefits involves considerable uncertainty, but simulations suggest that they can be more than twice the static gains (World Bank 2002). Factors likely to enhance productivity in tradable goods include:

- Increased investment embodying new technology, to expand capacity and take advantage of greater export opportunities.

- Transfers of technology and management, known to come in through greater openness.

- Greater economies of scale, from the increase in production and the access to larger markets.

Liberalizing services can enhance these productivity gains. For example, lower-cost telecommunications and networking services, following the liberalization of the ICT sector, are likely to boost connectivity, computer penetration, and the use of ICT business applications. This can dramatically improve the efficiency of the business sector—as the acceleration of productivity growth in the United States since the mid-1990s shows.

Looking Ahead

Once it is decided that deep integration, covering both goods and services, is the preferred strategy, a related issue is deciding what trading partners to integrate with. There are three choices: integrating with other, similarly placed economies within the region; integrating with a large economic zone, such as the EU or the United States; or integrating with the world as a whole through multilateral negotiations under the WTO.

In ideal conditions the third option would be the most desirable. It typically offers the greatest trade and welfare gains, as many quantitative studies attest. But MENA countries face some hurdles along this path. Not all of them are members of the WTO, and the accession process has in recent years acquired a broad range of politically difficult and time-consuming preconditions. And with many countries involved, with a higher possibility for deadlocks, WTO negotiations move rather slowly.

There are two reasons why integration agreements with the EU might offer a faster route. First, liberalizing services typically requires the movement of labor (both professional and unskilled), more easily agreed with a cohesive block (such as the EU) than with a larger, more fractious set of countries (such as the WTO). Such agreements are also more likely if the prospective size and sources of labor inflow can be contained, as with a geographically restricted RIA. Second, liberalizing services requires agreements on quality standards that typically require a process of mutual recognition or a protocol of harmonization to achieve common standards. This too is easier within an RIA than with a more diverse group of countries.

With service liberalization an important item on the deep integration agenda, and with time of the essence for domestic structural reforms, it might be best for the MENA countries to proceed on a dual track—one with the WTO, the other with the EU. If it proves possible to move faster along the second track, the opportunity should be taken. Recent developments provide grounds for optimism that RIAs with the EU could be revitalized along the lines suggested in this chapter. Proposals have been floated within the EU calling for a "new neighborhood policy" under which eastern and southern neighbors should be brought into a tighter economic relationship featuring freer flows of not only goods but also services, capital, and labor.

At the same time, it would help to push intraregional integration, which could prepare the ground for deeper integration beyond the region in two ways. First, it could stimulate additional investment. Today, outside investors treat the region as several different markets. To service these markets they find it most effective to set up investments in a European location. If intraregional trade in goods and services begins to flow more freely, there will be less reason for this sort of "hub-and-spoke" approach. It is more likely, then, that investment will take place in the region—to gain access to other countries in the region.

Second, deeper intraregional integration could provide opportunities for learning by doing in harmonizing standards and reducing barriers to the movement of technical and professional staff. If such integration improves productivity in MENA countries, this should make it easier for them to contemplate deeper links with Europe and the rest of the world.

Although the intraregional and interregional options for deep integration offer a speedier path to substantial welfare gains, it is important to note that the size of the gains is typically larger for multilateral liberalization. A preferred strategy would thus be to negotiate goods and services liberalization agreements within the region as well as with the EU (or the United States, if that is an option)—and having done so to offer the same terms and conditions to the rest of the world on a most favored nation basis.

Notes

1. Other measures of impact, such as inflows of foreign investment or convergence of incomes per capita, lead to similar conclusions (Diwan and others 2003).

2. Antidumping and other safeguard practices of the EU could also dampen trade with MENA, an aspect not explored here.

3. Recent declarations at the regional level give some hope for greater political commitments to liberalizing services. For example, recent Euro-Mediterranean Ministerial Conferences on Trade have called for working groups to accelerate discussions related to the liberalization of tourism, transport, and telecommunications.

4. A recent study of the Africa Growth and Opportunity Act estimates that stringent rules of origin limit the value of trade between the United States and African countries to less than US$140 million, from

an unconstrained potential of US$540 million (Subramanian, Mattoo, and Roy 2002).

5. A 1996 study of the Egyptian standards system estimated that compliance added costs equal to as much as 90 percent of the value of the goods for food products (Nathan Associates study referred to in Kheir-El-Din [2000]). Since then, however, Egypt has taken steps to reduce such costs by accepting some foreign certificates of compliance, allowing some importers with good records to bypass compliance, and improving coordination among multiple standards-checking authorities.

6. Sometimes regional trade agreements are pursued as precursors to multilateral agreements on the grounds that they might make the latter more politically defensible. But each regional agreement involves some adjustment costs as businesses and labor respond to new price incentives. Accordingly, trade-diverting RIAs that precede multilateral agreements could well imply double doses of adjustment, making the multilateral agreements politically more difficult.

7. This was done, for example, in Bulgaria as the country attempted to accelerate the harmonization of its standards with those of the EU (Brenton and Manchin 2003).

8. The discussion on standards applies to both industrial and agricultural goods. Even if the EU granted greater market access, MENA exporters would still have to meet sanitary and phytosanitary standards for agricultural products.

9. The extension of liberalization to services, capital, and labor flows is sometimes referred to as "widening" integration, while the term "deep" integration is reserved for the harmonization of product standards and customs procedures (Schiff and Winters 2003).

Statistical Appendixes

Data Definitions

| 1 | Population, total | Table 1 | Total population is based on the de facto definition of population, which counts all residents regardless of legal status or citizenship—except for refugees not permanently settled in the country of asylum, who are generally considered part of the population of their country of origin. |

2   GDP per capita, PPP (current international $)   Table 1   GDP per capita based on purchasing power parity (PPP). PPP GDP is gross domestic product converted to international dollars using purchasing power parity rates. An international dollar has the same purchasing power over GDP as the U.S. dollar has in the United States. GDP is the sum of gross value added by all resident producers in the economy plus any product taxes and minus any subsidies not included in the value of the products. It is calculated without making deductions for depreciation of fabricated assets or for depletion and degradation of natural resources. Data are in current international dollars.

3   GDP (current US$)   Table 1   GDP is the sum of gross value added by all resident producers in the economy plus any product taxes and minus any subsidies not included in the value of the products. It is calculated without making deductions for depreciation of fabricated assets or for depletion and degradation of natural resources. Data are in current U.S. dollars. Dollar figures for GDP are converted from domestic currencies using single-year official exchange rates. For a few countries where the official exchange rate does not reflect the rate effectively applied to actual foreign exchange transactions, an alternative conversion factor is used.

4   GDP (constant 1995 US$)   Table 1   GDP is the sum of gross value added by all resident producers in the economy plus any product taxes and minus any subsidies not included in the value of the products. It is calculated without making deductions for depreciation of fabricated assets or for depletion and degradation of natural resources. Data are in constant 1995 U.S. dollars. Dollar figures for GDP are converted from domestic currencies using 1995 official exchange rates. For a few countries where the official exchange rate does not reflect the rate effectively applied to actual foreign exchange transactions, an alternative conversion factor is used.

5   Consumer price index (1995 = 100)   Table 1   Consumer price index reflects changes in the cost to the average consumer of acquiring a fixed basket of goods and services that may be fixed or changed at specified intervals, such as yearly. The Laspeyres formula is generally used.

6   Current account balance (current US$)   Table 1   Current account balance is the sum of net exports of goods, services, net income, and net current transfers.

7   Overall budget balance, including grants (current US$)   Table 1   Overall budget balance is current and capital revenue and official grants received, less total expenditure and lending minus repayments. Data are shown for central government only.

8	Merchandise exports (current US$)	Table 2	Merchandise exports show the FOB value of goods provided to the rest of the world valued in U.S. dollars. Data are in current U.S. dollars.
9	Oil exports (current US$)	Table 2	Fuels are SITC section 3 (mineral fuels).
10	Ores and metals exports (current US$)	Table 2	Ores and metals are the commodities in SITC sections 27 (crude fertilizer, minerals), 28 (metalliferous ores, scrap), and 68 (nonferrous metals).
11	Agricultural exports (current US$)	Table 2	Agricultural exports are the commodities in SITC 00+01+02+04−27−28.
12	Merchandise imports (current US$)	Table 3	Merchandise imports show the CIF value of goods received from the rest of the world valued in U.S. dollars. Data are in current U.S. dollars.
13	Manufacturing imports (current US$)	Table 3	Manufactures are the commodities in SITC sections 5 (chemicals), 6 (basic manufactures), 7 (machinery and transport equipment), and 8 (miscellaneous manufactured goods), excluding division 68 (nonferrous metals).
14	Agricultural imports (current US$)	Table 3	Agricultural imports are the commodities in SITC 00+01+02+04−27−28.
15	Service exports (balance of payments [BoP], current US$)	Table 4	*Services* (previously nonfactor services) refer to economic output of intangible commodities that may be produced, transferred, and consumed at the same time. International transactions in services are defined by the IMF's *Balance of Payments Manual* (1993), but definitions may nevertheless vary among reporting economies. Data are in current U.S. dollars.
16	International tourism receipts (current US$)	Table 4	International tourism receipts are expenditures by international inbound visitors, including payments to national carriers for international transport. These receipts should include any other prepayment made for goods or services received in the destination country. They also may include receipts from same-day visitors, except in cases where these are so important as to justify a separate classification. Data are in current U.S. dollars.
17	Service imports (BoP, current US$)	Table 4	*Services* (previously nonfactor services) refer to economic output of intangible commodities that may be produced, transferred, and consumed at the same time. International transactions in services are defined by the IMF's *Balance of Payments Manual* (1993), but definitions may nevertheless vary among reporting economies. Data are in current U.S. dollars.
18	Foreign direct investment net inflows (BoP, current US$)	Table 5	Foreign direct investment is net inflows of investment to acquire a lasting management interest (10 percent or more of voting stock) in an enterprise operating in an economy other than that of the investor. It is the sum of equity capital, reinvestment of earnings, long-term capital, and short-term capital as shown in the balance of payments. This series shows net inflows in the reporting economy. Data are in current U.S. dollars.
19	Workers' remittances, receipts (BoP, current US$)	Table 5	Workers' remittances are current transfers by migrants who are employed or intent to remain employed for more than a year in another economy in which they are considered residents. Some developing countries classify workers' remittances as a factor income receipt (and thus as a component of GNI). The World Bank adheres to international guidelines in defining GNI, and its classification of workers' remittances may therefore differ from national practices. This item shows receipts by the reporting country. Data are in current U.S. dollars.
20	Aid per capita (current US$)	Table 5	Official development assistance and net official aid record the actual international transfer by the donor of financial resources or of goods or services valued at the cost to the donor, less any repayments of loan principal during the same period. Grants by official agencies of the members of the Development Assistance Committee are included, as are loans with a grant element of at least 25 percent, and technical cooperation and assistance. Aid per capita includes both official development assistance and official aid, and is calculated by dividing total aid by the midyear population estimate.

Data Sources

1	Population, total	Table 1	World Bank staff estimates from various sources, including the United Nations Statistics Division's Population and Vital Statistics Report, country statistical offices, and Demographic and Health Surveys from national sources and Macro International.
2	GDP per capita, PPP (current international $)	Table 1	World Bank, International Comparison Programme database.
3	GDP (current US$)	Table 1	World Bank national accounts data and OECD National Accounts data files.
4	GDP (constant 1995 US$)	Table 1	World Bank national accounts data and OECD National Accounts data files.
5	Consumer price index (1995 = 100)	Table 1	International Monetary Fund, *International Financial Statistics* and data files.
6	Current account balance (current US$)	Table 1	Current account balance is the sum of net exports of goods, services, net income, and net current transfers.
7	Overall budget balance, including grants (current US$)	Table 1	International Monetary Fund, *International Financial Statistics* and data files, and World Bank and OECD GDP estimates.
8	Merchandise exports (current US$)	Table 2	World Trade Organization.
9	Fuel exports (current US$)	Table 2	World Bank staff estimates from the COMTRADE database maintained by the United Nations Statistics division.
10	Ores and metals exports (current US$)	Table 2	World Bank staff estimates from the COMTRADE database maintained by the United Nations Statistics division.
11	Agricultural exports (current US$)	Table 2	World Bank staff estimates from the COMTRADE database maintained by the United Nations Statistics division.
12	Merchandise imports (current US$)	Table 3	World Trade Organization.
13	Manufacturing imports (current US$)	Table 3	World Bank staff estimates from the COMTRADE database maintained by the United Nations Statistics division.
14	Agricultural imports (current US$)	Table 3	World Bank staff estimates from the COMTRADE database maintained by the United Nations Statistics division.
15	Service exports (BoP, current US$)	Table 4	International Monetary Fund, *Balance of Payments Statistics Yearbook* and data files, and World Bank staff estimates.
16	International tourism, receipts (current US$)	Table 4	World Tourism Organization, *Yearbook of Tourism Statistics* and data files.
17	Service imports (BoP, current US$)	Table 4	International Monetary Fund, *Balance of Payments Statistics Yearbook* and data files, and World Bank staff estimates.
18	Foreign direct investment net inflows (BoP, current US$)	Table 5	International Monetary Fund, Balance of Payments Statistics and Balance of Payments databases, and World Bank, *Global Development Finance.*
19	Workers' remittances, receipts (BoP, current US$)	Table 5	International Monetary Fund, *Balance of Payments Statistics Yearbook* and data files, and World Bank staff estimates.
20	Aid per capita (current US$)	Table 5	Development Assistance Committee of the OECD and World Bank population estimates.

APPENDIX TABLE 1

Selected Macro–Indicators

Region/ country	Population Million 1998– 2000[a]	Population % growth 1990– 2000	GDP per capita US$ PPP 1998– 2000	GDP per capita US$ 1998– 2000	GDP per capita % growth 1990– 2000	GDP Billion US$ 1998– 2000[a]	GDP % growth 1990– 2000	Rates of inflation % 1990– 2000	Fiscal balance % to GDP 1998– 2000	Current account balance % to GDP 1998– 2000
MENA	**264.2**	**2.1**	**4,937**	**2,451**	**1.2**	**647**	**3.3**	**8.2**	**−1.9**	**9.5**
Non-GCC	*235.7*	*2.1*	*4,177*	*1,463*	*1.6*	*345*	*3.8*	*14.3*	*−1.9*	*1.4*
Algeria	30.0	2.0	5,113	1,650	−0.3	49	1.7	16.3	1.8	4.9
Djibouti	0.6	3.0	2,012	862	−3.9	1	−1.0	3.5	−1.8	−7.2
Egypt, Arab Rep. of	62.8	2.0	3,432	1,437	2.3	90	4.3	9.0	−3.0	−2.0
Iran, Islamic Rep. of	62.8	1.6	5,641	1,611	2.5	101	4.2	24.0	1.0	5.9
Jordan	4.7	4.4	3,901	1,726	0.6	8	5.1	3.5	−4.7	2.0
Lebanon	4.3	1.8	4,274	3,847	5.3	16	7.2	20.5	−19.7	−22.0
Morocco	28.2	1.8	3,518	1,233	0.4	35	2.2	3.9	−4.5	−0.8
Syrian Arab Republic	15.8	2.9	3,470	1,026	2.1	16	5.2	6.2	0.8	5.9
Tunisia	9.5	1.6	5,984	2,126	3.1	20	4.7	4.5	−2.5	−3.2
Yemen, Rep. of	17.1	4.0	770	453	1.5	8	5.5	25.4	−0.1	20.3
GCC	*28.5*	*2.7*	*10,597*	*10,615*	*−0.3*	*303*	*2.5*	*1.2*	*—*	*18.8*
Bahrain	0.7	3.2	—	10,385	2.9	7	5.5	0.6	—	9.8
Kuwait	1.9	−0.7	15,684	16,104	—	31	—	2.3	—	40.9
Oman	2.3	3.9	—	7,647	0.6	18	4.6	0.3	—	17.3
Qatar	0.6	1.9	—	21,772	—	12	—	2.7	—	22.2
Saudi Arabia	20.2	2.7	10,968	8,850	−0.5	179	2.2	1.0	—	7.6
United Arab Emirates	2.8	4.7	17,935	19,819	—	56	—	1.6	—	43.2
Non–MENA	**3,702.9**	**1.4**	**4,109**	**1,323**	**2.5**	**4,898**	**4.0**	**41.8**	**−2.7**	**0.5**
LAC	*402.1*	*1.6*	*6,251*	*4,126*	*1.7*	*1,659*	*3.3*	*87.2*	*−1.5*	*−3.2*
Argentina	36.6	1.3	12,423	7,902	3.2	289	4.5	14.9	−2.3	−3.1
Bolivia	8.1	2.4	2,376	1,025	1.3	8	3.8	9.0	−4.6	−5.3
Brazil	168.2	1.4	7,248	3,786	1.3	637	2.7	199.9	—	−4.1
Chile	15.0	1.5	9,001	4,688	4.9	70	6.5	9.4	0.1	−1.4
Colombia	41.5	1.9	5,987	2,141	0.8	89	2.7	20.3	—	0.4
Costa Rica	3.7	2.3	8,338	4,095	2.9	15	5.2	15.9	−1.3	−4.8
Ecuador	12.4	2.1	3,214	1,405	−0.3	17	1.8	42.5	—	6.8
El Salvador	6.2	2.1	4,377	2,039	2.5	13	4.6	8.3	1.6	−3.3
Guatemala	11.1	2.7	3,715	1,707	1.4	19	4.1	11.0	—	−5.5
Jamaica	2.6	0.9	3,619	2,876	−0.4	7	0.3	24.8	−1.6	−5.0
Mexico	96.6	1.6	8,470	5,113	1.8	494	3.5	18.3	−1.3	−3.1
EAP	*1,663.8*	*1.2*	*4,072*	*1,083*	*6.0*	*1,801*	*7.3*	*6.9*	*−3.4*	*3.4*
China	1,252.7	1.1	3,658	803	8.9	1,006	10.1	7.2	—	1.9
Indonesia	207.0	1.7	2,922	624	2.7	129	4.2	13.3	—	5.2
Korea, Rep. of	46.9	1.0	15,851	8,428	5.2	395	6.2	5.1	—	2.7
Malaysia	22.7	2.5	8,356	3,534	4.4	80	7.0	3.5	—	9.4
Philippines	74.2	2.2	3,833	971	0.5	72	2.9	8.5	−4.1	11.3
Thailand	60.3	0.9	6,157	1,973	3.5	119	4.4	4.5	−3.0	7.7

APPENDIX TABLE 1 (continued)

Selected Macro–Indicators

Region/ country	Population Million 1998– 2000[a]	Population % growth 1990– 2000	GDP per capita US$ PPP 1998– 2000	GDP per capita US$ 1998– 2000	GDP per capita % growth 1990– 2000	GDP Billion US$ 1998– 2000[a]	GDP % growth 1990– 2000	Rates of inflation % 1990– 2000	Fiscal balance % to GDP 1998– 2000	Current account balance % to GDP 1998– 2000
SAR	*1261.3*	*1.9*	*2,123*	*432*	*3.3*	*545*	*5.2*	*8.7*	*–5.3*	*–0.7*
Bangladesh	128.8	1.8	1,509	355	3.0	46	4.8	5.2	—	0.0
India	997.7	1.8	2,239	440	3.6	439	5.4	9.0	–5.2	–0.6
Pakistan	134.8	2.5	1,856	451	1.4	61	3.9	9.2	–5.5	–2.0
ECA	*283.4*	*0.2*	*7,901*	*2,575*	*–1.1*	*730*	*–0.9*	*56.5*	*–2.2*	*2.7*
Bulgaria	8.2	–0.7	5,290	1,488	–1.1	12	–1.7	109.0	0.6	–5.6
Czech Republic	10.3	–0.1	13,431	5,261	0.2	54	0.1	7.6	–3.0	–5.2
Hungary	10.2	–0.2	11,473	4,589	1.0	47	0.8	20.0	–3.5	–2.8
Poland	38.7	0.1	8,522	4,062	3.5	157	3.7	27.0	0.3	–6.3
Russian Federation	146.3	–0.2	7,666	1,677	–3.9	245	–4.0	79.0	3.9	18.2
Turkey	64.3	1.5	6,705	3,019	2.0	194	3.6	76.1	–11.4	–4.9
Slovak Republic	5.4	0.2	10,734	3,715	0.1	20	0.3	9.2	–3.0	–3.5
Africa	*92.3*	*2.3*	*5,198*	*1,765*	*–0.4*	*163*	*1.9*	*9.1*	*–2.1*	*–1.0*
Cameroon	14.6	2.5	1,616	613	–1.1	9	1.4	4.8	—	–1.7
Côte d'Ivoire	15.6	3.1	1,624	769	–0.5	12	2.6	6.0	–1.5	–2.3
Ghana	18.9	2.5	1,879	356	1.8	7	4.3	25.6	—	–8.3
Mauritius	1.2	1.2	9,257	3,621	3.8	4	5.1	6.7	–1.4	–0.8
South Africa	42.1	2.0	9,134	3,112	–0.2	131	1.7	8.9	–2.2	–0.4

— Not available.

Note: All indicators are three-year averages for 1998–2000 unless otherwise indicated. EAP = East Asia and Pacific region; ECA = Europe and Central Asia region; GCC = Gulf Cooperation Council; GDP = gross domestic product; LAC = Latin America and the Caribbean region; MENA = Middle East and Northern Africa region; and SAR = South Asia region.

a. Group figures in the column are totals, not averages.

Sources: *WDI*; live database.

APPENDIX TABLE 2

Merchandise Exports

Region/ country	Total merchandise exports			Oil exports		Nonoil exports			Ores and metals exports		Agricultural exports	
	Billion US$ 1998– 2000	US$ per capita 1998– 2000	% to GDP 1998– 2000	Billion US$ 1998– 2000[a]	% to GDP 2000	Billion US$ 1998– 2000[a]	US$ per capita 1998– 2000	% to GDP 2000	Billion US$ 1998– 2000[a]	% to GDP 2000	Billion US$ 1998– 2000[a]	% to GDP 2000
MENA	**186**	**704**	**28.7**	**130.8**	**23.0**	**55.2**	**132**	**9.7**	**114.3**	**19.6**	**5.9**	**1.0**
Non-GCC	*61*	*261*	*17.8*	*38.8*	*11.9*	*22.6*	*95*	*6.9*	*40.5*	*11.8*	*5.0*	*1.4*
Algeria	15	494	29.9	14.3	28.9	0.5	17	1.0	14.4	29.1	0.0	0.1
Djibouti	0	34	3.9	—	—	—	—	—	—	—	—	—
Egypt, Arab Rep. of	4	60	4.2	1.3	1.4	2.5	40	2.8	1.5	1.6	0.5	0.6
Iran, Islamic Rep. of	21	332	20.6	17.6	17.4	3.2	52	3.2	17.8	17.6	1.0	0.9
Jordan	2	389	22.5	0.0	0.0	1.8	389	22.5	0.4	5.1	0.2	2.6
Lebanon	1	160	4.2	—	—	0.7	—	4.2	0.04	0.2	0.1	0.9
Morocco	7	259	21.0	0.2	0.5	7.1	252	20.5	0.9	2.5	1.7	4.9
Syrian Arab Republic	4	232	22.6	2.5	15.2	1.2	76	7.4	2.5	15.5	0.7	4.3
Tunisia	6	616	29.0	0.5	2.5	5.3	563	26.5	0.6	2.9	0.6	3.0
Yemen, Rep. of	3	157	34.6	2.5	32.2	0.2	11	2.4	2.5	32.3	0.1	1.0
GCC	*125*	*4,366*	*41.1*	*92.0*	*38.3*	*32.6*	*472*	*13.6*	*73.8*	*30.7*	*0.9*	*0.4*
Bahrain	4	6,554	63.1	2.9	42.0	1.5	—	21.1	—	—	0.0	0.2
Kuwait	14	7,156	44.4	10.9	35.1	2.9	1,506	9.4	10.9	35.2	0.0	0.1
Oman	8	3,349	43.8	6.0	33.2	1.9	808	10.6	6.1	33.7	0.3	1.9
Qatar	8	14,055	64.6	7.2	58.2	0.8	1,387	6.4	7.2	58.3	0.0	0.0
Saudi Arabia	56	2,758	31.2	49.5	27.7	6.3	309	3.5	49.6	27.8	0.5	0.3
United Arab Emirates	35	12,386	62.5	15.6	27.9	19.3	—	34.6	—	—	—	—
Non–MENA	**1,154**	**312**	**23.6**	**98.4**	**2.0**	**1,055.6**	**285**	**21.6**	**144.7**	**3.0**	**136.1**	**2.8**
LAC	*263*	*654*	*15.9*	*20.8*	*1.3*	*242.1*	*602*	*14.6*	*36.5*	*2.2*	*53.9*	*3.2*
Argentina	25	693	8.8	3.3	1.1	22.1	604	7.6	4.1	1.4	12.6	4.4
Bolivia	1	139	13.5	0.1	1.2	1.0	126	12.3	0.4	4.5	0.4	5.1
Brazil	51	306	8.1	0.5	0.1	50.9	302	8.0	5.6	0.9	16.1	2.5
Chile	16	1,079	23.0	0.1	0.2	16.1	1,072	22.9	7.2	10.2	5.8	8.3
Colombia	12	285	13.3	4.4	4.9	7.4	179	8.4	4.5	5.0	3.5	3.9
Costa Rica	6	1,604	39.2	0.0	0.2	6.0	1,596	39.0	0.1	0.5	2.0	13.4
Ecuador	5	365	26.0	1.6	9.0	3.0	239	17.0	1.6	9.0	2.5	14.1
El Salvador	3	428	21.0	0.1	0.9	2.5	409	20.1	0.2	1.4	0.6	4.4
Guatemala	3	231	13.5	0.1	0.5	2.5	222	13.0	0.1	0.7	1.6	8.4
Jamaica	1	493	17.2	0.0	0.0	1.3	492	17.1	0.1	1.0	0.3	4.0
Mexico	140	1,450	28.4	10.6	2.2	129.5	1,340	26.2	12.8	2.6	8.5	1.7
EAP	*593*	*357*	*32.9*	*32.4*	*1.8*	*560.8*	*337*	*31.1*	*43.4*	*2.4*	*49.4*	*2.7*
China	209	167	20.8	5.8	0.6	203.5	162	20.2	10.0	1.0	14.8	1.5
Indonesia	53	257	41.2	12.0	9.3	41.3	199	31.9	14.4	11.2	7.7	5.9
Korea, Rep. of	149	3,189	37.8	6.6	1.7	142.8	3,048	36.2	8.8	2.2	4.2	1.1

APPENDIX TABLE 2 (continued)

Merchandise Exports

Region/ country	Total merchandise exports			Oil exports		Nonoil exports			Ores and metals exports		Agricultural exports	
	Billion US$ 1998–2000	US$ per capita 1998–2000	% to GDP 1998–2000	Billion US$ 1998–2000[a]	% to GDP 1998–2000	Billion US$ 1998–2000[a]	US$ per capita 1998–2000	% to GDP 1998–2000	Billion US$ 1998–2000[a]	% to GDP 1998–2000	Billion US$ 1998–2000[a]	% to GDP 1998–2000
Malaysia	85	3,754	106.2	6.4	8.0	78.9	3,471	98.2	7.4	9.2	8.9	11.1
Philippines	35	475	49.0	0.3	0.4	35.0	471	48.5	0.9	1.2	2.0	2.8
Thailand	61	1,007	51.0	1.3	1.1	59.4	986	49.9	1.9	1.6	11.8	9.9
SAR	*51*	*41*	*9.4*	*0.2*	*0.0*	*51.3*	*41*	*9.4*	*1.1*	*0.2*	*7.9*	*1.4*
Bangladesh	6	44	12.3	0.0	0.0	5.6	44	12.3	0.01	0.0	0.5	1.0
India	37	37	8.5	0.1	0.0	37.0	37	8.4	1.0	0.2	6.2	1.4
Pakistan	9	64	14.3	0.1	0.1	8.6	64	14.1	0.1	0.2	1.2	2.0
ECA	*209*	*739*	*28.7*	*41.1*	*5.6*	*168.1*	*593*	*23.0*	*55.7*	*7.6*	*17.3*	*2.4*
Bulgaria	4	532	35.7	0.3	2.6	4.0	493	33.1	0.8	6.3	0.7	5.8
Czech Republic	27	2,629	50.0	0.8	1.5	26.2	2,552	48.5	1.3	2.5	1.9	3.5
Hungary	25	2,482	54.1	0.4	0.9	24.9	2,440	53.2	1.0	2.0	2.6	5.4
Poland	29	753	18.5	1.5	0.9	27.6	714	17.6	2.9	1.8	3.2	2.0
Russian Federation	85	584	34.8	37.4	15.2	48.0	328	19.6	47.9	19.5	3.9	1.6
Turkey	27	421	14.0	0.3	0.2	26.8	417	13.8	1.0	0.5	4.4	2.3
Slovak Republic	11	2,028	54.6	0.5	2.3	10.5	1,941	52.2	0.9	4.3	0.7	3.3
Africa	*37*	*402*	*22.8*	*3.8*	*2.4*	*33.2*	*360*	*20.4*	*8.0*	*4.9*	*7.7*	*4.7*
Cameroon	2	117	19.1	0.6	6.4	1.1	78	12.7	0.7	7.5	0.8	8.5
Côte d'Ivoire	4	280	36.5	0.6	5.2	3.7	240	31.2	0.6	5.3	2.7	22.8
Ghana	2	93	26.2	0.1	1.4	1.7	88	24.8	0.3	4.5	0.7	10.7
Mauritius	2	1,332	36.8	0.0	0.0	1.6	1,332	36.8	0.0	0.1	0.4	8.6
South Africa	28	658	21.1	2.5	1.9	25.1	597	19.2	6.4	4.9	3.1	2.4

— Not available.
Note: All indicators are three-year averages for 1998–2000 unless otherwise indicated. EAP = East Asia and Pacific region; ECA = Europe and Central Asia region; GCC = Gulf Cooperation Council; GDP = gross domestic product; LAC = Latin America and the Caribbean region; MENA = Middle East and Northern Africa region; and SAR = South Asia region.
a. Group figures in the column are totals, not averages.
Source: *WDI*; live database.

APPENDIX TABLE 3

Merchandise Imports

Region/country	Total imports			Manufacturing imports			Agricultural imports		
	Billion US$ 1998–2000	US$ per capita 1998–2000	% to GDP 1998–2000	Billion US$ 1998–2000	US$ per capita 1998–2000	% to GDP 1998–2000	Billion US$ 1998–2000	US$ per capita 1998–2000	% to GDP 1998–2000
MENA	**155**	**588**	**24.0**	**84**	**324**	**14.4**	**24.3**	**93**	**4.1**
Non-GCC	*74*	*315*	*21.5*	*49*	*210*	*14.3*	*16.7*	*71*	*4.9*
Algeria	9	308	18.7	6	204	12.4	2.9	96	5.8
Djibouti	0	314	36.4	—	—	—	—	—	—
Egypt, Arab Rep. of	15	245	17.1	9	145	10.1	4.2	68	4.7
Iran, Islamic Rep. of	14	219	13.6	10	163	10.1	2.8	45	2.8
Jordan	4	850	49.2	3	540	31.3	0.9	194	11.3
Lebanon	7	1,523	39.6	4	921	23.9	1.3	315	8.2
Morocco	11	375	30.4	7	252	20.5	1.9	66	5.4
Syrian Arab Republic	4	244	23.8	2	152	14.8	0.8	54	5.2
Tunisia	8	895	42.1	7	700	32.9	1.0	106	5.0
Yemen, Rep. of	2	127	28.1	1	70	15.5	0.8	46	10.2
GCC	*81*	*2,845*	*26.8*	*35*	*1,403*	*14.6*	*7.6*	*295*	*3.1*
Bahrain	4	5,937	57.2	—	—	—	0.2	244	2.3
Kuwait	8	4,052	25.2	6	3,240	20.1	0.9	470	2.9
Oman	5	2,185	28.6	4	1,587	20.8	1.1	455	5.9
Qatar	3	5,630	25.9	3	4,501	20.7	0.3	455	2.1
Saudi Arabia	29	1,457	16.5	23	1,120	12.7	5.2	257	2.9
United Arab Emirates	32	11,236	56.7	—	—	—	—	—	—
Non–MENA	**1,097**	**296**	**22.4**	**814**	**220**	**16.6**	**100.9**	**27**	**2.1**
LAC	*292*	*727*	*17.6*	*240*	*596*	*14.5*	*24.2*	*60*	*1.5*
Argentina	27	748	9.5	24	661	8.4	1.7	47	0.6
Bolivia	2	228	22.2	2	189	18.5	0.2	28	2.7
Brazil	57	339	9.0	43	254	6.7	5.8	35	0.9
Chile	17	1,155	24.6	13	874	18.6	1.4	94	2.0
Colombia	12	296	13.8	10	234	10.9	1.8	43	2.0
Costa Rica	6	1,690	41.3	5	1,330	32.5	0.5	135	3.3
Ecuador	4	331	23.5	3	253	18.0	0.5	44	3.1
El Salvador	4	704	34.5	3	469	23.0	0.7	106	5.2
Guatemala	5	415	24.3	3	310	18.2	0.6	58	3.4
Jamaica	3	1,168	40.6	2	748	26.0	0.6	216	7.5
Mexico	154	1,595	31.2	132	1,368	26.8	10.4	107	2.1
EAP	*483*	*290*	*26.8*	*359*	*216*	*20.0*	*43.2*	*26*	*2.4*
China	177	141	17.6	140	112	13.9	15.3	12	1.5
Indonesia	28	137	21.9	18	86	13.7	5.3	26	4.1
Korea, Rep. of	125	2,657	31.5	78	1,663	19.7	11.0	235	2.8
Malaysia	68	3,015	85.3	58	2,558	72.4	4.4	194	5.5
Philippines	33	440	45.3	26	345	35.5	3.2	43	4.4
Thailand	52	859	43.5	40	665	33.7	4.0	67	3.4

APPENDIX TABLE 3 (continued)

Merchandise Imports

Region/country	Total imports			Manufacturing imports			Agricultural imports		
	Billion US$ 1998–2000	US$ per capita 1998–2000	% to GDP 1998–2000	Billion US$ 1998–2000	US$ per capita 1998–2000	% to GDP 1998–2000	Billion US$ 1998–2000	US$ per capita 1998–2000	% to GDP 1998–2000
SAR	**65**	**52**	**11.9**	**35**	**28**	**6.4**	**8.1**	**6**	**1.5**
Bangladesh	8	60	16.8	5	41	11.7	1.5	11	3.2
India	47	47	10.7	24	24	5.6	4.5	4	1.0
Pakistan	10	76	16.9	5	40	8.8	2.2	16	3.5
ECA	**218**	**771**	**29.9**	**153**	**541**	**21.0**	**22.0**	**78**	**3.0**
Bulgaria	6	690	46.4	3	421	28.3	0.4	53	3.6
Czech Republic	30	2,871	54.6	24	2,335	44.4	2.3	227	4.3
Hungary	29	2,798	61.0	24	2,363	51.5	1.4	138	3.0
Poland	47	1,224	30.1	38	972	23.9	4.1	107	2.6
Russian Federation	48	328	19.5	20	139	8.3	8.8	60	3.6
Turkey	47	731	24.2	34	535	17.7	3.9	61	2.0
Slovak Republic	12	2,286	61.5	9	1,743	46.9	1.0	182	4.9
Africa	**38**	**414**	**23.5**	**26**	**286**	**16.2**	**3.4**	**36**	**2.1**
Cameroon	1	95	15.4	1	60	9.9	0.3	19	3.1
Côte d'Ivoire	3	204	26.6	2	112	14.6	0.6	37	4.8
Ghana	3	159	44.7	2	103	28.8	0.4	22	6.3
Mauritius	2	1,818	50.2	2	1,332	36.8	0.4	318	8.8
South Africa	29	678	21.8	20	481	15.4	1.7	41	1.3

— Not available.

Note: All indicators are three-year averages for 1998–2000 unless otherise indicated. EAP = East Asia and Pacific region; ECA = Europe and Central Asia region; GCC = Gulf Cooperation Council; GDP = gross domestic product; LAC = Latin America and the Caribbean region; MENA = Middle East and Northern Africa region; and SAR = South Asia region.

Source: WDI; live database.

APPENDIX TABLE 4

Service Trade

Region/ country	Service exports Billion US$ 1998– 2000a	Service exports US$ per capita 1998– 2000	Service exports % to GDP 1998– 2000	Nontourism receipts Billion US$ 1998– 2000a	Nontourism receipts US$ per capita 1998– 2000	Nontourism receipts % to GDP 1998– 2000	Tourism receipts Billion US$ 1998– 2000a	Tourism receipts US$ per capita 1998– 2000	Tourism receipts % to GDP 1998– 2000	Service imports Billion US$ 1998– 2000a	Service imports % to GDP 1998– 2000
MENA	**29.6**	**114**	**5.1**	**16.8**	**65**	**3.0**	**12.5**	**49**	**2.2**	**46.6**	**7.9**
Non-GCC	*21.9*	*93*	*6.4*	*11.5*	*49*	*3.3*	*10.4*	*44*	*4.0*	*17.3*	*5.0*
Algeria	0.8	26	1.6	0.8	26	1.6	0.02	1	0.0	2.4	4.8
Djibouti	—	—	—	—	—	—	0.004	6	0.7	—	—
Egypt, Arab Rep. of	9.0	144	10.0	5.4	86	6.0	3.6	57	4.0	5.2	5.7
Iran, Islamic Rep. of	1.5	23	1.4	0.8	13	0.8	0.7	11	0.7	2.5	2.5
Jordan	1.7	357	20.7	0.9	196	11.4	0.8	161	9.3	1.3	15.4
Lebanon	1.3	301	7.8	0.4	95	2.5	0.9	206	5.3	0.5	2.8
Morocco	3.0	106	8.6	1.1	39	3.2	1.9	66	5.4	1.9	5.6
Syrian Arab Republic	1.7	106	10.3	0.7	42	4.1	1.0	64	6.2	1.6	9.8
Tunisia	2.8	298	14.0	1.3	135	6.4	1.5	163	7.7	1.2	6.2
Yemen, Rep. of	0.2	11	2.5	0.1	7	1.5	0.1	4	1.0	0.7	9.6
GCC	*7.7*	*307*	*3.3*	*5.4*	*235*	*2.5*	*2.1*	*92*	*1.0*	*29.3*	*9.7*
Bahrain	0.8	1,151	11.1	0.4	561	5.4	0.4	591	5.7	0.7	9.5
Kuwait	1.7	891	5.5	1.5	771	4.8	0.2	120	0.7	5.2	16.8
Oman	0.3	118	1.5	—	—	—	—	—	—	1.5	8.5
Qatar	—	—	—	—	—	—	—	—	—	1.6	12.7
Saudi Arabia	5.0	246	2.8	3.5	173	2.0	1.5	72	0.8	20.3	11.4
United Arab Emirates	—	—	—	—	—	—	—	—	—	—	—
Non–MENA	**210.4**	**57**	**4.3**	**116.6**	**31**	**2.4**	**93.9**	**25**	**1.9**	**233.1**	**4.8**
LAC	*36.6*	*91*	*2.2*	*16.8*	*42*	*1.0*	*19.9*	*49*	*1.2*	*53.1*	*3.2*
Argentina	4.5	124	1.6	1.7	46	0.6	2.9	78	1.0	8.9	3.1
Bolivia	0.2	30	2.9	0.1	9	0.9	0.2	21	2.0	0.5	5.4
Brazil	8.1	48	1.3	4.1	24	0.6	4.0	24	0.6	15.9	2.5
Chile	3.9	263	5.6	3.0	201	4.3	0.9	62	1.3	4.3	6.1
Colombia	2.0	47	2.2	1.0	24	1.1	1.0	23	1.1	3.3	3.7
Costa Rica	1.5	393	9.6	0.5	126	3.1	1.0	267	6.5	1.2	7.5
Ecuador	0.8	61	4.3	0.4	33	2.3	0.3	28	2.0	1.2	7.0
El Salvador	0.6	102	5.0	0.4	70	3.5	0.2	32	1.6	0.8	6.7
Guatemala	0.7	65	3.8	0.2	20	1.2	0.5	45	2.6	0.8	4.3
Jamaica	1.9	740	25.7	0.7	252	8.8	1.3	488	17.0	1.3	18.1
Mexico	12.4	128	2.5	4.7	49	1.0	7.7	79	1.6	14.9	3.0
EAP	*90.9*	*55*	*5.0*	*52.4*	*32*	*2.9*	*38.6*	*23*	*2.1*	*109.1*	*6.1*
China	26.9	21	2.7	12.5	10	1.2	14.3	11	1.4	31.4	3.1
Indonesia	4.8	23	3.7	0.0	0	0.0	4.9	24	3.8	12.8	9.9
Korea, Rep. of	27.5	588	7.0	20.8	444	5.3	6.8	144	1.7	28.4	7.2
Malaysia	12.4	546	15.4	8.9	391	11.1	3.5	155	4.4	14.9	18.5
Philippines	5.4	73	7.5	2.9	39	4.1	2.5	34	3.5	7.9	11.0
Thailand	13.9	230	11.7	7.3	121	6.1	6.6	109	5.5	13.7	11.5

APPENDIX TABLE 4 (continued)

Service Trade

Region/country	Service exports			Nontourism receipts			Tourism receipts			Service imports	
	Billion US$ 1998–2000ᵃ	US$ per capita 1998–2000	% to GDP 1998–2000	Billion US$ 1998–2000ᵃ	US$ per capita 1998–2000	% to GDP 1998–2000	Billion US$ 1998–2000ᵃ	US$ per capita 1998–2000	% to GDP 1998–2000	Billion US$ 1998–2000ᵃ	% to GDP 1998–2000
SAR	*18.1*	*14*	*3.3*	*14.9*	*12*	*2.7*	*3.2*	*3*	*0.6*	*15.9*	*2.9*
Bangladesh	0.8	6	1.6	0.7	5	1.5	0.1	0	0.1	0.6	1.2
India	15.9	16	3.6	12.8	13	2.9	3.1	3	0.7	13.0	3.0
Pakistan	1.4	11	2.3	1.3	10	2.2	0.1	1	0.1	2.3	3.7
ECA	*57.1*	*202*	*7.8*	*28.5*	*100*	*3.9*	*28.7*	*101*	*3.9*	*45.8*	*6.3*
Bulgaria	1.9	233	15.7	0.9	113	7.6	1.0	121	8.1	1.5	12.4
Czech Republic	7.1	686	13.0	3.8	374	7.1	3.2	312	5.9	5.7	10.5
Hungary	5.9	581	12.7	2.5	244	5.3	3.4	337	7.3	4.3	9.2
Poland	9.9	255	6.3	3.1	81	2.0	6.7	174	4.3	7.5	4.8
Russian Federation	10.5	72	4.3	3.3	23	1.3	7.2	49	2.9	15.8	6.4
Turkey	19.7	307	10.2	13.1	203	6.7	6.7	104	3.4	9.0	4.6
Slovak Republic	2.1	397	10.7	1.7	312	8.4	0.5	85	2.3	2.0	9.9
Africa	*7.7*	*83*	*4.7*	*4.1*	*44*	*2.5*	*3.6*	*39*	*2.2*	*9.2*	*5.7*
Cameroon	0.6	38	6.2	0.5	35	5.7	0.0	3	0.4	0.8	8.8
Côte d'Ivoire	0.5	35	4.6	0.4	28	3.7	0.1	7	0.9	1.4	11.7
Ghana	0.5	25	7.0	0.2	9	2.6	0.3	16	4.4	0.6	9.6
Mauritius	1.0	859	23.7	0.5	395	10.9	0.5	464	12.8	0.7	17.2
South Africa	5.1	121	3.9	2.5	59	1.9	2.6	62	2.0	5.7	4.3

— Not available.

Note: All indicators are three-year averages for 1998–2000 unless otherwise indicated. EAP = East Asia and Pacific region; ECA = Europe and Central Asia region; GCC = Gulf Cooperation Council; GDP = gross domestic product; LAC = Latin America and the Caribbean region; MENA = Middle East and Northern Africa region; and SAR = South Asia region.

a. Group figures in the column are totals, not averages.

Source: *WDI*; live database.

APPENDIX TABLE 5

Financial Flows

Country/region	FDI			Workers' remittances, receipts			Aid flows		
	Million US$ 1998–2000[a]	US$ per capita 1998–2000	% to GDP 1998–2000	Million US$ 1998–2000[a]	US$ per capita 1998–2000	% to GDP 1998–2000	Million US$ 1998–2000[a]	US$ per capita 1998–2000	% to GDP 1998–2000
MENA	**5,476**	**21.0**	**0.9**	**9,648**	**62.9**	**4.1**	**4,139**	**15.7**	**0.6**
Non-GCC	*2,242*	*9.5*	*0.7*	*9,609*	*57.2*	*4.4*	*4,022*	*17.1*	*1.2*
Algeria	7	0.2	0.0	934	31.2	1.9	216	7.2	0.4
Djibouti	4	5.9	0.7	—	—	—	76	122.4	14.2
Egypt, Arab Rep. of	1,125	17.9	1.2	3,746	59.7	4.2	1,626	25.9	1.8
Iran, Islamic Rep. of	33	0.5	0.0	—	—	—	152	2.4	0.2
Jordan	342	72.1	4.2	1,684	355.2	20.6	464	97.9	5.7
Lebanon	249	58.4	1.5	—	—	—	210	49.1	1.3
Morocco	8	0.3	0.0	2,037	72.1	5.8	543	19.2	1.6
Syrian Arab Republic	94	6.0	0.6	482	30.5	3.0	181	11.4	1.1
Tunisia	584	61.8	2.9	727	76.9	3.6	208	22.0	1.0
Yemen, Rep. of	−205	−12.0	−2.7	—	—	—	345	20.2	4.5
GCC	*3,234*	*129.1*	*1.3*	*39*	*16.6*	*0.2*	*117*	*4.1*	*0.0*
Bahrain	—	—	—	—	—	—	33	50.1	0.5
Kuwait	49	25.6	0.2	—	—	—	5	2.8	0.0
Oman	48	20.6	0.3	39	16.6	0.2	43	18.4	0.2
Qatar	—	—	—	—	—	—	2	4.0	0.0
Saudi Arabia	3,136	155.2	1.8	—	—	—	28	1.4	0.0
United Arab Emirates	—	—	—	—	—	—	4	1.4	0.0
Non–MENA	**148,535**	**40.1**	**3.0**	**36,043**	**10.2**	**0.8**	**16,884**	**4.6**	**0.3**
LAC	*69,155*	*172.0*	*4.2*	*12,672*	*31.5*	*0.8*	*1,850*	*4.6*	*0.1*
Argentina	14,314	391.3	5.0	34	0.9	0.0	87	2.4	0.0
Bolivia	902	110.8	10.8	79	9.7	0.9	560	68.7	6.7
Brazil	31,089	184.8	4.9	1,089	6.5	0.2	282	1.7	0.0
Chile	5,845	389.2	8.3	449	29.9	0.6	76	5.0	0.1
Colombia	2,224	53.5	2.5	1,120	26.9	1.3	219	5.3	0.2
Costa Rica	564	151.0	3.7	107	28.6	0.7	11	3.0	0.1
Ecuador	738	59.5	4.2	1,065	85.8	6.1	159	12.8	0.9
El Salvador	507	82.3	4.0	1,488	241.7	11.9	182	29.5	1.4
Guatemala	353	31.8	1.9	495	44.6	2.6	263	23.7	1.4
Jamaica	450	172.9	6.0	712	273.9	9.5	2	0.9	0.0
Mexico	12,171	126.0	2.5	6,036	62.5	1.2	10	0.1	0.0
EAP	*54,813*	*32.9*	*3.0*	*3,171*	*1.9*	*0.2*	*5,391*	*3.2*	*0.3*
China	40,301	32.2	4.0	396	0.3	0.0	2,191	1.7	0.2
Indonesia	−2,550	−12.3	−2.0	1,086	5.2	0.8	1,745	8.4	1.4
Korea, Rep. of	8,010	170.9	2.0	69	1.5	0.0	−101	−2.1	0.0
Malaysia	1,792	78.9	2.2	675	29.7	0.8	134	5.9	0.2
Philippines	1,630	22.0	2.3	144	1.9	0.2	636	8.6	0.9
Thailand	5,631	93.5	4.7	802	13.3	0.7	785	13.0	0.7

ANNEX TABLE 5 (continued)

Financial Flows

Country/ region	FDI			Workers' remittances, receipts			Aid flows		
	Million US$ 1998– 2000ᵃ	US$ per capita 1998– 2000	% to GDP 1998– 2000	Million US$ 1998– 2000ᵃ	US$ per capita 1998– 2000	% to GDP 1998– 2000	Million US$ 1998– 2000ᵃ	US$ per capita 1998– 2000	% to GDP 1998– 2000
SAR	*3,038*	*2.4*	*0.6*	*13,556*	*10.7*	*2.5*	*3,581*	*2.8*	*0.7*
Bangladesh	217	1.7	0.5	1,727	13.4	3.8	1,217	9.5	2.7
India	2,373	2.4	0.5	10,651	10.7	2.4	1,530	1.5	0.3
Pakistan	449	3.3	0.7	1,178	8.7	1.9	833	6.2	1.4
ECA	*20,028*	*70.7*	*2.7*	*6,592*	*48.1*	*1.4*	*3,921*	*13.8*	*0.5*
Bulgaria	782	95.2	6.4	240	29.2	2.0	274	33.4	2.2
Czech Republic	4,865	473.2	9.0	737	71.6	1.4	404	39.3	0.7
Hungary	1,902	186.0	4.1	35	3.4	0.1	247	24.2	0.5
Poland	7,659	198.1	4.9	758	19.6	0.5	1,153	29.8	0.7
Russian Federation	2,929	20.0	1.2	—	—	—	1,530	10.5	0.6
Turkey	902	14.0	0.5	4,815	74.8	2.5	117	1.8	0.1
Slovak Republic	990	183.4	4.9	7	1.4	0.0	196	36.3	1.0
Africa	*1,500*	*16.3*	*0.9*	*53*	*0.9*	*0.0*	*2,142*	*27.7*	*4.0*
Cameroon	40	2.8	0.5	—	—	—	414	28.4	4.6
Cote d'Ivoire	270	17.3	2.3	—	—	—	537	34.5	4.5
Ghana	76	4.0	1.1	31	1.6	0.5	641	34.0	9.5
Mauritius	109	92.9	2.6	—	—	—	35	29.5	0.8
South Africa	1,005	23.9	0.8	22	0.5	0.0	514	12.2	0.4

— Not available.
Note: All indicators are three-year averages for 1998–2000 unless otherwise indicated. EAP = East Asia and Pacific region; ECA = Europe and Central Asia region; GCC = Gulf Cooperation Council; GDP = gross domestic product; LAC = Latin America and the Caribbean region; MENA = Middle East and Northern Africa region; and SAR = South Asia region.
a. Group figures in the column are totals, not averages.
Source: *WDI*; live database.

References

The word *processed* describes informally reproduced works that may not be commonly available through libraries.

Chapter 1

Assad, R., and F. El-Hamidi. Forthcoming. "Female Labor Supply in Egypt: Participation and Hours of Work." In *Population Challenges in the Middle East and North Africa: Towards the 21st Century*. New York: Macmillan.

Beaumont, P., G. Blake, and J. M. Wagstaff. 1988. *The Middle East, a Geographical Study*. London: David Fulton.

Ben-David, D., H. Nordstrom, and A. Winters. 1999. "Trade, Income Disparity and Poverty." Special Studies 5. World Trade Organization, Geneva.

Coe, D., E. Helpman, and A. Hoffmaister. 1995. "North-South R&D Spillovers." *Economic Journal* 107 (January).

Dasgupta, D., J. Keller, and T. G. Srinivasan. 2002. "Reforms and Elusive Growth in the Middle East—What Has Happened in the 1990s?" Working Paper 25. World Bank, Washington, D.C.

Diwan, I., M. Nabli, A. Coulibaly, and S. Johansson. 2003. "Economic Reforms and People Mobility for a More Effective EU-MED Partnership." In Chibli Mallat, ed., *Union Européenne et Moyen Orient, état des lieux*. PUSJ Press.

Dollar, D., and Kraay, A. 2001. "Trade, Growth and Poverty." Working Paper 2615. World Bank, Washington, D.C.

Edwards, S. 1997. "Openness, Productivity and Growth: What Do We Really Know?" NBER Working Paper 5978. National Bureau of Economic Research, Cambridge, Mass.

El-Kogali, S., and E. Nizalova. 2003. "Does Trade Liberalization Have Gender-Differentiated Effects?" World Bank, Washington, D.C. Processed.

Fasano, U. 2002. "With Open Economy and Sound Policies, U.A.E. Has Turned Oil 'Curse' into a Blessing." *IMF Survey*, October 21.

Fontana, M., S. Joekes, and R. Masika. 1998. "Global Trade Expansion and Liberalisation: Gender Issues and Impacts." Institute of Development Studies, Department for International Development (DfID), Brighton, U.K.

Frankel, J. A., and D. Romer. 1999. "Does Trade Cause Growth?" *American Economic Review* 89(3):379–99.

Hoekman, B., and P. Messerlin. 2002. *Harnessing Trade for Development and Growth in the Middle East and North Africa.* New York: Council on Foreign Relations.

Hourani, A. H. 1991. *A History of the Arab Peoples.* Cambridge, Mass.: Harvard University Press.

IMF (International Monetary Fund). 2003. "United Arab Emirates: Selected Issues and Statistical Appendix." Country Report 03/67. Washington, D.C.

Iqbal, F. 2002. "The Impact of Deregulation on the Manufacturing Sector." In F. Iqbal and W. E. James, eds., *Deregulation and Development in Indonesia.* Westport, Conn.: Praeger Publishers.

Joekes, S., and A. Weston. 1994. *Women and the New Trade Agenda.* New York: United Nations Development Fund for Women.

Martin, Will, and Suphat Suphachalasai. 1990. "Effects of the Multi-Fiber Arrangements on Developing Country Exporters: A Simple Theoretical Framework." In C. B. Hamilton, ed., *Textiles Trade and the Developing Countries: Eliminating the Multi-Fiber Arrangement in the 1990s.* Washington, D.C.: World Bank.

Ministry of Information and Culture UAE. 2002. *United Arab Emirates Yearbook, 2002*. London: Trident Press.

Nabli, M. K., and J. Keller. 2002. "The Macroeconomic Outcomes in MENA over the 1990s: How Growth Has Failed to Keep Pace with a Burgeoning Labor Market." Paper presented at the Fourth Annual Mediterranean Development Forum, Amman, Jordan, October 6–9.

Nabli, M., and M.-A. Veganzones-Varoudakis. 2002. "Exchange Rate Regime and Competitiveness of Manufactured Exports: The Case of MENA Countries." MENA Working Paper 27. World Bank, Washington, D.C.

Nugent, J. B. 2002 "Why Does MENA Trade So Little?" Background paper for the trade report. University of Southern California, Department of Economics, Los Angeles, Calif.

Rama, M. 2001. "Globalization, Inequality, and Labor Market Policies." Paper for the European on-line Annual World Bank Conference in Development and Economics (ABCDE-Europe), Washington, D.C.

Schiff, M. W. 1994. "How Trade, Aid and Remittances Affect International Migration." Policy Research Working Paper 1376. World Bank, Washington, D.C.

————. 1996. "South-North Migration and Trade: A Survey." Policy Research Working Paper 1696. World Bank, Washington, D.C.

UNCTAD (United Nations Conference on Trade and Development). Various years. *TRAINS Database*.

UNDP (United Nations Development Programme). 2002. *Arab Human Development Report: Creating Opportunities for Future Generations*. Amman, Jordan: UNDP Arab Fund for Economic and Social Development and National Press.

UNIFEM (United Nations Development Fund for Women). 2002. *Annual Report*. New York: United Nations.

World Bank. 2002. "Globalization, Growth and Poverty." World Bank Policy Research Report. Washington, D.C.

World Bank. 2003a. *World Development Indicators*. Washington, D.C.

World Bank. 2003b. *Accompanying Reports for Dubai Meetings*. Washington, D.C.

Chapter 2

Al-Atrash, H. M., and T. Yousef. 2000. "Intra-Arab Trade: Is It Too Little?" Working Paper 00/10. International Monetary Fund, Washington, D.C.

Auty, Richard M., ed. 2001. *Resource Abundance and Economic Development*. United Nations University, World Institute for Development Economics Research, Studies in Economic Development. New York: Oxford University Press.

Bordo, M. D., and M. Flandreau. 2001. "Core Periphery, Exchange Rate Regimes and Globalization." NBER Working Paper 8584. National Bureau of Economic Research, Cambridge, Mass.

Chase-Dunn, C., Y. Kawano, and B. Brewer. 2000. "Trade Globalization since 1795: Waves of Integration in the World System." *American Sociological Review* 65:77–95.

Diwan, I., M. Nabli, A. Coulibaly, and S. Johansson. 2003. "Economic Reforms and People Mobility for a More Effective EU-MED Partnership." In Chibli Mallat, ed., *Union Européenne et Moyen Orient, état des lieux*. PUSJ Press.

Ghezali, S., and M. Lowi. 2001. "DECRG Project: Case Study of Algeria." Paper presented at the World Bank, Oslo Conference, June 11–12.

Girgis, M. 2002. "The GCC Factor in Future Labor Migration." Paper prepared for the Fourth Mediterranean Development Forum, Amman, Jordan, October 6–9. Processed.

Gupta, S., B. J. Clements, R. Bhattacharya, and S. Chakravarti. 2002. "Fiscal Consequences of Armed Conflict and Terrorism in Low and Middle Income Countries." Working Paper 02/142. International Monetary Fund, Washington, D.C.

Havrylyshyn, O., and P. Kunzel. 2000. "Intra-industry Trade of Arab Countries: An Indicator of Potential Competitiveness." In B. Hoekman and J. Zarrouk, eds., *Catching Up with Competition*. Ann Arbor, Mich.: University of Michigan Press.

Heidelberg Institute of International Conflict Research. 2003. *Kosimo Database*. Available at http://www.hiik.de/en/index_e.htm

IMF (International Monetary Fund). Various years. *Balance of Payments Statistics Year Book*. Washington, D.C.

———. *International Financial Statistics*. Various years. Washington, D.C.

———. 2001. *Direction of Trade Statistics Year Book*. Washington, D.C.

Maddison, Angus. 2001. "The World Economy: A Millennial Perspective." Development Centre Studies. Organisation for Economic Co-operation and Development, Paris.

McGormick, B., and J. Wahba. 1997. "Return Migration and Entrepreneurship in Egypt?" Background paper presented at the Economic Research Forum Fourth Annual Conference on Regional Trade Finance and Labor Markets in Transition, Beirut, Lebanon, September 7–9.

Mesquida, C., and N. Wiener. 2001. "Young Men and War: Could We Have Predicted the Distribution of Violent Conflicts at the End of the Millennium?" *PECS News* 3(2).

Murdoch, J. C., and T. Sandler. 2002. "Economic Growth, Civil Wars, and Spatial Spillovers." *Journal of Conflict Resolution* 46(1).

Nabli, M. K., and A. I. de Kleine. 2000. "Managing Global Integration in the Middle East and North Africa." In Bernard Hoekman and Hanaa Kheir-El-Din, eds., *Trade Policy Developments in the Middle East and North Africa*. Washington, D.C.: World Bank.

OECD (Organisation for Economic Co-operation and Development). 2001. "Trend in International Migration." Paris.

O'Rourke, K. H., and J. G. Williamson. 1999. "The Heckscher-Ohlin Model between 1400 and 2000: When It Explained Factor

Price Convergence, When It Did Not, and Why?" NBER Working Paper 7411. National Bureau of Economic Research. Cambridge, Mass.

Ranis, G. 1991. "Towards a Model of Economic Development." In L. B. Krause and K. Kihwan, eds., *Liberalization in the Process of Economic Development*. Berkeley: University of California Press.

Sachs, Jeffrey D., and A. Warner. 1995. "Economic Reform and the Process of Global Integration." *Brookings Papers on Economic Activity* 1:1–118.

———. 1999. "Natural Resource Intensity and Economic Growth." In J. Meyer, B. Chambers, and A. Farooq, eds., *Development Policies in Natural Resource Economies*. Cheltenham, U.K.: Elgar.

U.N. (United Nations). Various years. *UN COMTRADE Statistics*. Geneva.

———. 2002. "International Migration." United Nations Population Division, Department of Economic and Social Affairs, New York.

UNCTAD (United Nations Conference on Trade and Development). 1997. *Handbook of Statistics*. Geneva.

———. 2000. *Handbook of Statistics*. Geneva.

UNCTAD and World Bank. 2002. *World Integrated Trade Solution Database*. Washington, D.C.

World Bank. 2002. *Global Development Finance*. Washington, D.C.

———. 2003. *World Development Indicators*. Washington, D.C.

WTO (World Trade Organization). 2001. *Annual Report*. Geneva.

Yeats, A. P., and F. Ng. 2000. "Beyond the Year 2000: Implications of the Middle East's Recent Trade Performance." In B. Hoekman and J. Zarrouk, eds., *Catching up with Competition*. Ann Arbor, Mich.: University of Michigan Press.

Chapter 3

Anderson J., and P. Neary. 1996. "A New Approach to Evaluating Trade Policy." *Review of Economic Studies* 63(1):107–125.

Dasgupta, D., J. Keller, and T. G. Srinivasan. 2002. "Reform and Elusive Growth in the Middle-East—What Has Happened in the 1990s?" Middle East and North Africa Working Paper 25. World Bank, Washington, D.C.

Devlin, J., and P. Yee. 2002. "Global Links to Regional Networks: Trade Logistics in MENA Countries." Paper presented at the Fourth Annual Mediterranean Development Forum, Amman, Jordan, October 6–9.

Djankov, Simeaon, Rafael La Porta, Florencio Lopez de Silanes, and Andrei Shleifer. 2001. "The Regulation of Entry." Working Paper 2661. World Bank, Washington, D.C.

Galal, A. 2000. "Incentives for Economic Integration in the Middle East." In B. Hoekman and H. Kheir-El-Din, eds., *Trade Policy Developments in the Middle East and North Africa*. Washington, D.C.: World Bank Institute.

Galal, A., and S. Fawzy. 2002. "Egypt's Export Puzzle." Egyptian Center for Economic Studies, Cairo.

Hamdouch, B. 1998. "Adjustment, Strategic Planning, and the Moroccan Economy." In N. Shafik, ed., *Economic Challenges Facing Middle Eastern and North African Countries: Alternative Futures*. Economic Research Forum for the Arab Countries, Iran and Turkey. London: Macmillan.

IMF (International Monetary Fund). 2002. "Trade Issues in the Maghreb and the Mashreq." Washington, D.C. Processed.

Karshenas, M. 1998. "Structural Adjustment and the Iranian Economy." In N. Shafik, ed., *Economic Challenges Facing Middle Eastern and North African Countries: Alternative Futures*. Economic Research Forum for the Arab Countries, Iran and Turkey. London: Macmillan.

Lahouel, M. H. 1998. "Competition Policies and Deregulation in Tunisia." In N. Shafik, ed., *Economic Challenges Facing Middle Eastern and North African Countries: Alternative Futures.* Economic Research Forum for the Arab Countries, Iran and Turkey. London: Macmillan.

Lall, S. 1999. "Competing with Labor: Human Capital in a Globalizing World." International Labour Office, Geneva.

Levy-Yayati, E., F. Sturzenegger, and E. Reggio. 2003. "On the Endogeneity of Exchange Rate Regimes." *International Monetary Fund Seminar Series (International).* 2003:04[1]–25.

Mayda, A. M., and D. Rodrik. 2001. "Why Are Some People (and Countries) More Protectionist than Others?" NBER Working Paper 8461. National Bureau of Economic Research, Cambridge, Mass.

Nabli, M. K. 1990. "The Political Economy of Trade Liberalization in Developing Countries." *Open Economies Review* 1:111–45.

Nabli, M. K., and M. A. Veganzones-Varoudakis. 2002. "Exchange Rate Regime and Competitiveness of Manufactured Exports: The Case of MENA Countries." MENA Working Paper 27. World Bank, Washington, D.C.

Nash, J., and S. Andriamananjara. 1997. "Have Trade Policy Reforms Led to Greater Openness in Developing Countries?" Working Paper 1730. World Bank, Washington, D.C.

Nashashibi, K., P. Alonso-Gamo, S. Bazzoni, A. Feler, N. Laframboise, S. P. Horvitz, and P. Horvitz. 1998. "Algeria: Stabilization and Transition to Market." International Monetary Fund Occasional Paper 165. Washington, D.C.

Nicita, A., and M. Olarreaga. 2001. "Trade and Production, 1976–99." Paper accompanying the eponymous database from the Development Research Group's Trade Unit. World Bank, Washington, D.C.

Oliva, M. A. 2000. "Estimation of Trade Protection in Middle East and North African Countries." Middle Eastern Department, International Monetary Fund Working Paper 00/27. Washington, D.C.

Petri, A. 1997. "Trade Strategies for the Southern Mediterranean." OECD Development Centre, Technical Paper 127. Paris.

Tybout, J. 1997. "Manufacturing Firms in Developing Countries: How Are They Different and Why?" Georgetown University, Department of Economics, Working Paper (U.S.) No. 97-19.

UNCTAD (United Nations Conference on Trade and Development). Various years. *TRAINS Database.*

World Bank. 2001. "Iran: Trade and Foreign Exchange Policies in Iran: Reform Agenda, Economic Implications and Impact on the Poor." Report 22953-IRN, November 1. Washington, D.C.

———. 2002a. "Syrian Arab Republic Economic Review." Washington, D.C.

———. 2002b. "Economic Growth in the Republic of Yemen: Sources, Constraints, and Potentials." World Bank Country Study. Washington, D.C.

———. 2003a. "Global Economic Prospects and the Developing Countries: Investing to Unlock Global Opportunities." Washington, D.C.

———. 2003b. *World Development Indicators.* Washington, D.C.

———. 2003c. "Iran: Medium-Term Framework for Transition: Converting Oil Wealth to Development." Country Economic Memorandum. Report 25848-IRN, April 30. Washington, D.C.

———. 2003d. *Doing Business Indicators.* Available at http://rru.world bank.org/DoingBusiness/default.aspx.

WTO (World Trade Organization). *Trade Policy Reviews* for various years and countries.

Zarrouk, J. 2003. "A Survey of Barriers to Trade and Investment in Arab Countries." In A. Galal and B. Hoekman, eds., *Arab Economic Integration: Between Hope and Reality.* Egyptian Center for Economic Studies. Washington, D.C.: Brookings Institution.

Chapter 4

Agenor, P. R., and P. J. Montiel. 2001. "Sequencing and Speed of Reforms." World Bank Institute Course Material on Development Macroeconomics. World Bank, Washington, D.C.

Alamgir, Jalal. 1999. "Strategic Rivalry and Tariff Rate Reforms in India." *Brown Economic Review* (Spring): 54–56.

Bannister, G. J., and K. Thugge. 2001. "International Trade and Poverty Alleviation" International Monetary Fund Working Paper 01/54. Washington, D.C.

Bhattarcharya, A. N., and M. Pangestu. 1993. *Indonesia: Development, Transformation, and Public Policy.* Washington, D.C.: World Bank.

Chaherli, N. 2002. "Agricultural Trade Liberalization: Main Issues for the MENA Region." Background paper for *Trade and Investment Report.* World Bank, Washington, D.C.

Currie, Janet, and A. Harrison. 1997. "Sharing the Costs: The Impact of Trade Reform on Capital and Labor in Morocco." *Journal of Labor Economics* 15:S44–71.

Dasgupta, D., E. Hulu, and B. Das Gupta. 2002. "The Determinants of Indonesia's Non-oil Exports." In F. Iqbal and W. E. James, eds., *Deregulation and Development in Indonesia 2002.* Westport, Conn.: Praeger.

Dessus, S., and A. Suwa-Eisenmann. 1998. "Trade Integration with Europe, Export Diversification, and Economic Growth in Egypt." Technical Paper 135. OECD Development Centre, Paris.

Hoekman, B., and J. Roy. 2000. "Benefiting from WTO Accession and Membership." In B. Hoekman and J. Zarrouk, eds., *Catching Up with the Competition.* Ann Arbor: University of Michigan Press.

Hufbauer, G. C. and J. J. Schott. 1993. "NAFTA: An Assessment." Institute for International Economics, Washington, D.C.

Jadresic, E. 2002. "On a Common Currency for the GCC Countries." International Monetary Fund Policy Discussion Paper 02/12, December 1.

Lucke, B. 2001. "Fiscal Impact of Trade Liberalization: The Case of Syria." University of Hamburg.

Nugent, J. B. 2002. "Why Does MENA Trade So Little?" Background paper for the *Trade Report.* University of Southern California, Department of Economics, Los Angeles.

Rama, M. 2001. "Globalization, Inequality, and Labor Market Policies." Paper for the European on-line Annual World Bank Conference in Development and Economics (ABCDE-Europe), Washington, D.C., June 20.

Someya, M. 2001, "Yemen External Competitiveness." Background paper prepared for the World Bank Country Study, "Economic Growth in the Republic of Yemen: Sources, Constraints, and Potentials." Washington, D.C.

Tarr, D., and S. J. Matusz. 1999. "Adjusting to Trade Policy Reform." Working Paper 2142. World Bank, Washington, D.C.

Thomas, V., J. Nash, and S. Edwards. 1991. *Best Practices in Trade Policy Reform*. New York: Oxford University Press.

Wood, A. 1997. "Openness and Wage Inequality in Developing Countries: The Latin American Challenge to East Asian Conventional Wisdom." *World Bank Economic Review* 11:33–57.

World Bank. 2000. "Progress toward the Unification of Europe." Washington, D.C.

———. 2001. "Iran: Trade and Foreign Exchange Policies in Iran: Reform Agenda, Economic Implications and Impact on the Poor." Report 22953-IRN. Washington, D.C.

———. 2002a. "Jordan Development Policy Review: A Reforming State in a Volatile Region." Report 24425-JO. Washington, D.C.

———. 2002b. "Economic Growth in the Republic of Yemen: Sources, Constraints, and Potentials." World Bank Country Study. Washington, D.C.

———. 2003. *World Development Indicators*. Washington, D.C.

Chapter 5

Arndt, Sven, and H. Kierzkowski. 2001. "Introduction." In S. Arndt and H. Kierzkowski, eds., *Fragmentation: New Production Patterns in the World Economy*. Oxford and New York: Oxford University Press.

Barth, J., G. Caprio Jr., and R. Levine. 2001. "Banking System around the Globe: Do Regulations and Ownership Affect Performance and Stability?" In F. S. Mishkin, ed., *Prudential Supervision: What Works and What Doesn't*. Chicago: University of Chicago.

Boylaud, Olivier, and G. Nicoletti. 2000. "Regulation, Market Structure and Performance in Telecommunications." Economics Department Working Paper 237. Organisation for Economic Co-operation and Development. Paris.

Bureau van Dijk. Various years. *BankScope Database*.

Clarke, G. R., R. Cull, and M. S. Martinez Peria. 2001. "Does Foreign Bank Penetration Reduce Access to Credit in Developing Countries? Evidence from Asking Borrowers." Policy Research Working Paper 2716. World Bank, Washington, D.C.

Cowhey, P., and M. M. Klimenko. 2000. "Telecommunications Reform in Developing Countries after the WTO Agreement on Basic Telecommunications Services." *Journal of International Development* 12:265–81.

Harris, C. 2003. "The Beginning of the End or the End of the Beginning? A Review of Private Participation in Infrastructure in Developing Countries." Private Sector Advisory Services. World Bank, Washington, D.C.

Kessides, I. 2002. "Regulatory Reform in Network Utilities in the MENA Region." Background paper for the MENA Trade Intensification Study. World Bank, Washington, D.C.

Klein, M. 2003. "Where Do We Stand Today with Private Infrastructure?" *Development Outreach* 5(1).

Konan, D. E., and K. E. Maskus. 2002. "Quantifying the Impact of Services Liberalization in a Developing Country." World Bank, Washington, D.C.

Lee, J. 2002. "Financial Liberalization and Foreign Bank Entry in MENA." Background paper for the MENA Trade Intensification Study. World Bank, Washington, D.C.

Mathieson, D. J., and J. E. Roldòs. 2001. "The Role of Foreign Banks in Emerging Markets. Paper presented at the World Bank, International

Monetary Fund, Brookings Institution Third Annual Financial Markets and Development Conference, New York, May 19–21. Processed.

Mattoo, A., R. Rathindran, and A. Subramanian. 2001. "Measuring Services Trade Liberalization and Its Impact on Economic Growth: An Illustration." Policy Research Working Paper 2655. World Bank, Washington, D.C.

Muller-Jentsch, D. 2002. "Transport Policies for the Euro-Mediterranean Free Trade Area: An Agenda for Multimodal Transport Reform in the Southern Mediterranean." World Bank and European Commission Programme on Private Participation in Mediterranean Infrastructure. World Bank, Washington, D.C.

Nashashibi, K., M. Elhage, and A. Fedelino. 2001. "Financial Liberalization in Arab Countries." In Z. Iqbal, ed., *Macroeconomic Issues and Policies in the Middle East and North Africa*. Washington, D.C.: International Monetary Fund.

NASSCOM–McKinsey. 2002. NASSCOM-McKinsey Study—India Information Technology Strategies. Hyderabad, India.

Newbery, D. M. G. 1999. *Privatization, Restructuring, and Regulation of Network Utilities*. Cambridge, Mass.: MIT Press.

OECD (Organisation for Economic Co-operation and Development). 2000. "A New Economy: The Changing Role of Innovation and Information Technology in Growth." Paris.

Rosotto, C. M., K. Sekkat, and A. Varoudakis. 2003. "Opening up Telecommunications to Competition and MENA Integration in the World Economy." World Bank, Washington, D.C.

UNCTAD (United Nations Conference on Trade and Development). 2001. *World Investment Report*. Geneva.

UNDP (United Nations Development Programme). 2002. "Arab Human Development Report: Creating Opportunities for Future Generations." UNDP Arab Fund for Economic and Social Development, New York.

University of Napoli Federico II. 2001. "The MENA Region: Overview of the Information Technology Sector and Investment Opportunities." DIEG–Department of Business and Managerial Engineering, Napoli, Italy (research report funded by the International Finance Corporation).

Varoudakis, A., and C. M. Rosotto. 2001. "Regulatory Reform and Performance in Telecommunications: Unrealized Potential in the MENA Countries." World Bank, Washington, D.C. Processed.

World Bank. 1998. "Egypt in the Global Economy: Strategic Choices for Savings, Investments, and Long-Term Growth." World Bank Middle East and North Africa Economic Studies. Washington, D.C.

World Bank. 2001a. "Finance for Growth: Policy Choices in a Volatile World." Washington, D.C.

———. 2001b. "Global Economic Prospects and the Developing Countries." Washington, D.C.

———. 2001c. "Republic of Tunisia: Information and Communications Technology Strategy Report." Washington, D.C.

———. 2002a. "Global Economic Prospects and the Developing Countries." Washington, D.C.

———. 2002b. *Global Development Finance: Financing the Poorest Coutries.* Washington, D.C.: World Bank.

WTO (World Trade Organization). 2000. *GATS Database.*

———. 2001. *Annual Report.* Geneva.

———. 2002. *Annual Report.* Geneva,

Yeats, Alexander J. 1998. "Just How Big Is Global Production Sharing?" Policy Research Working Paper 1871. World Bank, Washington, D.C.

Chapter 6

Agricultural Market Access Database. 2001. Available at www.amad.org.

Allan, J. A. 1997. "'Virtual Water': A Long-Term Solution for Water Short Middle Eastern Economies?" Paper presented at the 1997

British Association Festival of Science, University of Leeds, September.

———. 2001a. "Virtual Water—Economically Invisible and Politically Silent—A Way to Solve Strategic Water Problems." *International Water & Irrigation* 21(4):39–41.

———. 2001b. *The Middle East Water Question: Hydropolitics and the Global Economy*. London: I. B. Tauris.

Anderson, K., B. Hoekman, and A. Strutt. 2001. "Agriculture and the WTO: Next Steps." *Review of International Economics* 9(2):192–214.

Anderson, K., and P. Morris. 2000. "The Elusive Goal of Agricultural Trade Reform." *Cato Journal* 19(3):385–96.

Barthelemy, F. 1993. "Water for Sustainable Human Nutrition: Inputs and Resources Analysis in Arid Areas." *Ecole Nationale du Génie Rural, des Eaux et Forêts, mémoire de fin d'études*. Montpellier, France.

Cockburn, J., B. Decaluwe, and B. Dostie. 1998. "Les leçons du mariage entre les modèles d'equilibre général calculable et la nouvelle théorie du commerce international: Application à la Tunisie." Centre de Recherche en Économie et Finance Appliquées (CREFA), Université Laval, Quebec, Canada.

DAI (Development Alternatives, Inc.). 2002. "Assessment of Egypt's Agricultural Sector Competitiveness." Report by Abt Associates, Inc., and DAI for the United States Agency for International Development. Bethesda, Maryland.

Diao, X., T. Roe, and A. Somwaru. 2002. "Developing Country Interests in Agricultural Reforms under the World Trade Organization." Discussion Paper 85. International Food Policy Research Institute, Trade and Macroeconomics Division, Washington, D.C.

DEFRA (Department for Environment, Food and Rural Affairs). 2002. *Milk Statistics*. Available at http://www.defra.gov.uk/esg.

Diwan, I., M. Nabli, A. Coulibaly, and S. Johansson. 2003. "Economic Reforms and People Mobility for a More Effective EU-MED Partnership." In Chibli Mallat, ed., *Union Européenne et Moyen Orient, état des lieux*. PUSJ Press.

Elbehri, A., and S. Leetmaa. 2002. "How Significant Are Export Subsidies to Agricultural Trade? Trade and Welfare Implications of Global Reforms." Paper presented at the Fifth Annual Conference on Global Economic Analysis, Taipei, Taiwan, June 5–7.

Elshennawy, A. 2001. "The Euro-Mediterranean Free Trade Agreement: An Inquiry into the Cost of Adjustment to Tariff Liberalization for the Egyptian Economy—An Inter-temporal General Equilibrium Analysis." Forum Euro-Méditerranéen des Instituts Economiques (FEMISE) and Economic Research Forum (ERF). Available at http://www.femise.org (updated March 20, 2002).

FAO (United Nations Food and Agriculture Organization). 1996. "World Food Summit—Food Production: The Critical Role of Water." Available at http://www.fao/org/documents..

———. 2002a. AQUASTAT. Available at http://www.fao.org/waicent/portal/statistics_en.asp.

———. 2002b. FAOSTAT. Available at http://www.fao.org/waicent/portal/statistics_en.asp.

Fontana, M. 2003. "Modeling the Effects of Trade on Women, at Work and at Home: A Comparative Perspective." Discussion Paper 110. International Food Policy Research Institute, Trade and Macroeconomics Division, Washington, D.C.

Gehlhar, M., and J. Wainio. 2002. "A Re-evaluation of Tariffs Facing Exporters of Processed Food: Implications for Trade Liberalization." Paper presented at the Fifth Annual Conference on Global Economic Analysis, Taipei, Taiwan, June 3–7. Downloaded on May 15, 2003 from http://www.gtap.agecon.purdue.edu/resources/download/1159.pdf.

Gleick, Peter H. 2000. *The World's Water 2000–2001*. Washington, D.C.: Island Press.

Government of Ontario, Canada, Ministry of Agriculture. 1992. "Water Requirements of Livestock." Available at http://www.gov.on.ca/OMAFRA/english/engineer/facts/86-053.htm.

Hakimian, H. 2003. "Water Scarcity and Food Imports: An Empirical Investigation of the 'Virtual Water' Hypothesis in the MENA Region." University of London, School of Oriental and African Studies.

Downloaded on May 15, 2003 from www2.soas.ac.uk/Geography/WaterIssues/OccasionalPapers.

Kasnakoglu, Z. 1999. "Women and Agricultural Development in the Near East." Paper presented at the Seventh International Interdisciplinary Congress on Women, Tromsø, Norway, June 20–26.

Newberry, D. M. G., and J. E. Stiglitz. 1981. *The Theory of Commodity Price Stabilization: A Study in the Economics of Risk.* Oxford: Clarendon Press.

OECD (Organisation for Economic Co-operation and Development). 2000. "The European Union's Trade Policies and Their Economic Effects." Paris.

Rutherford, T. F., E. E. Rutstrom, and D. G. Tarr. 1997. "Morocco's Free Trade Agreement with the EU: A Quantitative Assessment." *Economic Modeling* 14(2):237–69.

U.N. (United Nations). 2001. *UN COMTRADE Database.* New York.

Wilson, J. S. 2002. "Liberalizing Trade in Agriculture: Developing Countries in Asia and the Post-Doha Agenda." Working Paper 2804. World Bank, Washington, D.C.

World Bank. 2002. "Project Appraisal Document on a Proposed Learning and Innovation Loan in the Amount of US$5 Million to the Hashemite Kingdom of Jordan for a Horticultural Exports Promotion and Technology Transfer Project." Report 24428-JO, June 25. Washington, D.C.

———. 2003. *World Development Indicators.* Washington, D.C.

WTO (World Trade Organization). 2002. *EU-Trade Policy Review.*

Chapter 7

Al-Atrash, H. M., and T. Yousef. 2000. "Intra-Arab Trade: Is It Too Little?" Working Paper 00/10. International Monetary Fund, Washington, D.C.

Brenton, P., and M. Manchin. 2003. "Raising Barcelona: Economic Policy Scenarios." Trade Department, World Bank, Washington, D.C. Processed.

Chaherli, N., and M. El-Said. 2000. "Impact of the WTO Agreement on MENA Agriculture." Economic Research Forum, Cairo.

Diwan, I., M. Nabli, A. Coulibaly, and S. Johansson. 2003. "Economic Reform and People Mobility for a More Effective EU-MED Partnership." In Chibli Mallat, ed., *Union Européenne et Moyen Orient, état des lieux.* PUSJ Press.

Fawzy, S. 2003. "The Economics and Politics of Arab Economic Integration." In A. Galal and B. Hoekman B., eds., *Arab Economic Integration: Between Hope and Reality.* Egyptian Center for Economic Studies. Washington, D.C.: Brookings Institution.

Gasiorek, M., P. Augier, C. Lai-Tong, D. Evans, and P. Holmes. 2001. "The EU and the Southern Mediterranean: The Impact of Rules of Origin." Institute for Development Studies, Sussex, U.K. Processed.

Hoekman, B., and P. Messerlin. 2002. *Harnessing Trade for Development and Growth in the Middle East and North Africa.* New York: Council on Foreign Relations.

Herin, J. 1986. "Rules of Origin and Differences between Tariff Levels in EFTA and in the EC." Occasional Paper 13. Economic Affairs Department, European Free Trade Association, Geneva.

Kheir-El-Din, H. 2000. "Enforcement of Product Standards as Barriers to Trade: The Case of Egypt." In B. Hoekman and H Kheir-El-Din, eds., *Trade Policy Developments in the Middle East and North Africa.* Washington, D.C.: World Bank.

Schiff, M., and L. A. Winters. 2003. *Regional Integration and Development.* London: Oxford University Press.

Subramanian, A., A. Mattoo, and D. Roy. 2002. "The Africa Growth and Opportunity Act and Its Rules of Origin: Generosity Undermined?" Working Paper 2908. World Bank, Washington, D.C.

UNESCWA (United Nations Economic and Social Commission for West Africa). 2001. "Free Trade Areas in the Arab Region: Where Do We Go from Here?" United Nations, New York.

World Bank. 2002. "Global Economic Prospects: Making Trade Work for the World's Poor." Washington, D.C.

Zarrouk, J. 2003, "A Survey of Barriers to Trade and Investment in Arab Countries." In A. Galal and B. Hoekman, eds., *Arab Economic Integration: Between Hope and Reality.* Egyptian Center for Economic Studies. Washington, D.C.: Brookings Institution.

Background Papers

Chaherli, N. 2002. "Agricultural Trade Liberalization: Main Issues for the MENA Region." World Bank, Washington, D.C. Processed.

Dasgupta, D., and F. Iqbal. 2003. "Trade, Investment Climate, and Jobs in the Middle East and North Africa Region: Some Emerging Issues." World Bank, Washington, D.C. Processed.

Dasgupta, D., J. Keller, and T. G. Srinivasan. 2001. "Reform and Elusive Growth in the Middle-East: What Has Happened in the 1990s?" Paper for the MEEA Conference on Global Change and Regional Integration: The Redrawing of the Economic Boundaries in the Middle East and North Africa, London, July 20–22.

Dasgupta, D., M. K. Nabli, C. Pissarides, and A. Varoudakis. 2002. "Making Trade Work for Jobs: International Evidence and Lessons for MENA." World Bank, Washington, D.C. Processed.

Dasgupta, D., M. K. Nabli, T. G. Srinivasan, and A.Varoudakis. 2003. "The Post-Doha Agenda: Issues and Implications for the MENA Region." World Bank, Washington, D.C.

Lee, J. 2002. "Financial Liberalization and Foreign Bank Entry in MENA." World Bank, Washington, D.C. Processed.

Nabli, M. K., and J. Keller. 2002. "The Macroeconomic Outcomes in MENA over the 1990s: How Growth Has Failed to Keep Pace with a Burgeoning Labor Market." World Bank, Washington, D.C. Processed.

Nabli, M., and M.-A. Veganzones-Varoudakis. 2002. "Exchange Rate Regime and Competitiveness of Manufactured Exports: The Case of MENA Countries." MENA Working Paper 27. World Bank, Washington, D.C.

Nugent, J. B. 2002. "Why Does MENA Trade So Little?" World Bank, Washington, D.C. Processed.

Roy, J., and J. Zarrouk. 2002. "The World Bank Completing the GCC Customs Union." World Bank, Washington, D.C.

Sekkat, K. 2002. "Trade, FDI and 'Backbone' Services in the MENA Region." World Bank, Washington, D.C. Processed.

Someya, M., H. Shunnar, and T. G. Srinvasan. 2002. "Textile and Clothing Exports in MENA: Past Performance, Prospects and Policy Issues in Post-MFA Context." World Bank, Washington, D.C. Processed.

Yee, P. H. J. 2003. "Trade Logistics in Egypt and Jordan." World Bank, Washington, D.C. Processed

Index

Abu Dhabi, FDI, 148
administrative barriers, 7
agricultural exports, 180–181, 186
    Egypt, 195
    job creation, 58–60
    Jordan, 195
agricultural products
    market access, 216–217
    water cost, 192
    water requirements, 190
agricultural sector, distortion,
        185–186, 194
agricultural trade, water and,
        189–193, 179–205
agricultural trade liberalization,
        133
    food importers and, 185–187
    gains, 188
    losses, 187
    policies, 201
    results, 196–197
    transition, 201–204
agricultural water productivity,
        181, 189
agriculture, 126
    dynamic, 15–16
    GDP, 180, 181
    main messages, 179–180
    marketing, 203
    prices, 205*n*.11
    production, 182

support programs, 216
    see also crops
aid, 19
    declines, 27–29
    inflows, 28
    to GDP ratio, 31
air transport, 158–160, 161
    cargo, 159
    international efficiency stan-
        dards, 160
Algeria
    air transport, 160
    banks, 11, 172
    exchange rate misalignment,
        110
    gradual reforms, 98
    import duties, 144
    job loss, 132
    oil, 28
    production structure (2000),
        127
    quantitative restrictions, 103
    state-owned and -operated
        activities, 144
    tariffs, 144
    telephone service, 10
    trade and investment, 25
    trade policy reforms, 139–146
    trade reforms, 9–11, 132
    transition, 1
    valuation, 105